GW00889077

SEA BATTLES IN CLOSE-UP:
THE AGE OF
NELSON

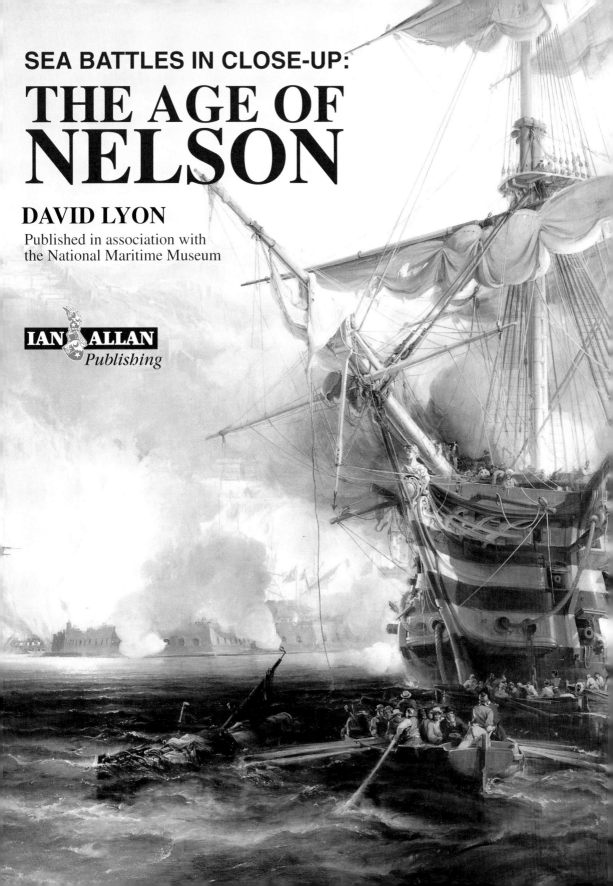

SEA BATTLES IN CLOSE-UP:
THE AGE OF
NELSON

DAVID LYON

Published in association with
the National Maritime Museum

IAN ALLAN
Publishing

First published 1996

ISBN 0 7110 2283 6

All rights reserved. No part of this book may be reproduced or transmitted in any form or by any means, electronic or mechanical, including photocopying, recording or by any information storage and retrieval system, without permission from the Publisher in writing.

© National Maritime Museum 1996

Published by Ian Allan Publishing

an imprint of Ian Allan Ltd, Terminal House, Station Approach, Shepperton, Surrey TW17 8AS.
Printed by Ian Allan Printing Ltd, Coombelands House, Coombelands Lane, Addlestone, Weybridge, Surrey KT15 1HY.

Front cover: The drama of naval warfare in the age of Nelson is typified in this painting by Pocock of *HMS Defence* in battle, 1 June 1794. *NMM neg no. BUC 0474*

Back cover: Portrait of Nelson by Abbott. *NMM neg no. E989*

CONTENTS

Foreword

by ALEXANDER KENT

The great interest in this country's maritime past is not surprising when we consider the centuries of ships, sailors and events which give it such colour and depth. For a thousand years, vessels of every kind have left these shores to explore, to discover other lands, and to foster trade, with the necessary means to protect it. From those early and hazardous days, and the foundation of the Cinque Ports by Edward the Confessor to form the first Royal Navy, to the lines of battered ships in convoy through two world wars, we have observed the expansion of fleets and development of weapons to a degree that would have seemed incredible even a few years ago. Today we see a modern navy with weapons so advanced and overwhelming that they have already outpaced the minds of those who might yet be called upon to commit them to open conflict.

Perhaps because of this, and the inability of most people to fully comprehend a seemingly uncontrollable situation, our interest returns again and again to the days of fighting sail and the men who, from choice or enforcement, served in those ships and keep them vividly alive in our minds. So firmly engrained is that maritime history in our lives that we take for granted the day-to-day language which, if often used out of its correct context, is very much a part of those times. *'First-rate', 'third-rate', 'taken aback', 'between the devil and the deep',* or even *'letting the cat out of the bag',* are all as much a part of that sailing navy as the timber, canvas and cordage that kept them afloat. Even today, it is like hearing voices of those same seamen, reminding us of the heritage they have bequeathed to us.

From the letters I receive, some from people who have rarely seen the ocean except from a high-flying jet, I believe this unwavering fascination with all things maritime is the result of two factors: the mystique of those fine, brutal ships and the men who lived and died in them, and the knowledge that we will never see their like again; and also because they represented the last days of true independence and self-reliance. Everything carried or rigged in a ship of that period had to be repaired or replaced with whatever materials were readily to hand: masts and spars, boats, sails, even the food, water and basic supplies that were needed to sustain any fighting ship, large or small. Once out of sight of land, and particularly when sailing without company, a ship was only as strong as those who served her, and as strong as the man in command.

Tactics when fighting an enemy at sea changed little over time, and relied less on strategy than on the ability of one captain to exploit any weakness or lack of vigilance on the part of his adversary, which would permit him to lay his ship as close as possible to another for the first, and often decisive, broadside.

Only the marines were trained ashore in their barracks. For the rest, from captain to midshipman, from nimble-footed topman to some dazed and frightened landman dragged aboard by the press gang, it was all a question of leadership by example, with the trained and seasoned men ready, if need be, to put a rope into a novice's fingers, if only to avoid a break in the vital chain of command.

One man will always stand out as the personification of courage and the finest qualities of leadership during this entire period of fighting sail. Horatio Nelson inspired all those he met, and many others who knew him only by reputation. So great was the influence of the little admiral, and his power over the imaginations of his commanders, that he won his greatest victory by inspiration alone, even after he had fallen, mortally wounded.

One of the last sea-fights under sail was the battle of Lissa in 1811. The hero and victor of that battle was Captain William Hoste. It is worth noting that Hoste originally went to sea at the age of 12, to serve under Nelson in his old *Agamemnon.* Like several youngsters on board, all from Nelson's home county of Norfolk, Hoste was quick to learn, and to benefit from that experience.

When he sailed into battle at Lissa against daunting odds, Hoste flew one significant signal, *'Remember Nelson'.* It was enough. For his men, and so, too, for us.

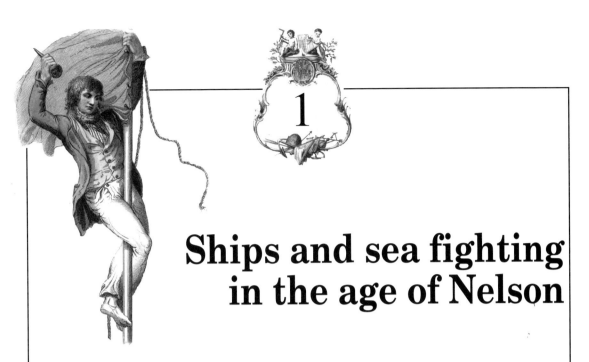

Ships and sea fighting in the age of Nelson

For the purposes of this book, the 'Age of Nelson' is that between his birth in 1758 and the end of the Napoleonic War in 1815. Nelson of course died at Trafalgar in 1805, having only then been a significant naval figure since rocketing to fame as a fighting commander at the Battle of Cape St Vincent in 1797. Moreover, his 'age', in the sense of the influence he exerted, lasted well beyond the end of the Napoleonic period.

In strictly chronological terms it is then more accurate to say that, excepting Quiberon Bay in 1759, what follows here are case-studies of sea warfare in the age of George III, who came to the throne in 1760 and died in 1820. In some respects it would also be more appropriate to do so. For his reign saw the two great political revolutions — in America and France — which made the 'Nelsonic navy' such a vital arm of national policy and defence at this time, as well as the first wave of Britain's pioneering industrial revolution. This too, with the social upheavals and administrative changes it brought, had marked effects on many aspects of naval life, technology and organisation. Nelson was at least as much a product of these events as a contributor to them and this brief introductory chapter is intended to give some background to the types of ships that fought in his period and how they did so.

Until at least the mid-19th century, navies were the most complicated and expensive arms of government, just as ships were the largest and most complicated artefacts produced by human ingenuity. The largest ships were moving towns, supporting community life for months on end, and capable of surviving the worst the sea could throw at them. They carried more and heavier cannon than accompanied whole armies. The dockyards and arsenals that supported them were the largest economic organisations of the day. Navies required a very large economic outlay and a big bureaucratic effort to set up and support, though, as the examples of the Netherlands and Britain showed, it was one that could pay off handsomely in the long run.

Navies also required large numbers of skilled men to run them. A navy could not be created quickly. Both officers and at least a reasonable proportion of the men needed to be trained professionals. The Russians throughout this period made considerable use of foreign officers, importing their expertise, and both Russia and Sweden sent young officers to serve with the British navy and learn their business there. For all navies at this time manning was always a major problem, usually the chief problem. There were never enough volunteers in time of war, when higher rates of pay in merchant ships and the attractions of privateering lured men away from the hardship, discipline and danger of naval employment. The French and Spanish operated, not very successfully,

The Progress on the Works at His Majesty's said Yard the Week past.

NMM neg no: A107

national registers of seamen and a conscription system. Britain relied on the archaic and haphazard system of chance conscription by the press gang to make up the deficiencies of her crews. However, it must always be remembered that a fair proportion, up to half, of these crews were volunteers and not pressed men — the press gang was not the only way of getting men for the navy. Impressment was almost always only for men who were sailors already, for the navy only accepted landsmen with extreme reluctance and at times of crisis — and these were either volunteers or jailbirds, the latter particularly unwelcome. Some navies, the Spanish and Russian for example, made up their deficiencies by drafting in soldiers, but this was never a satisfactory answer. The Swedes relied on a peasant militia to man the gunboats and galleys of their inshore flotilla, but these were local men who were used to their boats, a sensible answer to a particular problem and not a temporary expedient.

Above: Navies were the most complex of government organisations in this period. The dockyards and arsenals that kept them going were the biggest and most advanced technological establishments of the day. They required efficient, well-organised management and bureaucratic arrangements. Inevitably there was much paperwork. Here we have an example (and notice that the work is done on a printed form). This is a 'progress sheet' — a weekly report from a yard (in this case Portsmouth) to the administrative centre of the Navy (the Navy Board, which coped with the day-to-day work of running the fleet and yards). The date is May 1780, during the height of the crisis of the War of American Independence. It shows what is being done to each ship under repair or building, together with labour and material costs. *NMM neg no: A107*

Men were required in large numbers (the biggest warships needed up to a thousand to be fully manned) because both motive power and firepower depended on human muscle: sails and their rigging, guns and oars were all operated by manpower. As we will see time and again in the stories of the battles that follow, it was the state of training of this manpower that made the difference. From Quiberon Bay to the Nile and from Lissa to the *Shannon/Chesapeake* action it was the best trained officers and crews that won, even against quite considerable numerical and material odds. It bears repeating that naval warfare is a game for professionals.

So much for the men; what about the ships? In this period nearly all warships were basically built to the same pattern, ship-shaped wooden boxes into which men, stores and individual cannon could be loaded. The cannon would be mounted on individual mountings, which could be moved about on the small solid wheels known as trucks, and were controlled and kept in place by ropes. These guns would fire through holes (ports) cut in the ship's side, and, although a few guns could be placed to fire forwards from the bow or aft from the stern ('chasers'), the main firepower of the ship's armament could only be developed to one side or another, with only a very limited amount of training (pointing to one side or the other) possible. Improvements in the Royal Navy's rope 'tackles', which trained the guns round and permitted a small increase in the angle forward or abaft the beam on which the guns could fire, was one of those small detail improvements which made a great deal of difference in action. The ability to open fire five minutes earlier on an enemy you were approaching at an angle, or to get in an extra broadside when passing on opposite courses, might make the difference between winning or losing.

At the end of the 1770s the Royal Navy introduced a short-ranged, light weapon firing a heavy cannonball, in the form of the carronade. These were usually mounted in a different way, on a pivoted 'slide', a form of mounting which was also used for some of the more conventional 'long guns' (a term which was developed to distinguish them from carronades). Both long guns and carronades fired either cannonballs (solid shot) for general use or a group of the smaller balls known as 'grapeshot' or tin boxes of musket balls ('canister') to kill men. At close range various forms of 'dismantling shot' — chain, bar, star, etc — could be used to cut up rigging and deprive a ship of her motive power, but this was, by its nature, even more inaccurate than the cannonballs. Guns were short-ranged anyway, and only accurate at very close quarters. Sights were rarely used, and the means of training or elevating were both primitive and imprecise. Gunpowder and shot were expensive and rarely used for practice.

Below: View of Portsmouth — a watercolour by an unknown artist, probably done early in the 19th century. The larger ships are, right to left, a hulked two-decker, with a frigate alongside, a three-decker and another frigate. *NMM neg no: 6256*

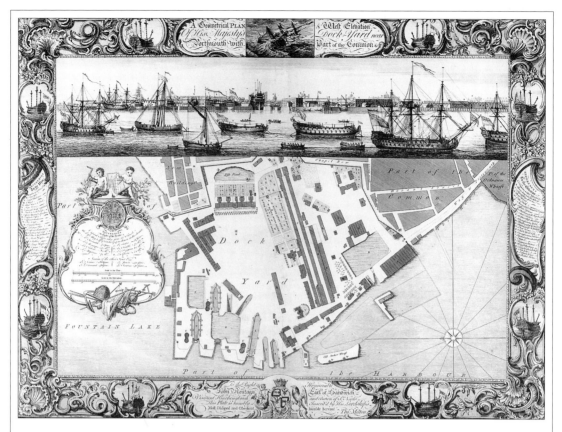

Above: This general view and plan of Portsmouth Dockyard was done by T. Milton in 1754. It emphasises just how large dockyards were; the largest, most complex, most expensive and most sophisticated establishments of their day. The odd-looking craft second from the left in the picture is a sheer hulk, an old two-decker cut down to take an enormous pair of sheer legs to act as a floating crane to hoist masts into and out of ships. The print is dedicated to the Earl of Sandwich who, contrary to legend, was a very effective and conscientious political head of the Navy. He had a particular concern with the organisation and expansion of the dockyards. *NMM neg no: 6258*

Left: A sailing warship carried numbers of young boys, who would play their part in action, be wounded or killed. Some were trainee officers like this fresh-faced midshipman, James Allen, painted when he was some 10 years old. Born in 1805, he died in 1852. Artist unknown. *NMM neg no: 3317*

Right: Cruikshank's splendid and lively representation of the licensed saturnalia of the crossing the line ceremony — performed to initiate those who had not yet paid tribute to King Neptune — was published in 1825, but still is totally relevant to the seamen of the period covered in the age of Nelson. A close look at the antics shows that little has changed when crossing the equator, even in the 20th century. *NMM neg no: 8278*

Right: A cat-o'-nine-tails: one of the standbys of naval discipline at this time, its use (or lack of it) depended very much on the individual captain. It is notable that when both Royal and US navies finally came to abolish (or at least abandon) the lash half-way through the 19th century it was the petty officers and long-serving ratings who objected the most. This was on the grounds that they were the ones who had to live with the 'hard cases' and unruly elements in the crew, and the lash was the only restraint on such antisocial people. Fortunately these fears proved to be ill-grounded. *NMM neg no: A6070*

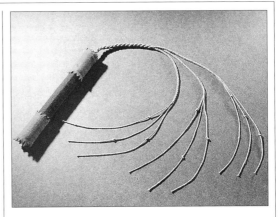

The Royal Navy tended to rely on a high rate of fire at close quarters, which was why it was so keen on carronades, and only a few captains paid much attention to long-range marksmanship until the American victories of 1812 put a new emphasis on it. As a general rule, British ships fighting the French tended to fire into the hull to kill the crew, whilst their opponents tended to fire into the masts and rigging to make the ship unmanoeuvrable or immobile. This tendency was accentuated by the fact that the British ships usually engaged from the windward side. This meant that they were leaning towards their enemy, so that the guns were pointing low because of the heel of the ship, whilst the opposite was true of their opponents, whose guns would naturally be tilted upwards on the side on which they were fighting.

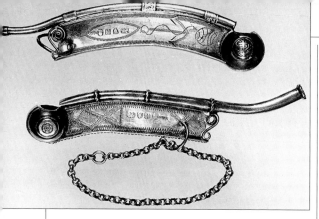

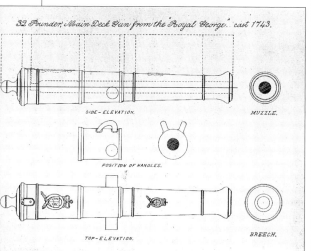

32 Pounder, Main Deck Gun from the "Royal George" cast 1743.

SIDE - ELEVATION.

MUZZLE.

POSITION OF HANDLES.

TOP - ELEVATION.

BREECH.

Left: The standard way of passing orders aboard ship was, and remains, by the high pitched, attention-grabbing pipe of bosun's 'calls'. This carries well over the hubbub of crowded messdecks, the crash of gunfire and the noise of wind and waves. The design of this variant of the whistle has changed little over the centuries, the pitch of the sound made by blowing down the pipe being varied by opening or closing the fist around the bowl. A whole code of different sound signals indicates the various orders to be passed. The two calls shown here were used during the 1790s aboard ships of the Royal Navy. One dates from 1792/3, the other was used aboard the *Monarch* during the Battle of Camperdown (1797). *NMM neg no: 4142*

Centre left: This drawing shows a 32-pounder gun raised from the wreck of the *Royal George* at Spithead in the 1830s. By the time this ship foundered at her moorings in 1782 the original 42-pounders on her lowest deck had been replaced by guns of this type. The reason was that the greater ease with which guns and shot could be handled, and therefore the increased rate of fire and accuracy possible, more than compensated for a reduction in the weight of the broadside that could be fired. 42-pounder shot and guns were really too heavy for convenient use aboard ship, and the 32-pounder was the heaviest long gun in regular use by the Royal Navy in the Great French War (1793–1815). 42-pounders continued to be used as fortress guns. *NMM neg no: 3208*

Below: A standard 'truck' carriage for a long gun, the normal way of mounting a cannon in a ship. The small, solid wheels are the 'trucks'. The drawing is taken from Muller's *A treatise of Artillery* of 1768. *NMM neg no: A1138*

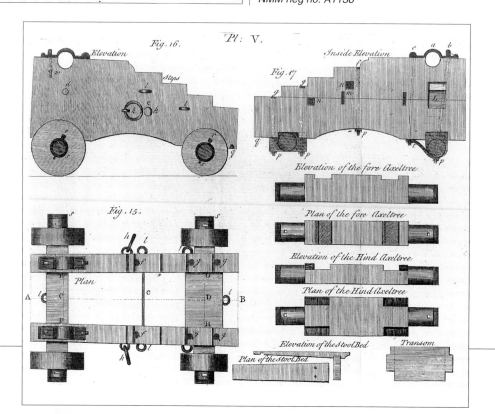

Pl: V.

Fig. 16.

Elevation

Steps

Inside Elevation

Fig. 17.

Elevation of the fore Axeltree

Plan of the fore Axeltree

Elevation of the Hind Axeltree

Plan of the Hind Axeltree

Fig. 15.

Plan

Elevation of the stool Bed

Transom

Plan of the stool Bed

Above: This photograph of a model of a 68-pounder carronade as fitted on the forecastle or quarterdeck of the *Royal William* shows one of the two 'secret weapons' which assisted the Royal Navy to stave off defeat in the American War of Independence. The other was the coppering of ships' bottoms which meant that they could stay faster for longer than ships which had nothing to stop fouling of their bottoms by marine growth with a subsequent increase in resistance. The carronade was a short-range, short-barrelled, lightly-built gun firing a heavy shot with a light charge of gunpowder. This meant that weapons firing a very heavy ball could be mounted on the light upperworks of a ship and fired by a small gun crew. This made for a great increase in actual firepower at short ranges, a very attractive idea to the Royal Navy. The carronade was invented by (or at least for) the Scottish iron foundry at Carron, after which the weapon was named. The original weapons, which first appeared in the late 1770s, were very short indeed. They looked like dustbins mounted on their sides. The weapon seen here was a later development, with a slightly lengthened muzzle to decrease the danger of muzzle flash spreading to the rigging. Carronades were not usually mounted on wheeled ('truck') carriages and elevated by a primitive arrangement of wedges as were normal 'long guns'. Instead, as here, they were mounted on specially developed pivoting slides, giving much greater control in traverse (side to side movement). The screw at the breech was also a much more effective and precise way of controlling the elevation and depression of the gun. A final note on the ship concerned is justified. The *Royal William* was built as a 100-gun First Rate and launched in 1719, but was laid up immediately and never served as such. It was not until 1756 that she was brought out of reserve and cut down to an 86-gun Second Rate. As such she had a successful career till the early 1780s. Hulked in 1790 she did not leave this second-line service till broken up in 1813. *NMM neg no: A9516*

Above: A fine picture by Pyne of shipmates carousing. This gives a good idea of an individual mess, with their living and eating space between two guns on the gun deck. The mess table hangs from the deckhead (sailor's word for the ceiling) and can be tied up there when not in use. This is a generation or more before the introduction of uniform for ordinary sailors. *NMM neg no: B8413*

Left: A fine picture of a young sailor in action — this is Jack Crawford, the seaman who nailed the flag to the mast-head aboard the *Venerable*, Duncan's flagship at the Battle of Camperdown (1797) against the Dutch. The few portraits of named sailors we do have are mostly of them in old age as Greenwich pensioners or the like, so the existence of this particular print is especially pleasing. *NMM neg no: A8108*

Above right: Death of Lord Manners at the Battle of the Saintes. This engraving of Stothard's picture of the death of a captain on his quarterdeck seems to owe more to the theatre than to reality. It does tell us something about the way the 18th century saw death in action; pointing up its heroic aspects rather than the reality of pain, mutilation and gore; as well as about the naval dress of the period. The seaman on the left is wearing the garment known as a 'seaman's frock'. *NMM neg no: A6955*

Right: A later stage in the fiercely-fought Dogger Bank action of 1781 as shown in a Dutch engraving. The British fleet having come angling down on the Dutch line have now turned on to a parallel course and the two sides are slugging it out in line ahead formation. This is a classic, indecisive line ahead action. Neither side lost ships, though both lost a large number of men. The convoy the Dutch were escorting had to turn back, whilst the British convoy got through, so one could say that the British won on points, but in most respects this was a drawn battle. *NMM neg no: X1930*

hn Cranford, of   *Sunderland, D*

ilor who nailed the Flag to   *the Main Top Gallant mai*
rd the Venerable, Lord   *Duncan's Ship,*
t away by the Dutch Adm.   *de Winter.*

by M.Came on board for the Express   *purpose of Introducing*
f L.d Duncan's Victory now Engraving by   *Subscription & which inc*
nirals & Officers who so Gloriously   *Distinguished themselve*
morable 11.th of October 1797.

An aspect of the fighting power of ships that should not be ignored is the use of small arms, and other man-killing weapons like hand grenades, swivel guns and small mortars. We will see a number of cases, particularly John Paul Jones' *Bonhomme Richard* and Lucas' *Redoubtable*, where small arms training made a great difference to the outcome of particular fights. This was especially so when, as in both the examples quoted, intelligent use was made of the advantages of height given by fighting from the tops, the platforms on the masts. Also, most battles were eventually won by boarding the enemy with cutlass, boarding pike, axe, sword, pistol and clubbed musket, in a murderous but mercifully short close-quarters scrimmage. Ships were very rarely sunk in battle, though they might occasionally catch fire or blow up. In battles close to shore, grounding — either accidental or deliberate — was another possibility.

The fact that the main firepower of ships of this time could only be used to one side or another made a long line of ships, head to stern, the obvious way of fighting. To be able to fight in that line ships had to be of a certain size and power, big enough and strong enough to have a chance of standing up to the biggest ships around. This concept of 'being fit to stand in the line of battle' produced the 'line of battle ship' or 'ship of the line', the capital ship of the day. In the 1750s the smallest of these were of 60 guns, but this was an obsolete type even then, and the limit soon moved up to the 64-gun ship. Even though there were some of these at Trafalgar they were by then considered rather weak for the task, none had been built for some years, and by 1815 the type was no longer in front-line service. The Royal Navy had kept them rather longer than the French because, with its world-wide responsibilities, numbers of ships were always more important than their individual power. 64s were cheaper to build and man than the standard 74-gun ships which provided the majority of the line of battle ships at this time.

Both the 64 and the 74 were types originally developed by the French and Spanish navies at a time when British ship design was going through a very conservative phase (and from which the popular, but over-simplified and largely inaccurate, legend of the inferiority of British warships dates). They were both 'two-deckers' (ie ships with two continuous gun decks one on top of the other) as were all ships of the line except the largest. The French had larger two-deckers of 80 guns, but these were expensive to man and to build, especially

Above: The greatest warship designer of the age, Sir Thomas Slade, who, as Surveyor of the Navy (chief designer for the Royal Navy) from 1755 to 1771, produced an extremely successful series of designs for various types of ship from the 100-gun *Victory* through 74s like *Bellona* to frigates (eg the long-lived *Southampton*) and smaller vessels. Some of his designs were being built a generation after his death. *NMM ref: BHC3030*

because their length was nearing the limits possible with the methods of construction of wooden hulls then in use. All ships had other decks; the unarmed orlop and platforms below the waterline, and the armed quarterdeck and forecastle above the upper deck — but none of these were both continuous and armed. Hulls were constructed of large numbers of relatively short pieces of timber. The length of these pieces of timber was conditioned by the size of the trees available, which is the explanation why the Spaniards, building in Cuba with exceptionally tall trees available, could build the enormous *Santisima Trinidad*. Around 1800, new methods of construction, involving girder-type structures and increased use of iron, made it possible to build longer ships, though the full benefits of these developments were not to be seen until after the end of the Napoleonic War.

The biggest ships of all were the cumbersome but powerful three-deckers, which

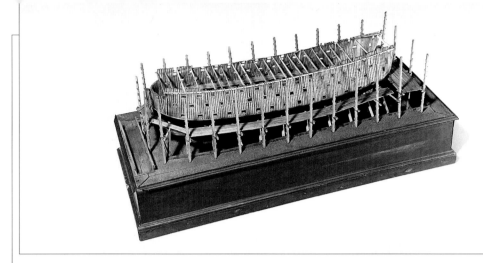

Above: This model shows what the hull of a late 18th century three-decker ship of the line (in this case actually *Victory*) looked like before being planked. As you can see, the thick transverse frames already present a nearly solid side. Thick sides like this would exclude most cannonballs, but also required very large amounts of timber that had grown into the right curves. The shortage of suitable timber for these frames was a major problem for all European navies at this time. *NMM neg no: B9355*

Below: This detailed small-scale plan shows the 120-gun line of battle ship *Nelson* launched at Woolwich Dockyard on the Thames in 1814. The largest type of ship to serve in the Royal Navy at this period, but only at the very end of it; before that 100-gun ships were the largest. This particular vessel had a long career. In 1858 she completed a conversion to steam propulsion. In 1867 she was presented to the Victorian (Australia) government for local defence and training sailors. Hulked from 1887, she was sold, still as a hulk, in 1898, and not scrapped until 1928. *NMM neg no: A4808*

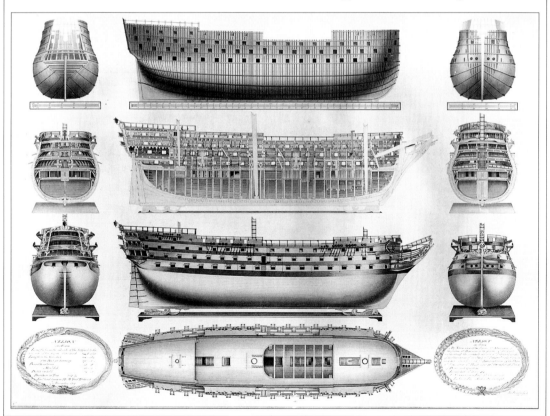

were usually the fleet flagships. In the 1750s only the British of the major navies had any in service. The Royal Navy always seems to have liked the gun power and protection that these towering ships gave. They were, however, expensive to build and man, so the Royal Navy had very few of the largest type, the ship of 100 guns, in service, but usually had more of the shorter, more cumbersome but cheaper 90s (classed by the 1770s as 98s). By the 1770s both the French and Spanish had decided that the advantages of three-deckers outweighed the disadvantages but decided to 'go for broke' by building ships of 110 or more guns, much bigger than the biggest British ones — a trend the British finally had to follow.

It may at this stage be worth saying something about two major causes of confusion when referring to warship types at this period. The simplest way of designating a major warship is to refer to its number of guns — as a 74, a 32 and so on. At the beginning of our period this did correspond to the numbers

Below: This picture of *Victory* shows her off the tower of Belem on the Tagus, just below Lisbon, a port she often visited and used as a base. The creation of that greatest of 18th century warship designers, Sir Thomas Slade, she was that rare creature, a three-decker that sailed as well as the two-deckers that made up the main body of the fleets of the time. It was her performance that kept her as a favourite for flagship duty for half a century. It also ensured that a class of ships were built to her lines a generation after she first went to sea. *NMM neg no: B5502*

Right: This magnificent model of the British 74-gun ship *Bellona* shows her as she was when first coppered in 1779. She was not new at this stage, having been launched in 1760, and she was to last in service until broken up in 1814 — a very long life for a ship of her kind, and a distinguished one. Coppering was, with the carronade, a technological step forward introduced by the Royal Navy which gave it a vitally needed edge against the heavy odds it experienced during the American War of Independence. Coppering was expensive, but it gave British ships a performance advantage, by slowing marine growth on their bottoms, which was priceless in military terms. *NMM neg no: C1100*

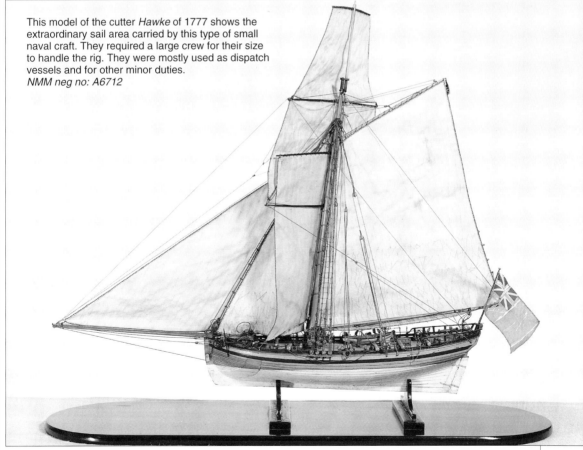

This model of the cutter *Hawke* of 1777 shows the extraordinary sail area carried by this type of small naval craft. They required a large crew for their size to handle the rig. They were mostly used as dispatch vessels and for other minor duties.
NMM neg no: A6712

actually aboard that ship. However, the introduction of the light carronade on the upper works of larger ships at the end of the 1770s complicated matters. These weapons were, usually, not replacing the long guns of the original armament but were supplementary to it. What they were actually replacing were the small guns, known as swivels, mounted on the bulwarks and the tops. Swivels were not counted in the total of guns, nor were carronades except on sloops and other unrated ships, or a few vessels equipped with an all-carronade armament). This actually makes a great deal of sense if we realise that from about 1780 the number of guns given is no longer the actual armament of a ship *but a description of the type*. So just as today we have Type-22 frigates, for example, there were then 38-gun frigates which, with carronades, actually carried 46 large weapons, but were a type originally developed to carry 38 guns. Similarly 74-gun ships might now carry 80 guns or more, but were the same dimensions, design and possibly the same ships as earlier 74s. Consistency is much better served by continuing to use these old designations and ignoring the reclassification of 1816, when the Royal Navy went over to including carronades in the official classification.

Another source of confusion is the rating system. Originally, in the mid-17th century, this referred to the rate of pay of the captain of a ship. However, since this necessarily coincided with the power and prestige of the ship it soon came to be synonymous with the number of guns carried.

The rates ran from first to sixth and referred only to ships commanded by captains (the rank, not the position); in effect ships of 20 guns or more. Smaller vessels were commanded by masters and commanders, or by lieutenants, and were 'unrated'. In the 18th and early 19th centuries the rates were approximately as follows: First Rates — 100 guns or more, Second Rates — 98 to 90 guns, Third Rates — 80 to 64 guns, Fourth Rates — 60 to 50 guns, Fifth Rates — 44 to 32 guns, Sixth Rates — 28 to 20 guns. The rating system actually cuts across a number of more precise and useful warship designations, such as frigate, and fails to distinguish between an 80 and a 64. It is not a very precise tool for determining warship types and I have made very little use of it in this book.

There were a couple of types of small two-deckers considered too weak to serve in the line of battle but which were built in some numbers for the Royal Navy and others like the Dutch who had need of convoy escorts, flagships overseas when a ship of the line was not needed and similar purposes vehicles. These were the 50-gun ships and the 44s. The former were still built in small numbers until the Napoleonic period, when we will find them serving as headquarters ships for groups of small vessels in the anti-invasion flotilla. The latter were never very satisfactory ships and were soon put into second-line service by the success of the much more effective true frigates. These ships and the small Sixth Rates of 20 or 24 guns were sometimes loosely referred to as 'frigates', but this is a very slovenly usage and has led to confusion in cases like that of the *Serapis* which was a 44-gun small two-decker, not a true frigate at all. All these ships could also be referred to as 'cruisers', a word which did not then refer to the type of ship at all, unlike its later usage. It simply meant any ship on detached duties and this could be anything from a 74 to a sloop.

Most ship type names can vary in their meaning according to who is using them, when, and in which context. In this book 'frigate' means the new type that had appeared in the Danish and French navies about 1740 and was later copied by the British from captured examples. The distinguishing feature was that these were two-decked ships but with only the top one, quarterdeck and forecastle, armed. The lower deck could therefore be a sort of 'tween deck' comfortably situated below the waterline, whilst the upper deck raised the guns up well above it. This made for a very seaworthy type of ship, the ideal type for cruising. The original frigates had a main armament of nine-pounder guns and were usually classed as 28s, though they were soon supplemented by 12-pounder 32s. During the American War of Independence the first 18-pounder frigates appeared. These were 36s and 38s and there were later a few smaller 32s as well. The final growth of the type in our period, heralded by the big American and Swedish

Right: One of the very few pictures to show the interior of a captain's cabin. This is by Chamberlin and shows the inventive Captain Bentick and his son (the latter in the uniform of the Royal Naval Academy at Portsmouth). The pulley blocks on the deck show one of the captain's inventions. It is interesting to see how bare and frugal the cabin is, though also notice the bell-pull to summon servants. The picture was painted in the late 1770s, shortly before the captain's death. *NMM ref: BHC2550*

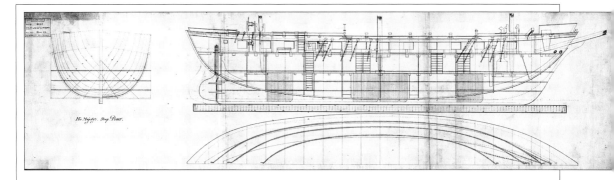

Above: Not every vessel built for the Royal Navy in this period was conventional. In the 1790s a whole series of unconventional designs were tried, of which the one shown in this Admiralty plan was amongst the most interesting. This is the *Dart* of 1797 which, with her sister *Arrow*, was designed and built by Samuel Bentham, the brother of the philosopher Jeremy Bentham. The shape, structure (the first use of watertight bulkheads in western craft) and armament (experimental 32-pounder carronades) and use of 'sliding keels' (dagger boards) were all totally unconventional. These two were classed as sloops, though the number (varying between 20 and 28) and power of guns carried made them much more formidable customers than any conventional sloop, which helps to explain why they were assigned to Nelson's force attacking Copenhagen in 1801. *Dart* had already distinguished herself in a cutting out raid on Dunkirk (see the picture of this action illustrated on page 102 . *NMM neg no: ADM 6060*

Above: This Dutch engraving shows how one line of battle could approach another by angling down. The fleet doing this from the windward position with their bows towards us here are British. Awaiting them in line ahead and going away from us is a Dutch fleet. Behind each fleet is a convoy of merchant ships. The date is 1781, and the two escorting squadrons are about to meet in the Battle of the Dogger Bank. This was one of the smaller fleet battles of the War of American Independence in terms of the size of the forces involved, but more men died and were wounded in this bloody little battle than in all the other battles of that war combined. *NMM neg no: 5625*

Above: Sailors were always a popular and picturesque subject, shown in all sorts of mediums. In this case we have the 'Sailor's adieu' on a creamware jug. *NMM neg no: B4416*

frigates and by the British 'cutting down' 64-gun line of battle ships, were the 'super frigates', with 24-pounders and anything up to 60 guns.

Below the frigates in the Royal Navy were the 24- and 20-gun Sixth Rates. The French had the rather more sensible classification of 'corvette', usually indicating a flush-decked vessel with all the guns on that one deck and which also included vessels of 14 to 18 guns of the type the British would call 'sloops'. The sloop of war was any vessel commanded by an officer of the rank immediately below captain, a rank which was coming to be known by the title of commander. A sloop could also be of almost any rig (three-masted ship, brig, ketch, even cutter) and would usually carry between 12 and 20 guns. A mercantile sloop was

Above: What a battle could do to a ship is shown by this print of a French 74 captured at the Glorious First of June 1794. All the masts have gone and light spars lashed to the stumps to take a jury rig of small sails. *NMM neg no: 7077*

different, being a simple, one-masted, fore- and aft-rigged craft.

In 1779 the Royal Navy built its first brig, a type with a two-masted, square sailed rig which required a smaller crew than a three-masted ship, and rapidly became the chief type of smaller vessel used by the service. All except the smallest were classed as 'brig sloops'. Below these were the schooners and cutters, both being types introduced to regular Royal Naval service in the 1760s which were used for communications duties and the like. Towards the end of the century increasing use was being made of rowing gun-boats and the other types of gun-boat and gun-brig we will meet in the chapter on the anti-invasion flotilla.

As has already been indicated, tactics in the age of sail were based on the fact that ships fought with their broadsides and were relatively ill-equipped for firing forward or backwards. They also depended nearly entirely on the presence and direction of the wind. Ships could be laboriously moved by towing with boats, or, with those up to the size of frigates, by using the long oars known as sweeps. Neither method was an effective means of propulsion in battle, though they might be useful for manoeuvring to bring the broadside into play. Possession of 'the weather gauge', being upwind of the enemy, enabled one to choose to engage the enemy, or to get away.

Another influence of ship construction on tactics was that bows and sterns were not only weakly armed but also, particularly the latter, weakly protected. The attractive stern windows of the captain's and officers' accommodation offered no obstacle to cannonballs or grapeshot which might well be stopped by a ship's oak sides. So 'raking' a ship from end to end was the best possible way of causing her a great deal of damage, whilst being in a position where you could not only use all your broadside

A rigged model of one of Britain's first 74-gun ships, the 'workhorse' of the line of battle in the period between 1756 and 1816. This is the *Hercules*, built in 1759 and sold for breaking up in 1784.
NMM neg no: C1666

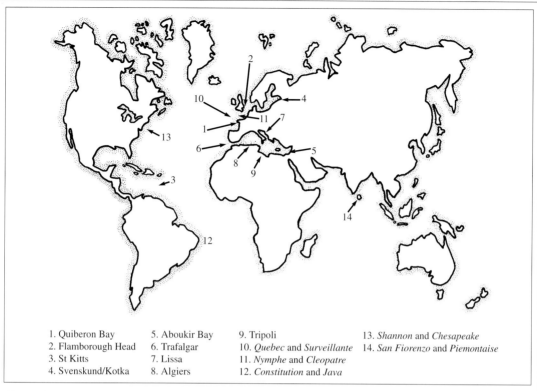

1. Quiberon Bay	5. Aboukir Bay	9. Tripoli	13. *Shannon* and *Chesapeake*
2. Flamborough Head	6. Trafalgar	10. *Quebec* and *Surveillante*	14. *San Fiorenzo* and *Piemontaise*
3. St Kitts	7. Lissa	11. *Nymphe* and *Cleopatre*	
4. Svenskund/Kotka	8. Algiers	12. *Constitution* and *Java*	

Above: Map of the world showing the location of the sea battles covered in this book. *Author*

Below: Plymouth Dock in 1816 in a contemporary illustration from the *Naval Chronicle*.
NMM neg no: 3044

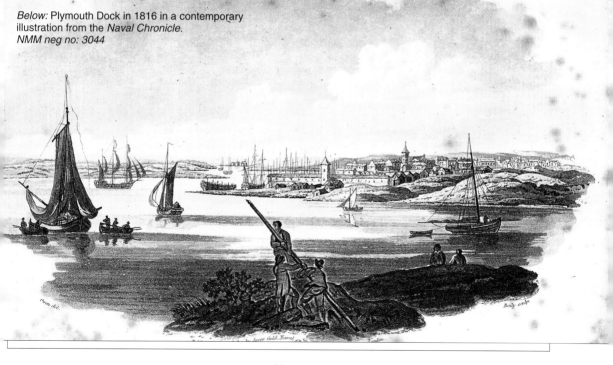

but where your enemy had little or no possibility of replying in kind.

If one body of ships was fighting another, both would normally be in line of battle. If both stayed that way and one side was not noticeably weaker than the other there was little chance of any decisive result. This was what happened in most of the battles of the American War of Independence, when the French Navy was at its best. Much was made by an earlier generation of naval historians of the 'tyranny of the fighting instructions', which made fighting in line obligatory, but unless there was some major advantage over the enemy in power, numbers or skill, there was little alternative.

'Breaking the line' of the enemy, breaking through, raking the enemy when doing so, and then isolating individual ships between two of your own ('doubling') and obtaining a local superiority enough to defeat part of the enemy fleet in detail before the other part could come to the rescue, was undoubtedly very attractive. Many students of Nelson's tactics at Trafalgar have tended to see it as a magic battle-winning formula and we will see what happened to a French commander who tried to utilise it at Lissa. The problem with this approach was that before you could break the enemy's line you had to approach it head on, exposing yourself to being raked before you could reply. This meant taking a gamble on the effectiveness of your enemy's fire, and his other skills. It would come off against a rattled, less efficient or flying enemy, as Hawke showed at Quiberon Bay and Nelson did at Trafalgar; but it could also prove costly or fatal, as it did when tried by Byron against the French fleet of the late 1770s, or Dubordieu against the British frigates at Lissa. Nelson's tactics were appropriate for dealing with a French navy still heavily damaged by its experience in the French Revolution and kept off-balance by constant pressure from the Royal Navy which at this time was noticeably more effective man for man and ship for ship.

Another development in our period which has been given a great deal of prominence by naval historians is the increasingly sophisticated codes of signals adopted, making it easier for admirals to communicate their intentions to their captains. This was important but I would suggest that what was a good deal more so was the ability of certain admirals — Hawke at Quiberon, Hood at St Kitts, Nelson at the Nile — to talk with and train their captains so they knew what to do in a whole series of contingencies, knew their leader's mind, and exercised intelligent initiative with the minimum need for signalling. The most impressive victories described here were the results of well-prepared, well-trained, well-motivated teamwork. Nelson's peculiar genius lay in his brilliance in leading an already extremely good team against a less good one. His success owed as much to that team as to his ability to use it.

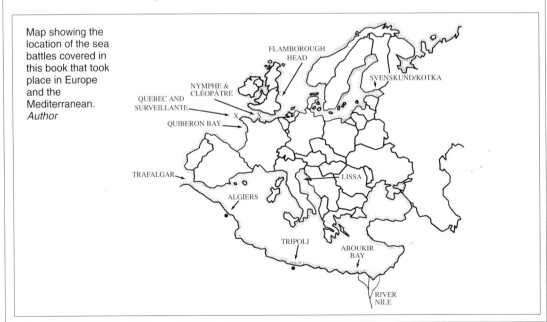

Map showing the location of the sea battles covered in this book that took place in Europe and the Mediterranean. *Author*

FLAMBOROUGH HEAD

SVENSKUND/KOTKA

NYMPHE & CLÉOPÂTRE

QUEBEC AND SURVEILLANTE

QUIBERON BAY

TRAFALGAR

LISSA

ALGIERS

TRIPOLI

ABOUKIR BAY

RIVER NILE

Above: This drawing shows an incident during the mutiny in the British fleet in 1797. The 38-gun *Clyde*, in the right foreground, is escaping from the mutinous fleet at the Nore. *NMM neg no: A8577*

Below: Chiffonne, a typical 36-gun frigate of the period, was captured from the French by the British in 1801. *NMM neg no: A1580*

Below: Illustration from the *Naval Chronicle* showing the coast near Brest at half-tide. *NMM neg no: B3045*

O.T. 1813

London, Published Sept. 30, 1816, by Joyce Gold, Naval Chronicle Office, 103 Shoe Lane, Fleet Str.t

Baily sc.t

Plate CCCCLXVIII. *La Parquette Rock, near Brest, at half tide.*

Quiberon Bay, 1759

In terms of sheer drama and scenic grandeur no battle under sail can rival that of Quiberon Bay.

It took place late on a November day, with the light going from the sky, a gale blowing, and amongst the rocky islands and shoals of the ironbound French coast between the mouth of the Loire and Belle-Ile. Most battles under sail were fought in light winds and comparatively calm seas and sinkings were rare, but here two ships sank, mostly because of the weather, and others were wrecked.

The background of the battle was that in late 1759 the French were threatening invasion of Britain as a last, desperate, attempt to reverse the trend of British victories. Transports had been collected in the Bay of Morbihan in Southern Brittany and the troops they were intended to carry billeted nearby. The over-complicated invasion plan had already had a major reverse, as the French Mediterranean fleet coming from Toulon to join

Left: An engraving of Monamy Swaine's painting of Boscawen's victory against a French squadron won off Lagos, Portugal in August 1759 — a victory, adequate in itself, which was the prelude to the greater triumph of Quiberon Bay, later the same year. Lagos and Quiberon were the main naval contributions (if one ignores amphibious triumphs such as Quebec) to what became known as 'the year of victories'.
NMM neg no: B9265

the Brest fleet had been defeated by Boscawen at a battle off Lagos on the Portuguese coast earlier that year. The French king, Louis XV, still wanted the invasion attempt to be made, which left the onus on the French commander at Brest, Conflans, to break out and escort the invasion fleet. There were, however, major difficulties in his way.

The chief of these was that he was the victim of the first really successful sustained blockade of a hostile naval base. This blockade was made possible by the combination of Anson at the Admiralty and Hawke in command of the blockading fleet. Between them they set up the organisation which kept the British fleet supplied with provisions and water, munitions and information. Brest was a very dangerous and difficult place to blockade, exposed to Atlantic gales and protected by a rock-girt coast. However, storms which would force the British ships to break their patrols off the entrance to Brest and force them to take shelter in Torbay would also pin the French inside the narrow entrance ('Goulet') to the roadstead of Brest. A change in the wind would, it was hoped, bring the British back to intercept before Conflans could collect the invasion transports from the Morbihan and this was indeed what actually happened.

The blockade had begun in May 1759 and it was not until November that Conflans took the opportunity offered to him by gales driving Hawke off station. In this time Hawke

Left: An engraving of Reynolds' portrait of Lord Anson (1697–1762). He sailed round the world in the *Centurion*, raiding the Pacific coast of South America and capturing the Manila galleon with huge amounts of treasure at the beginning of the War of Jenkins' Ear (1739–1748). Commanding the Western Squadron he won the first Battle of Finisterre (1747). He then became a most successful First Lord of the Admiralty, reorganising naval administration and being responsible for many of the successes of the Seven Years War (1757–1763). *NMM neg no: 471*

this battle). He also had no equivalent to the single 100-gun First Rate and the three 90-gun Second Rates which formed the fighting core of the British fleet and provided its flagships. It is significant that Hawke's flagship was the latest, largest and strongest of the Royal Navy's First Rates — the *Royal George* launched three years earlier. The French instead had four of their big 80-gun two-deckers as their largest and strongest ships and therefore as the flagships of the divisions of the fleet. The British had no equivalent, but it is interesting that they slightly outnumbered the French (seven to six) in what was to become the standard type of the ship of the line, 74-gun Third Rates. This is the more noticeable in that only 11 of the type had been launched before this date (*Torbay*, present at the battle, does not count in this total as she had been 'cut down' from a 90-gun three-decker, nor does the *Magnanime*, which had been captured from the French). So Hawke had a large proportion of the most modern and powerful ships available — which indicates the importance that was attached to his fleet and its task as the main defence against invasion. The French, however, considerably outnumbered the British (seven to two) in the slightly smaller 64-gun line of battle ships which were the descendants of the older 70-gun ships (of which the British had five and the French four). The 64 was already replacing the older and less well armed 60-gun ship as the smallest type of vessel fit to lie in the line of battle — the French had none of this latter type, though the British had five. It is appropriate that the British, with their liking for three-deckers and their great need for numbers, had the greater difference in force between the individual ships in their fleet.

The French were first sighted by the frigate *Maidstone*, one of two such ships placed on either bow of Hawke's fleet as scouts. She signalled 'fleet in sight' by the traditional method of letting fly (briefly releasing) her

had had the chance to train his fleet to a high degree of efficiency in gunnery and seamanship. He had managed to avoid the dangers of disease decimating his crews and, to some extent, of wear and tear reducing the effectiveness of his ships. Meanwhile Conflans suffered from the stagnation of his crews in port, and the shortages caused by the blockade. Brest was difficult to keep supplied with naval stores and could not feed itself, still less the men of a large fleet, from local resources. An effective blockade made the spectre of famine loom.

On 14 November weather conditions improved enough to let Hawke leave Torbay for his position off Brest. Two days later, information reached him that Conflans' fleet was out and the chase was on to intercept the French off Belle-Ile which shelters Morbihan Bay. Sure enough that is where the French fleet was, on the early morning of the 20th, in pursuit of the smaller British warships which had been blockading the invasion transports in the Morbihan. These vessels had been warned in time to escape by a little-used passage.

Conflans' fleet was numerically slightly weaker than Hawke's (21 to 23 ships of the line — the British also had available four small two-deckers of 50 guns but had no use for them in this battle — and both sides had five frigates or corvettes each, again of no significance in

topsail sheets (the ropes that controlled the bottom ends of the sail).

The Admiral then ordered the fleet 'to draw into a Line of Battle abreast at the distance of 2 cables asunder'. About an hour later the *Magnanime* made the signal for the fleet ahead to be that of the enemy. 'We ascertained them to be the French squadron of 21 ships of the line and 3 smaller ships and that they were then chasing Captain Duff's frigates and bombs, the destruction of which was one object of their destination. Upon their having a distincter view of our ships, they gave over the chase.' If the French were to be brought to action during the brief November day there was no time for the complicated manoeuvres of forming a line of battle, even if the enemy obliged by staying where he was, and he was more likely to run for shelter. 'In a short time after Sir Edward Hawke changed the signal for the line to one for a general chase, the enemy's ships (who were now within sight of our whole fleet) not being formed into any regular order, and by their motions seemingly confused. The whole English fleet gave chase accordingly, and at noon nine of our best sailing ships were in the pursuit advanced abreast of Belle Isle...' Aboard Commodore Duff's small British squadron, which had been losing its race to get away from its pursuers, the sight of Hawke's topsails coming above the horizon was a great relief, and cheering wildly, there was 'scarce a man but threw his hat overboard as a sort of defiance to the enemy'.

Above: Edward Hawke (1705–1781) as a rear-admiral, some years before his great victory at Quiberon Bay; an impressive man, straightforward, strong and likeable, also a brilliant seaman and commander. *NMM neg no: A1594*

Below: Wright's painting of the Battle of Quiberon Bay. Another artist wallowing in the dramatic possibilities of storm, gunfire and wreckage. *NMM ref: BHC0402*

QUARTER DECK

UPPER DECK

MIDDLE DECK

GUN DECK

32

On sighting Hawke's larger, better trained fleet Conflans stopped his pursuit of Duff's ships. He then formed his ships into a single line astern, turning them towards the entrance of Quiberon Bay. He thought he could get all his ships inside the bay before the British could reach him. Once he was inside it seemed unlikely that the British, without local knowledge, would dare to follow him into such a dangerous area in such extreme conditions. Even if they did he could hope to have enough time to form a strong defensive formation, and have every chance of beating them off. This was reasonable. The French commander could not know that the combination of an admiral determined to obtain a decisive victory and an equally determined and well-trained fleet would mean that his enemy was both bold and skilled enough to crack on enough sail to catch him before he reached sanctuary, and to dare to penetrate that sanctuary using the fleeing enemy as a guide. Furthermore, a fleet fleeing, keeping formation and necessarily tied to the speed of the slowest was necessarily slower than a pursuing force that had the nerve and confidence to pursue flat out without maintaining any sort of formation, with the fastest ships in the lead confident enough in their own fighting power and the support of their fellows not to hesitate in their chase.

Hawke described the resulting situation: 'All the day we had very fresh gales at NW and WNW, with heavy squalls, Monsieur Conflans kept going off under such sail as all his squadron could carry, and at the same time keep together; while we crowded after him with every sail our ships could carry.' In some cases with a little more than was practicable. At

Left: This cross-sectional model of the 1756 *Royal George* (Hawke's flagship at Quiberon) demonstrates what a three-decker's armament looked like: the heaviest cannon on the lowest continuous deck (42-pounders, later 32-pounders, on the lower, or gun deck), and then going up in stages (24-pounders on the middle or main deck, 12-pounders on the upper deck — the uppermost continuous deck — and six-pounders on the quarter-deck and forecastle, later supplemented or replaced by carronades). *NMM neg no: A1902*

Below: Serres' ship portrait of the *Royal George*, First Rate of 100 guns. Launched in 1756, she was Hawke's flagship at Quiberon Bay and continued a distinguished career until her loss in 1782. The cause of this dreadful accident at Spithead was very probably that she was heeled dangerously far over to get at a pipe, and as the poet Cowper put it: 'A land breeze shook her shrouds and she was overset'. *NMM ref: BHC3604*

9.30am the *Revenge* carried away her foretopsail-yard, and for the next few hours her crew worked frantically to get another one up. At 11am Howe's *Magnanime*, which had been crowding on sail and was the nearest to the enemy, lost her main topgallant-yard. Whilst the damage was being repaired, Howe told his men to be cool and collected and to attend very closely to their orders, 'and to keep back their fire till they could put their hands to the muzzles of the enemy's guns'.

Throughout the British fleet everyone worked hard at clearing for action. The crew of the *Burford* threw all the animals they carried: cows, pigs, goats, chickens, etc overboard in order to make a clean sweep of the decks; unremarked casualties of the battle even before it started. The crew of the *Magnanime* knocked a hole in their launch (the largest boat carried aboard) and flung it overboard to sink. About 10am the *Royal George* took out the last reef in her topsails and, not content with enlarging her sail area in this way, set her studding-sails as well (these were extra pieces of canvas boomed out on either side of the sails usually set, and were normally only used in light winds; setting them in the strong winds prevailing this day took great seamanship and a great deal of nerve, as an enormous strain was put on masts and rigging). Soon after this bold act the lookouts sighted land ahead, which they reported as Belle-Ile. The Admiral made the signal for the headmost ships to form in a line as they came up with the enemy: 'I threw out the signal for the seven ships nearest to them to chase, and draw into line of battle ahead of me, and endeavour to stop them till the rest of the squadron should come up, who were also to form as they chased, that no time might be lost in the pursuit'. Despite the threatening weather, the *Royal George* set her topgallant-sails. An hour later they had got her topgallant-yard across and had taken in a reef in her topgallant-sails. About noon the *Magnanime, Torbay, Resolution,* and *Warspite* came up with the *Rochester* frigate and gave her three cheers, which her crew returned. 'We now could plainly discover the enemy's fleet to consist of 21 ships of the line, three frigates, and six small barks steering for that part of Quiberon Bay which lies between the rocks called the Cardinals and the Island of Dumet.' By midday Hawke's fleet was moving in towards the cliffs on the southward side of Belle-Ile. Surf breaking over rocks showed in the eastern distance where the Grand

Above left: Probably the most impressive, and the most convincing, of all the paintings of the Battle of Quiberon Bay is this tremendous one by Serres. The November storm, the dying day, the British fleet harrying the French and the ironbound coast are all there. The leading ships of the chasing fleet are exchanging shots with the French rearguard, and their companions are straining every nerve and pushing their seamanship to the utmost to come up. *NMM ref: BHC2266*

Above: Paton's painting of Quiberon Bay captures the moment that *Thésée* foundered under attack from the *Torbay. NMM ref: BHC0397*

Cardinals broke surface. The southern entrance to Quiberon Bay lay between these Cardinals and the Four shoal, a dangerous rocky bank about seven miles to the east-south-eastward. White water showed the presence of other dangerous rocks and shoals on either side of this approach.

As the afternoon drew on the wind increased and the *Royal George* was obliged to take in her topgallant-sails, though half an hour later she was able to set them again. It was blowing hard with frequent showers of rain and heavy squalls; and the British, led by *Magnanime,*

were gaining fast. Conflans, who had thought to get safely inside the bay, and then to form line of battle under shelter of the western shore, had reckoned without the headlong speed of Hawke's pursuit. Despite the rising gale, the heavy seas and a lee shore bristling with rocks and shoals, the British ships came on, with their spars bending and groaning with the strain. The severe training of the previous months' blockade was now reaping its reward, for without it, Conflans' defensive plan would probably have worked.

The French flagship, *Soleil Royal,* had almost reached the Cardinals and the *Royal George* was driving past the southernmost point of Belle-Ile. The long chase had caused the two fleets to be strung out for many miles astern of their respective vans but the gap between the four rearmost French ships — the *Formidable, Thésée, Héros* and *Superbe* — and the nine or 10 vessels heading the British line was rapidly diminishing. Conflans had no real idea what was happening to his rearmost ships, and made no attempt to return to their support until it was too late.

At 2pm a French ship, perhaps the Vice-Admiral's *Tonnant,* fired two guns (perhaps a ranging salvo?) at the leading British ships as

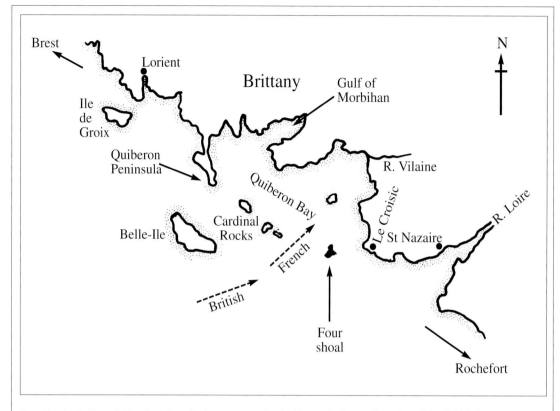

the first shots of the battle. It is uncertain whether it was at 2.30pm or as late as 2.45pm that the rear of the French and the British squadron began to engage. According to Hawke: 'We were then to the southward of Belle Isle and the French Admiral soon after led round the Cardinals.' The ships closest to the French at this stage 'in a close body, but not in any formed line' with the other British ships anything up to six miles astern, were *Torbay, Dorsetshire, Resolution, Warspite, Swiftsure, Revenge, Montague* and *Defiance*.

Shortly before 3pm the *Revenge* engaged the *Formidable,* 80, flagship of the French Rear Admiral, du Verger; and later she 'shot ahead of her' and fought for ¾hr with a 74-gun ship, apparently the *Magnifique,* which had lost her foretopmast and foreyard. About the same time the *Dorsetshire* and *Defiance* stood 'along the French line to windward, receiving the fire of every ship they passed, without making any return, intending to stop and engage the van of the enemy'. The other British leading vessels likewise stood on down the enemy's line, leaving the French laggards to be dealt with by the rest of Hawke's fleet.

Shortly after the action had begun a heavy rain-squall struck the opposing fleets. The

Above: Quiberon Bay c3pm. The British fleet pursues the French into Quiberon Bay — names shown include (direction of) Brest and Rochefort, L'Orient (now Lorient), Gulf of Morbihan, Rivers Vilaine and Loire, Ile de Groix, Quiberon Peninsula, Belle-Ile, Cardinal Rocks, Four shoal and St Nazaire. *Author*

Temple was forced to double reef her topsails reducing their area and her speed. The *Dorsetshire* and *Torbay* were forced over so far that water started flooding the lower deck through open gun ports and urgent measures were necessary to prevent capsizing: 'At this time we received so much water in at the lee ports, we were obliged to bring the ship up in the wind.' It was the same very heavy squall from the north that 'carried away the *Chichester's* foretopsail-yard and three of our ships ran foul of each other and carried away their jib-booms and spritsail yards' (the outer parts of their bowsprits). This accident only briefly delayed the three ships leading the pursuit, *Magnanime, Montague* and *Warspite*. On the *Magnanime's* getting clear she bore down on the *Formidable* and engaged her. She was shortly after joined by Sir John Bentley in the *Warspite,* and in half an hour they made a

Above: 'Admiral Hawke did bang/Monsieur Conflans' as a contemporary popular song put it. This engraving of Monamy Swaine's painting of Quiberon Bay shows (in the middle of the picture) Hawke's three-decker flagship *Royal George* at the moment when the *Superbe* foundered; her stern can be seen going down just behind the British ship's stern. Behind that still is the flagship of the French admiral Conflans, the *Soleil Royal*, which had been Hawke's target and which the *Superbe* had intervened to protect. In front of, and behind, the two flagships other British ships harry the fleeing French. *NMM neg no: 5639*

Below: Pocock's version of Quiberon Bay. Presumably this is meant to represent the two flagships firing at one another, but while *Royal George* (the nearest ship to the left) was a three-decker, the *Soleil Royal* was not, nor was any other French ship, and the ship shown flying the French admiral's flag certainly seems to be both a three-decker and rather larger than her opponent (which also was not the case). Admittedly the artist must have been painting this picture quite a few years after the event. *NMM ref: BHC0399*

dreadful havoc in the *Formidable,* whose fire began to slacken. The *Dorsetshire,* recovering from the squall, showed similar aggressiveness: she 'bore away and engaged five of the enemy's ships at different times and continued chasing the van ships when our rear ships came up'.

The *Formidable,* du Verger's flagship, took the chief brunt of this initial onslaught and fought stubbornly on as ship after ship came up to fire into her and then pass by. As one witness put it: 'Her starboard side was pierced like a cullender [colander] by the number of shot she received in the course of the action.' About 4pm the *Torbay,* came alongside her and gave her two broadsides, followed by *Resolution,* which continued to bombard her till her surrender. At 4.30pm she lost her foretopmast and fell away from the French line. Du Verger had been wounded and then had himself placed in a chair on the quarterdeck until he was killed. His brother (the flag-captain) succeeded to the command but was killed soon afterwards. The second captain also lost his life. Eventually, battered into a wreck, the *Formidable* surrendered to *Resolution.*

Having turned in round the Cardinals soon after 2.30pm, Conflans had heard the sound of distant gunfire but he had no clear idea of what was happening as he went well into the bay with his van followed by the centre. The squalls had increased the strength of the wind and that had made the British advance more rapid, and the shift in direction of the wind had not helped the French in maintaining their line formation, which was now in considerable disorder. *Magnanime,* closely followed by other British ships, came bursting into the bay mingled with the sternmost enemy ships who were showing them the safe passage in. A French eyewitness in one of the ships in the van wrote: 'The confusion was awful when the van tried to go about. Some could not manage to do so. We were in a sort of funnel, all on top of each other, with rocks on one side of us and ships on the other.'

Nearly 50 ships of the line were attempting to crowd into an anchorage which was surrounded by rocks, islets and shoals with poor visibility worsened by gunpowder smoke and the rapid onset of evening. No one had tried to fight a battle in conditions as bad as this before. Matters were made worse by another heavy squall; men were already being killed in numbers through cannon fire, now more would die because of the weather. The new French 74-gun ship *Thésée* had been fighting the *Torbay* and had her lower deck gunports open and guns run out (the heavier guns were on the lower decks; shutting lower deck gunports deprived you of the most powerful part of your broadside). The squall quickly laid on her beam ends (pushed her on her side) and she filled and sank with shocking speed, taking 600 men down with her. *Torbay* narrowly escaped a similar fate, but managed to hoist out all her boats and sent them to save as many as they could, but there were only 22 survivors. About the same time the *Magnanime* and the *Chatham* went after the *Héros,* 74, which had lost her fore and mizzen topmast and was now escaping southward. Swiftly overhauling her, the *Magnanime* came close to her stern and raked her. Soon after, as the *Chatham* approached, the *Héros* — which had 'lost every officer on board down to a midshipman, and had near 400 killed and wounded' surrendered. She anchored, but it was blowing too hard to get a prize-crew aboard in a boat.

Conflans' attempt to make a satisfactory defence in the anchorage had failed. He therefore tried to lead the fleet out to sea again. Accompanied by two other ships he made for the entrance. Several of the British ships were now trapped between two opponents. The *Swiftsure* 'received some damage from each of them, and by the last fire from the French admiral's ship had her tiller rope shot and her foretopsail-yard carried away in the slings, which occasioned her broaching-to, and she for some time lay muzzled, by which accident she was left out of further action, and being at the same time near the Island of Dumet. She wore and lay-to under a mizzen, the only sail she then had to set.' Meanwhile, the *Royal George* had got round the Cardinals shortly before 4pm and was making all the sail that she could bear in order to overhaul the French flagship, which was then steering for the entrance of the bay. In the fast-failing light and rising wind and sea Hawke ordered his ship to be laid alongside the *Soleil Royal.* The master (the warrant officer in charge of navigating the ship and the chief expert on sailing her) pointed out the dangers. There are various versions of what the admiral said in return, but the gist of it went down into legend. One version has him saying: 'You have done your duty in this remonstrance; now obey my orders, and lay me alongside the French admiral.' The French admiral seemed to be equally keen to engage his British counterpart. One eyewitness remarked that 'it was a glorious sight to behold the blue and white flags, both at the main topmast-head bearing down to each other'. The *Royal George* passed by the *Torbay,* at this stage still doing battle with the ill-fated *Thésée;* while on the other side the *Magnanime* was battering the *Héros.* 'At 35min after four we got up with four sail of the enemy ships who all wore and gave us their broadsides; we then began to engage. The two flagships were now approaching one another; and they fired two or three broadsides at each other. But after two or three exchanges other ships intervened, such was the confused nature of the fight owing to the tempestuous state of the weather, and the rival flags had no further contest. Several other French ships in succession had the honour of engaging the English Admiral as they passed; but the fifth ship fared not so well.' This was the *Superbe* which suddenly sank after *Royal George* had fired two broadsides at her. She is more likely to have been another victim of sudden flooding through open gunports than of the gunfire. The weather was too bad and the fighting too general for help to be given to the wretched survivors. 'The *Royal George's* gave a cheer, but it was a faint one; the honest sailors were touched at the miserable state of so many hundreds of poor creatures.' In a gallant gesture the *Intrépide,* which had been following the *Soleil Royal,* steered between the two flagships. Astern of the *Royal George,* Sir Charles Hardy in the *Union,* 90, with the *Mars*, *Hero* and several other ships, was pressing on to support the admiral.

Conflans' manoeuvring to avoid being raked by the *Royal George* meant that the *Soleil Royal* fell to leeward and, in trying to tack, collided with two of the ships following her, with the result that she was unable to get round the Four shoal. His plan to break out into the open sea had been frustrated and he had to turn back and anchor off Croisic.

It was now 5pm and nearly dark. The gale was still increasing and the wind coming round to the north again. This forced the French fleet to bear round. The rest of the British ships were pouring into the bay and the fighting spread. Seven French ships led by Villars de la Brosse in the *Glorieux,* manoeuvring between their enemy and the rocks, fell deeper and deeper into the depths of the bay, a cul-de-sac leading only towards the estuary of the River Vilaine. The ebb tide was now running out against the wind and causing a wicked sea to rise. At 5.30pm Hawke hauled down the signal for action, though sporadic fighting continued for another half hour in the gloom, with it becoming increasingly difficult to tell friend from foe and ships having narrow escapes

from going on to the rocks. 'Night was now come and being on a part of the coast of which we were totally ignorant, without a pilot, as was the greatest part of the squadron, and blowing hard on a lee shore, I made the signal to anchor, and came-to in 15-fathom...'

Like their admiral, most of the British fleet anchored between Dumet Island and the Cardinals. The signal to anchor by night at this time was two guns fired from the flagship, hardly one to be easily distinguished as the battle still spluttered on. Only those ships which happened to be near the Admiral noticed that he had anchored; the others made out to sea, or anchored wherever they found themselves. The *Temple* had to tack to avoid shoal water, and then did notice the signal to anchor. The *Magnanime* was close into shore and anchored as a sensible precaution. She signalled her prize, the *Héros,* to do the same, but still was unable to send a boat to board her. The shattered prize, deliberately or not, moved further away in the course of the night, and was seen aground the next morning.

Some British ships, repairing their damage, with pumps going and the sounding lead in constant use, crept carefully out to sea and anchored when clear of the land. For example, the *Swiftsure* had set her foresail as night fell and, 'having a windward tide, endeavoured to stand out to sea, making more sail as the damages she had received could be repaired'. The *Revenge, Dorsetshire* and *Defiance* also got safely out to sea in a similar way. About 10pm, however, while trying to rejoin the main body of the fleet, the *Resolution* ran on the Four shoal. Despite desperate attempts to save her, she struck twice again 'very hard' and was 'bulged' (ie bilged — her bottom was pierced and she would no longer float if she was got off). There was little anyone could do till morning, and both commanders were left, literally, in the dark about the state of their respective fleets. As Hawke put it: 'In the night we heard many guns fired, but, blowing hard, want of knowledge of the coast, and whether they were fired by a friend or enemy, prevented all means of relief.'

Bauffremont, the second-in-command of the French fleet, was warned by his pilot of the risks they were running in lying where they did surrounded by reefs and shoals. He decided that it made sense to break out to sea, and it seemed reasonable to expect that his commander, no longer in sight, would do the same. Several other French ships took the same decision and stood out of the bay, making for the shelter of the Basque Roads, southward along the coast, which they would reach the next day.

Morning dawned to show that Conflans was left with only eight ships. Hawke could see that *Resolution* was aground on the Four shoal, 'with all her masts gone and firing guns of distress'. Wind and weather prevented the *Royal George* coming to her assistance. Conflans' own *Soleil Royal* was found to be at anchor surrounded by British ships, so proceeded to cut her cables and run for the shore where she grounded to the westward of Croisic, on the Rouelle shoal. Hawke signalled *Essex* to slip her anchor and pursue but she, too, ran upon the Four shoal. Early in the afternoon she lost her fore and main masts, and despite the assistance of two frigates, also proved to be a total loss. 'Both she and the *Resolution* are irrecoverably lost, notwithstanding that we sent them all the assistance that the weather would permit.' Fortunately the gale moderated later in the day and both crews were saved.

Meanwhile Hawke attempted to attack the French ships off the mouth of the Vilaine, but was frustrated by the gale. The French ships found that the combination of spring tides and the onshore gale had raised the level of water over the shallow bar at the entrance to the river. By dint of throwing all of their guns and much other gear over the side they could lighten themselves enough to get over the bar into the river, where they were safe from British attack. However, this was at the cost of being stuck there until similar unusual meteorological conditions combined with a slackening of the inevitable British blockade to permit them to emerge.

The crew of the *Juste* had been busy all the night repairing shattered rigging and stopping leaks. They got under way for the mouth of the Loire, intending to go to St Nazaire, but came too close inshore and grounded on a falling tide. Attempts to save her failed, only 250 of the crew managing to get away in the boats as the ship broke up. The *Tonnant* and *Magnifique* joined the *Orient, Northumberland, Dauphin Royal, Solitaire* and *Bizarre* arrived in Aix Roads to find, much to their surprise, no sign of Conflans or the rest of the fleet.

For the British ships the 21st was a day of high winds and seas, with crews working to repair battle damage. The ships that had left the bay during the night rejoined their admiral. However, nothing more warlike could be done till the weather moderated, which it did on the next day. It was then that Hawke sent in three of his smaller and lighter draft ships, all of

Above: This wooden figure (presumably a stern carving, it is much too small for the figurehead of such a large vessel) was removed from the grounded and blazing wreck of the French flagship *Soleil Royal* by the British boats' crews sent to see if they could save her. They were too late to put out the fires started by her crew when they abandoned her, but took this as a souvenir instead. *NMM neg no: A217*

them from Duff's command, to destroy the grounded *Soleil Royal* and *Héros*. As *Portland, Chatham* and *Vengeance* approached, her own crew set the flagship on fire whilst *Héros* was fired by the British. Later the British would try to raise guns from the wrecks, and being fired on from shore, would bombard Croisic in retaliation.

By the time Hawke had managed to work up to the anchorage off the mouth of the Vilaine the two French ships which had still been outside the bar at daybreak had managed to get over it. Duff was sent in boats supported by the cutter *Hazard* to reconnoitre: 'All the 23rd we were occupied in reconnoitring the entrance of that river, which is very narrow, and only 12ft water on the bar at low water. We discovered 7 if not 8 line of battle ships, about half a mile within, quite light, and two large frigates moored across to defend the mouth of the river. Only the frigates appeared to have guns in. By evening I had twelve long boats fitted as fireships ready to attempt burning them under cover of the *Sapphire* and *Coventry*. But the weather being bad, and the wind contrary, obliged me to defer it till at least the latter should be favourable. If they can by any means be destroyed it shall be done.' It never was, and all but one of these trapped French ships were, eventually, to escape. Hawke then sent a detachment under Keppel to check on the French ships that had fled to Rochefort. Keppel would eventually return to report that they, like the ships in the Vilaine, had withdrawn beyond the reach of easy attack. Meanwhile Hawke, a widower, summed up the battle for a friend in an informal letter sent at the same time as his official dispatches:

'*Dear Sally,*
My express is just going away for England, and I have only time to tell you that we got up with the French off this place, and have beat and dispersed their fleet.

Below: Quiberon Bay: the end of the battle, showing where *Thesée* and *Superbe* foundered, *Juste* was wrecked and *Soleil Royal* and *Héros* were grounded and lost. *Resolution* and *Essex* were lost at Four shoal, the anchor symbols in the Bay indicate where the British fleet anchored overnight and the arrows indicate where the French ships escaped into the Loire and Vilaine and to Rochefort (Basque Roads). *Author*

We have burnt two of their ships of seventy-four and eighty-four guns; we sank two (one of 74 and another of 70 guns) and we have taken the *Formidable,* a ship of eighty guns. In the evening near dark, and blowing fresh and bad weather, some of them ran away clear out. Seven of them with two frigates anchored so near the shore, that we could not get at them; and the second day they flung everything overboard (for fear the weather should moderate, and that we should be able to get at them); and they got into a little harbour near the place where they were lying. There they must remain this winter at least, without anything in, and can be of no service to the French till we please to permit them. Two of our ships had the ill luck to run ashore; but these accidents can't be helped on such occasions; for it was next a-kin to a miracle that half our ships were not ashore in the pursuit of an enemy upon their own coast, which we were unacquainted with, besides its blowing strong and squally, and having no pilots. I thank God I am very well, though almost starved with cold. I hope to be allowed to go home soon, for I have had a long and tiresome service of it. Write to my children, the instant you receive this, and give my love and blessing to them. Make my compliments to all my neighbours, and believe me truly your sincere friend,

Edward Hawke'

British losses in the Battle of Quiberon Bay were the two ships wrecked on the Four and

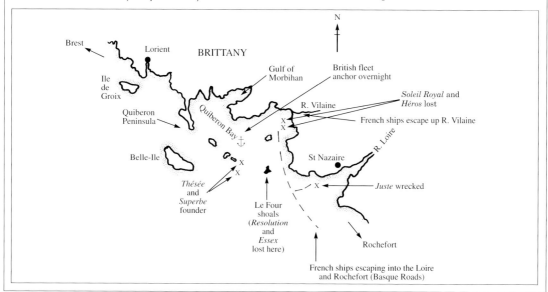

300–400 men; while their enemy had lost six ships, including the two flagships, the *Soleil Royal* and *Formidable*, and about 2,500 men, the great majority of whom were drowned. The loss bore heavily on Brittany, which had supplied the crews for the two ships which foundered. Only a small part of Conflans' fleet had been closely engaged. The division which got away to the Basque Roads, and then to Rochefort, had done very little fighting and had suffered very few casualties. The ships which escaped up the Vilaine had suffered even fewer casualties. However, one of these ships, the *Inflexible*, was lost as a result of entering that river, and the others were going to be out of action for well over a year. Eventually a young French officer would make his name by the combination of seamanlike skill, audacity and careful timing with which he got them away to sea. However, both these ships and their precious, jettisoned, guns (the French navy was always desperately short of cannon at this period — poor gun supply was to remain a major problem for that navy till nearly the end of the century) were taken away from the French war effort for the time being.

For the French side, the heroic stand made by Rear-Admiral Saint-André du Verger in the face of hopeless odds has redeemed an otherwise unsatisfactory story. To quote one (British) historian: 'Preoccupied above all else with the necessity of picking up the transports in the Morbihan, Conflans' one idea was to avoid a general action. At the crucial juncture, off Belle-Ile, he appears to have lost his head. First he stood towards the enemy; then he fled from them in such haste as to leave his rear unsupported; next he decided to take refuge in Quiberon Bay; and soon after he wanted to get out again. Admittedly the hand that Conflans had to play on the 20th was a poor one. Impossible to deny that he played it very badly. The conduct of Vice-Admiral the Chevalier de Bauffremont was no less deserving of censure. Bauffremont had been strictly enjoined not to lose sight of the flagship. Notwithstanding these orders, he had made off in the hours of

Below: D. Turner's view of prisoner-of-war hulks (many of them themselves captured) in the upper reaches of Portsmouth harbour is seen from near Portchester, looking at Portsmouth and its dockyard in the middle background, Gosport to the right, and in between these the entrance to Portsmouth Harbour and beyond it the Isle of Wight. Virtually all the hulks have been roofed over and various shacks and other structures built on them. During the Napoleonic Wars many foreign sailors, and soldiers too, languished in these unhealthy hulls for years. *NMM ref: BHC1925*

darkness without even informing the other ships under his command.' However, it is unfair to blame Conflans for the general French doctrine of the 'objective' to be achieved even at the expense of losing a battle (in this case getting the troop transports out of the Morbihan), nor is it realistic to hold him up to ridicule for not expecting the unprecedented dash made by the British fleet at his ships. He had no real reason to expect either Hawke's daring, even foolhardy decision, nor the extreme competence and audacity with which it was carried out. The British charge knocked the French commanders off balance and kept them there.

Hawke risked his entire fleet to achieve a smashing victory, as he put it: 'When I consider the season of the year, the hard gales on the day of action, a flying enemy, the shortness of the day, and the coast they were on, I can boldly affirm that all that could possibly be done has been done. As to the loss we have sustained, let it be placed to the account of the necessity I was under of running all risks to break this strong force of the enemy. Had we had but two hours more daylight the whole had been totally destroyed or taken; for we were almost up with their van when night overtook us.' The victory was as much over a seaman's natural fears and the elements as over the French. Hawke, writing to Anson, the First Lord of the Admiralty, made the point, seaman talking to seaman: 'Indeed, my Lord, had you been in the action, I am of opinion [sic] that you would have thought it a miracle that half our ships were not on shore, they were all so keen in the pursuit of the enemy, in a winter's day and hard squalls, upon their own coast, which we were all unacquainted with. The loss of our two ships was owing to their not having the *Neptune François* on board [a superb set of charts, which set a new high standard in hydrographic publishing], and they had neither of them anything to direct them what to do...'

As a footnote to the story of this battle we may note that divers have been working for some years on the remains of the grounded French flagship *Soleil Royal*. More recently the remains of one of the foundered vessels (believed to be the *Superbe*) have been found, buried deep in sand and mud. It would appear that the hull is mostly intact, but the task of recording, raising and preserving her and her contents would be of daunting cost and complexity, not dissimilar to the case of the *Mary Rose*, but in much deeper, more exposed and less accessible circumstances.

Above: Portrait of Augustus Keppel (1725–1786) by Reynolds. As a midshipman aboard *Centurion* on Anson's voyage round the world, Keppel lost most of his teeth and hair as a result of scurvy. His false teeth help to explain his close-mouthed expression. He was one of Anson's most brilliant protégés, and had a very successful career, including commanding a ship at Quiberon Bay, up to the time he was placed in command of the Channel Fleet when France entered the war against Britain in 1778. The drawn Battle of Ushant resulted in a quarrel between Keppel and his second-in-command, considerably exacerbated by politics and the considerable hostility to the war in parts of British society. In the court martial which followed Keppel sided with the Parliamentary opposition and resigned his command. He had a brief spell as First Lord in 1782–1783. *NMM ref: BHC2823*

British: 23 ships of the line
French: 21 ships of the line

Three-deckers 100-gun one/nil
British: *Royal George* (Flagship of Sir Edward Hawke, Captain Campbell) — **one**
French: no equivalent — **nil**

Three-deckers 90-gun three/nil
British: *Union* (Flag — Sir Charles Hardy, Captain J. Evans), *Duke* (Thomas Graves),
           Namur (M. Buckle) — **three**
French: no equivalent — **nil**

Two-deckers 80-gun nil/four
British: no equivalent — **nil**
French: *Soleil Royal* (taken — Flagship of Marshal de Conflans, Captain Bidé de Chésac), *Orient*
(Flag of Chevalier de Guébridant Budes, Captain Chevalier Nogérée de la Fillière, snr),
           Tonnant (Flag of Chevalier de Bauffremont, Captain Saint-Victoret), *Formidable*
           (taken — Flag of Saint-André du Verger, Captain Saint-André, snr — taken) — **four**

Two-deckers 74-gun seven/six
British: *Mars* (Commodore James Young), *Warspite* (Sir John Bentley), *Hercules* (W. Fortescue),
           Torbay (Hon Augustus Keppel), *Magnanime* (ex-French — Lord Viscount Howe),
           Resolution (lost — H. Speke), *Hero* (Hon G. Edgecumbe) — **seven**
French: *Glorieux* (Villars de la Brosse), *Robuste* (Fragnier de Vienne), *Intrépide* (Chasteloger),
           Thésée (lost — Kersaint de Coëtnempren), *Magnifique* (Bigot de' Morogues), *Héros*
           (lost — Vicomte de Sanzay) — **six**

Two-deckers 70-gun five/four
British: *Swiftsure* (Sir Thomas Stanhope), *Dorsetshire* (P. Denis), *Burford* (G. Gambier),
           Chichester (W. S. Willet), *Temple* (Hon W. Shirley) — **five**
French: *Dauphin Royal* (Chevalier d'Urturbie Fagosse), *Northumberland* (Belingant de
           Kerbabut), *Superbe* (lost — Montalais), *Juste* (lost — Saint Allouarn, snr) — **four**

Two-deckers 64-guns two/seven
British: *Revenge* (J. Storr), *Essex* (lost — Lucius O'Brien) — **two**
French: *Dragon* (Le Vassor de la Touche), *Solitaire* (Vicomte de Langle), *Éveillé* (La Prevalais de
           la Roche), *Brilliant* (Keremar de Boischateau), *Inflexible* (lost — Tancrède, Chevalier de
           Caumont)), *Sphinx* (de Goyon, Chevalier de Coutance La Selle), *Bizarre* (Prince de
           Montbazon, Chevalier de Rohan) — **seven**

Two-deckers 60-gun five/nil
British: *Kingston* (Thomas Shirley), *Intrepid* (J. Maplesden), *Montague* (Joseph Rowley),
           Dunkirk (R. Digby), *Defiance* (P. Baird) — **five**
French: no equivalent — **nil**

Not in the line of battle
British: four x 50-gun small two-deckers, one x 36, two x 32 and two x 28-gun frigates
French: five x frigates or corvettes

The British had 23 of the line, the French 21, of which the former lost two and the latter seven (one of which was captured and so counts as a British gain). The total of guns carried by ships of the line was 1,666 against 1,532. In men the British would have had some 13,000 in the line of battle as against about 700 less on the French side. The British loss was 300 to 400 men against some 2,500 to the French.

The single 100-gun and three 90-gun three-deckers on the British side gave them an advantage in fighting power because of the extra height and protection of the additional deck which more than negated the French edge in the largest type of two-deckers. However, it was the British who had the smallest and weakest of the ships of the line in their five 60s — a type which was approaching obsolescence by this stage.

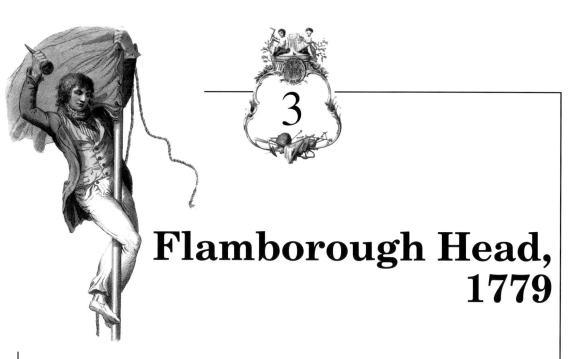

Flamborough Head, 1779

ehind the struggles of the battlefleets lay another, more basic, layer of naval warfare. This was the business of protecting your own trade and attacking that of the enemy. Trade in this context means merchant ships.

The main means of trade protection, tried and tested from the days of the German Hanse confederation in the late Middle Ages, was convoy. A group of merchant ships intended for the same destination would be assembled and provided with an escort. In 18th century usage, somewhat confusingly, 'convoy' could mean the escort as such, rather than the ships that were escorted. Convoys in the age of sail could be enormous. The Austro-German politician Metternich, when once asked what the most beautiful thing he had ever seen was, replied that when he was in exile during the Napoleonic Wars in the Isle of Wight, he had seen a British convoy escorted by ships of the Royal Navy, some 200 ships in all, setting sail simultaneously.

The destruction or capture of an entire convoy would be a major blow against any state, particularly those like Britain and the Netherlands whose economic strength relied so much on their maritime trade. It was not something that happened very often, and it usually required a considerable force, usually a substantial fleet, to produce this result. Most raiding warfare was done by individual raiders snapping up merchantmen sailing independently or separated from convoys. Some of this work was done by warships; much of it by privateers. The central figure of this chapter was and is often described as one of the latter, though in fact he was a commissioned naval officer, so it may be as well to be clear what a privateer was.

Attacking enemy merchant ships could be a profitable business. This was why it was the province of private war, of the privateers who raided enemy commerce for profit. They were not pirates. Pirates were totally private-enterprise sea-robbers, outlaws with no government support or justification — enemies of human-kind, as the old formula had it. A privateer was not a pirate, though some might behave like pirates. There could be a very grey area here between outright crime and legal warlike proceedings, particularly in regions like the West Indies. A privateer had a piece of paper from a government to justify his activities, though he was still working for private profit. That piece of paper could either be a 'letter of reprisal' or a 'letter of marque'. Usually in our period it would be the latter. The Napoleonic War was the last major European war in which privateering was a recognised means of waging war. All European nations practised it to a greater or lesser degree, and a specialised local variant of it was a way of life for many ports in North Africa, as we shall see in a later chapter. The French, fighting both the Dutch and the British, had

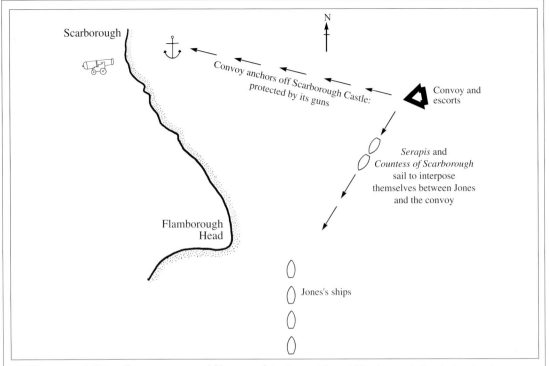

Scarborough

N

Convoy anchors off Scarborough Castle: protected by its guns

Convoy and escorts

Serapis and
Countess of Scarborough
sail to interpose
themselves between Jones
and the convoy

Flamborough
Head

Jones's ships

made a speciality of commerce raiding, and many of their greatest heroes of the age of sail (Jean Bart and Robert Surcouf being the best known) were raiders and privateers rather than regular naval officers. British and Dutch heroes of this kind (eg Francis Drake and Piet Heijn) come from a somewhat earlier period when both were attacking Spanish maritime ascendancy. However, both nations continued to produce plenty of less well publicised privateers in our period. Prior to the 1770s the British colonists in North America had become very effective privateers, and when the struggle for independence began, the decentralised, private-enterprise, self-financing struggle of the privateers was an obvious and inevitable way the colonists would fight the mother-country. Fighting for a rebellion, commissioned by a government that was not recognised, and extremely successful as a raider, it is not surprising that John Paul Jones was called a 'privateer' by his British enemies, European admirers and all too many modern historians alike. In fact he was a commissioned naval officer, one of the first to serve the new country.

John Paul (he added the Jones to his name when he moved to the American colonies) was born in Scotland and began his career as a merchant seaman sailing from British ports. He seems to have been a quarrelsome, prickly,

Above: Map of Flamborough Head showing the convoy and escorts appearing from the Baltic off Flamborough Head where John Paul Jones' force awaited them. On seeing them the two British escorts, *Serapis* and *Countess of Scarborough,* sailed to interpose themselves between Jones and the convoy whilst the latter anchored off Scarborough under the guns of that town's castle. *Author*

violent individual, very ambitious and with something of a chip on his shoulder. He was also a very competent seaman, and had soon risen to being master (ie captain). He was driven into removing himself to the North American colonies because of a quarrel in which he ran a subordinate through with a sword.

His brother was already established there as a merchant, and he was a useful contact for John Paul when war came and the infant United States began to consider setting up a navy, and providing that navy with officers. Jones established himself as an extremely competent commander and an excellent raider on a cruise in the *Providence* in 1776 and then as a bonny fighter into the bargain when he commanded the 18-gun sloop *Ranger* on a cruise in European waters in 1778 and defeated a vessel of the Royal Navy, the

Above: Bust of John Paul Jones after Houdon. This must be by far the best portrait of the American captain, and gives some impression of the force and character of the man. It also has a strong resemblance to the features of the body dug out of a French cemetery late in the 19th century (a difficult feat, as the cemetery had been built over and a tunnel had to be driven under a building to find the grave) and thought (probably rightly) to be Jones. The body is now buried in a crypt under the US Naval Academy's chapel at Annapolis in a wonderfully elaborate tomb.
NMM neg no: B3536

purchased sloop (ie converted merchantman) *Drake* of 16 guns, an inferior vessel to his own, but still a regular, commissioned warship of the Royal Navy. Benjamin Franklin, the American representative in France, took Jones under his patronage and organised him the command of a mixed Franco-American raiding squadron of seven ships. This sailed from the port of Lorient in France under the American flag with Jones as commodore in August 1779 (an earlier sailing had been thwarted by a collision between the flagship and the *Alliance*). Two French privateers soon separated from the squadron, as did the cutter

Cerf. This left Jones with his flagship, *Bonhomme Richard* (named in honour of Franklin and converted from the French indiaman *Duc de Duras*), the 36-gun American frigate *Alliance* commanded by a Frenchman Pierre Landais, who seems to have been somewhat unstable, the French 32- or 30-gun frigate *Pallas*, a converted merchantman, and the French brig *Vengeance* of 14 or 12 guns, also a converted merchantman.

The flagship was a curious ship and deserves a closer look if we are to understand her role in the forthcoming battle. The *Duc de Duras* was the result of an experimental policy of building ships for the French East India Company which were intended to be converted to ships of the line in time of war. The result was a somewhat unfortunate hybrid, not capacious enough to be a good merchantman, and over-expensive for this role, whilst producing a very inferior version of a 64-gun ship of the line in wartime. She was, however, available, and would provide the ship of force which would enable Jones' squadron to overpower the smaller ships the British would be using as convoy escorts. Unfortunately what were not available were the guns needed to arm her adequately. This is scarcely surprising. The French cannon founding industry was inadequate for the job of arming the rapidly-growing French Navy, still less of providing extra for a foreigner. In the end Jones had a job lot of varied guns, mostly old. The only armament on the lower (gun) deck were six old 18-pounders in the three aftermost gunports on each side. They seem to have been placed there because the ship needed extra weight in the stern to achieve a proper trim ('sit' in the water) so that she would sail and steer reasonably well. Without this weight right aft she 'trimmed by the head' (the bow was lower in the water) which made her 'gripe' (become difficult to steer). The main part of the gun armament was the row of 28 12-pounders on the upper deck. There were probably six eight-pounders on the quarterdeck, whilst a further two which had earlier been positioned on the forecastle seem to have been removed by the time she went on the raiding cruise. This gave her a total of 40 guns. A feature which was going to be of great, probably crucial, importance in her battle was that she had particularly large tops. She carried swivels, probably the miniature mortars known as 'coehorns' and plenty of small arms to fire from these tops.

Having sailed round the north of Scotland and captured a number of independently-

Above: Lieutenant John Crispo (1773–1841), with his command the hired cutter *Telemachus* in 1796, was one of the junior officers who never rose to high rank, but helped keep the navy going. During wartime numbers of merchantmen were hired to serve as minor or auxiliary warships — they usually kept their civilian crews, but were commanded by naval officers, like this one. *NMM ref: BHC2637*

sailing merchantmen, the squadron was off Flamborough Head by 23 September. There it was right in the path of the return convoy from the Baltic escorted by two British warships.

The Baltic was the main source of 'naval stores' for the navies and merchant marines of Western Europe, Britain included. Tall, straight, evergreen trees for masts and spars, the raw materials for ropes and sails, 'Stockholm tar' (which came mostly from Finland), which was the main protective coating used aboard ship; all these came principally from around the shores of the Baltic. The Baltic was, therefore, the vital source of strategic raw materials which made it an area of concern to the great powers of the day; not unlike the Persian Gulf is today. Equally the loss of the materials carried in a convoy from the Baltic would represent a major defeat to Britain, depriving her of the materials to build or repair both war and merchantships, as well as causing financial damage and giving a severe blow to morale, particularly if it happened within sight of the British coast.

Conspicuous headlands make ideal landfalls for ships which have to steer a course across oceans or seas, and Flamborough Head is the obvious point to steer for when sailing across

from the exit to the Baltic to Britain. Such landfalls are also obvious places for the raider to lurk in ambush, so his prey comes steering straight for him. There is no need to search the trackless wastes of the ocean for victims in these circumstances. So the 41 ships of the convoy returning from the Baltic appeared off the Head on that September morning. The escort consisted of two ships. One was a hired merchant ship of 20 guns called the *Countess of Scarborough*. Hired ships were not regular warships, but a convenient supplement to the Royal Navy in wartime. They were merchantmen which usually kept their crews, but were given a naval officer in command, and might have their original armament supplemented during the months they were hired for the Admiralty. They were useful for shepherding a convoy and usually adequate for

Above: A print, taken from a picture by Paton, and published in Augsburg, showing the Flamborough Head action, with *Serapis* and *Bonhomme Richard* slogging it out, with Landais' *Alliance* making her erratic contribution, and the *Countess of Scarborough* fighting her own gallant battle in the background. The place of publication of this print goes to show the great and widespread interest in this battle. *NMM neg no: X1935*

beating off a privateer (usually not keen on hard knocks and expensive damage on a voyage which had more to do with profit than with glory). They were not, however, considered the equal of even a small regular man-of-war. This sort of opposition would have to be dealt with by the other escort. This was a brand-new (launched that year) 44-gun small two-decker of the Fifth Rate, the *Serapis* commanded by Captain Pearson.

There are a number of misconceptions about the *Serapis* which appear in most accounts of this battle. She is usually described as a frigate, which is incorrect, except in so far as many naval officers used the term very loosely to describe any ship from 50 guns down to a sloop as a 'frigate'. By this time the true frigate was in service, a ship with a single continuous deck of guns above an unarmed 'tween deck'

and with guns also on quarterdeck and (usually) forecastle. This true frigate was a very seaworthy, fast sailing design, the best all-round cruising warship. Thanks to the tween deck the guns were carried high and were comparatively easy to work in bad weather. *Serapis* was one of the last of an earlier type of cruising warship, rapidly being rendered obsolete by the growth in size of the 'true' frigates, and soon to be replaced in active roles by the new 18-pounder armed 36- and 38-gun ships. The old '44s' of her type, small two-deckers, were short, slow, unsatisfactory fighting ships, unable to fight their lower deck guns in bad weather. However, they were proper warships. *Serapis* is sometimes described in terms better fitted to a 'crack' frigate, which she was not. She was a recently-commissioned ship with a relatively raw crew, assembled at a time when the rapid expansion of the Royal Navy to cope with the crisis of fighting with the two next biggest navies in Europe combined was causing great strains and difficulties in obtaining adequate numbers of men of any kind, still less of trained seamen. That having been said, there is also no sign that her crew was of bad quality or her captain other than competent. She was simply a rather run-of-the-mill vessel with a crew of average

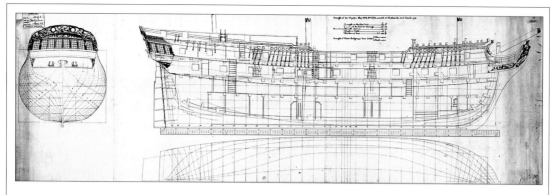

quality. Her armament comprised 20 18-pounders on the lower deck and, probably, 22 short 12-pounders rather than the nine-pounders she was designed for. Two six-pounders were carried on the forecastle.

The British escorts were warned that Jones' squadron was in the path of the convoy, so when Pearson saw its sails he sent his charges to take shelter under the guns of the shore batteries at Scarborough, whilst he stood towards the enemy. As a result of this action the convoy did not lose a ship, thus thwarting Jones' main intention. He attempted to form a line of battle with his ships, but seems to have had little collaboration from his captains. It is, however, worth remembering that he had a squadron of four ships at his disposal against the British two, and though the brunt of the battle against the *Serapis* was borne by his flagship, this really cannot be considered as a single-ship action in the same way as, for example, the *Constitution's* fight with the *Java*, or the *Shannon's* with the *Chesapeake* were. However, a comparison of the ships is still worth making, and shows that the British ship was slightly smaller (879 tons against 900+ tons, distinctly less well manned (264 men against 347), but rather more heavily armed (a broadside of 328lb against 246lb).

Commander Piercy in the *Countess of Scarborough* fought a fine two-hour battle against the *Pallas*, with Landais in the *Alliance* making some erratic contributions to the defeat of the smaller and less powerful British ship which did not surrender until 9.15pm. It is not entirely clear what the *Vengeance* was doing, but she seems to have made no particular contribution to any stage of the fight.

Meanwhile *Bonhomme Richard* and *Serapis* had opened fire on one another at 7.20pm. On her second broadside the American ship suffered a bad blow when one (often said to be two, but one seems more likely, in any case the

Above This attractive 'as built' plan of the 44-gun ship *Dolphin*, launched in 1781 was 'taken off' her hull whilst she was completing, and can therefore be taken as being reasonably accurate. It is included here because she was a sister of the *Serapis*, of the same class (*Roebuck* class) and built to the same plans. This, therefore, gives an excellent idea of what Pearson's ship looked like, though it is possible that *Serapis* had somewhat deeper stern windows and quarter galleries, making her look more like a ship of the line and less like a frigate. *NMM neg no: ADM 1693*

Above right: Flamborough Head, 1779 — a Perrot engraving. This purports to show the *Serapis* and *Countess of Scarborough* bearing down to engage the Franco-American squadron, with the Baltic convoy in the background. It is not likely to bear much relationship to what actually happened — for a start the *Serapis* is portrayed as a frigate rather than the small two-decker she actually was. This picture probably relied a good deal more on the artist's imagination than on any serious research or accurate information. *NMM neg no: 8820*

Right: The Flamborough Head action as depicted by Dodd, lit by the moon, flames and flashes of gunfire. This British artist probably had a much better idea what a Royal Navy 44 looked like than the French ships she was fighting, which probably explains why we can see the full length of the hull of the *Serapis* unobscured by gun smoke or other ships. Landais' *Alliance* is crossing her stern and raking her. Behind *Bonhomme Richard's* stern is the unequal battle between the *Pallas* and the hired ship *Countess of Scarborough*. *NMM neg no: 9790*

result was the same) of her 18-pounders blew up, killing and maiming the men in her lower battery and causing its abandonment. Shortly afterwards the *Bonhomme Richard* moved ahead, and Pearson seized the opportunity to cross her stern and rake her with three broadsides. He then came up alongside the American ship, fired another broadside and then turned to cross Jones' bow and rake him

from that end. However, the dying wind let him down and Jones then attempted to turn to rake his stern. Instead the American ship's bowsprit caught in the *Serapis's* shrouds. An attempt to board by the *Bonhomme Richard's* crew failed, and the two ships drifted apart again. More puffs of wind caused the ships to come together again, this time with Jones trying to cross Pearson's bow. Instead the British ship's bowsprit caught in the American's rigging, and Jones himself lashed it to his mizzen mast. The ships then swung together pointing in opposite directions, bow to stern, and though the *Serapis's* jib-boom had broken, the American crew had managed to get grappling lines across and lash the ships side to side.

For some time a situation of virtual stand-off had been developing. The British ship's 18-pounders on the lower deck, with no competition and crews protected by the deck over their heads, was steadily battering the hull of the *Bonhomme Richard*, smashing the sides in, and slowly reducing her to a sinking condition. The American's upper deck battery of 12-pounders had also suffered dreadfully. However, the battle was not going all the British ship's way. Jones had instructed his men in the tops, including an invaluable contingent of Irish soldiers from the French army, serving as marines, to concentrate on suppressing the fire from the British ship's tops before anything else. This they had successfully done, and were now shooting anyone who moved on the upper decks of the *Serapis*. This meant that only her upper deck guns under the quarterdeck and the forecastle could be kept in action. At the same time *Bonhomme Richard* was being restricted to her quarterdeck eight-pounders. Both ships caught fire and had to divert attention to trying to put the flames out. It was fast becoming a contest of endurance and Jones was losing because his ship had begun, very slowly, to sink under him.

By this time it was past 9pm and the errant *Alliance* came up and started raking fire. It appears that some of her shot arrived aboard her consort and caused casualties. However, her presence can hardly have encouraged Pearson, and certainly also caused him damage and loss.

Meanwhile the American ship's carpenter had found out she was sinking and reported this to the gunner. Both men, who were wounded, failed to locate the captain, and thinking they were the senior survivors tried to surrender the ship. Jones found them at it

and chased them. The carpenter escaped, but Jones tried to shoot the gunner. Perhaps fortunately his pistols were unloaded, but he flung one of them hard enough to knock out the unfortunate man. At this stage a confused Pearson hailed to ask whether he had surrendered. There is argument about

Above: Little provision was made for support of the seamen who fought so well for Britain in this period once they were paid off. A few were lucky enough to become Greenwich pensioners, given clothing, food, pay and accommodation for their old age in the magnificent buildings of the 'Royal Naval Hospital' at Greenwich. More recently these buildings, across the road from the National Maritime Museum, have been used as the Royal Naval College, but now (1995) their future is uncertain. This picture by F. Cruickshank shows one early 19th century Greenwich pensioner, John Lovell. *NMM neg no: 2723*

the reply, but it seems likely that 'I have not yet begun to fight' is a later embroidery. Certainly the alternative of 'No, I'll sink, but I'm dammed if I'll strike' sounds more likely and is better attested. The battle started all over again, but the stalemate continued, a British attempt at boarding being beaten back by Jones at the head of a party of his men.

The prisoners from British merchantmen captured earlier in the cruise were now released from their rapidly-flooding quarters, and pressed into operating the pumps. One of them managed to get away, crossed from one ship to the other and, finding Pearson, told him that he had only to endure a little longer and his opponent would sink. However, this was the stage that the final, and decisive, blow was struck. A seaman, apparently a Scot, named William Hamilton, in the main top of the *Bonhomme Richard* crawled out along the main yard and found himself in the ideal position to drop one of the hand grenades he was carrying down the partly-open main hatch of the *Serapis*. Down it dropped, on to the lower deck, where it exploded and set off a number of cartridges which were lying there. Perhaps 50 men were either killed or badly burned by the resulting explosion. The grenades and bullets continued to hail down; the lower deck guns were silenced, the convoy had escaped, the mainmast was shot through and about to fall (the *Bonhomme Richard's* eight-pounders had been concentrating on this for some time) and the *Alliance* seemed to be coming up to attack again. It was this that persuaded Pearson to ask for quarter to end the bloodshed at 10.30pm after three hours of desperate fighting.

The casualty list was appropriate to such a hard battle. Out of 347 men the *Bonhomme Richard* probably had about 49 killed and 67 wounded, whilst her opponent lost 54 and 75 respectively. The *Countess of Scarborough* had 24 killed or wounded out of a crew of 150, but it is not known what casualties, if any, the other ships of the Franco-American squadron suffered.

Both ships were fairly shattered, but whilst the British ship's hull was reasonably sound, the American's was not. She finally sank early on the morning of the 25th. Meanwhile Jones had transferred his command and his men to the *Serapis*. On her arrival in France she was sold to the French navy. She was still in that service when she was wrecked, some two years later, off Madagascar.

Pearson, who had fought a long and bloody battle against the odds and saved his convoy (his main duty) was knighted despite losing his ship. This seems fair in the circumstances. Jones, however, who had, by sheer force of character, turned probable defeat into victory, was never employed by the US Navy again. He was a fine fighting captain, but there are signs that there were flaws in his character (quite possibly the defects of his qualities) and he certainly does not seem to have made himself popular with any of his employers. It would certainly be interesting to know more about why his squadron did not collaborate as well as it should have done. He certainly should have been able to overwhelm and defeat the British escorts both faster and more easily than actually happened. Jones died a forgotten man, a failure and a pauper, and it would be a long time before he would be revered as the founding father of the US Naval tradition; but if any one person won a battle by personality and refusal to give in, it was he.

Right: 'I have not yet begun to fight': a splendidly heroic, if slightly piratical view of John Paul Jones by Notte.
NMM neg no: A3325

Left: Samuel Hood (1724–1816), later Lord Hood, as Rear-Admiral; portrait by Lawrence showing his appearance at the time of the Frigate Bay action. Second-in-command to Rodney in the West Indies, and to Graves at the Battle of the Chesapeake, he was a great one for seeing what should have been done, and saying it loudly, notably so at the victory of the Saintes which he thought could have been much more vigorously followed up, a view that has coloured most historians' opinions ever since. In 1793 he was in command of the Mediterranean Fleet when Toulon was handed over to him, but he had insufficient military resources to hold it against the young Napoleon's guns. *NMM neg no: 2142*

Below: Map of St Kitts showing the two islands of St Kitts and Nevis; the shallows, the line at which the sea bed falls away; Brimstone Hill fort and the town of Basse Terre. Stage (1) represents the French fleet moored off Basse Terre; stage (2) shows Hood coming from Antigua, rounding the south end of Nevis, and the French fleet sailing from off Basse Terre to meet him; and stage (3) shows the British fleet skirting Nevis and heading for the anchorage with the French fleet slanting down on it.
Author

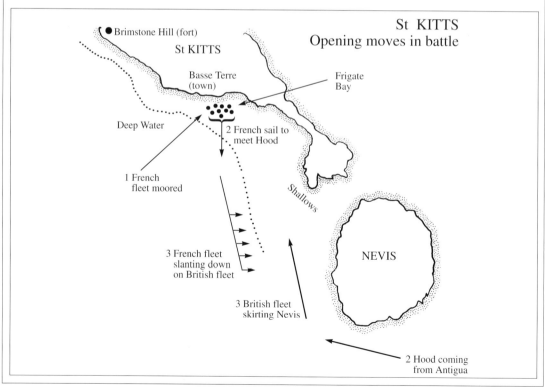

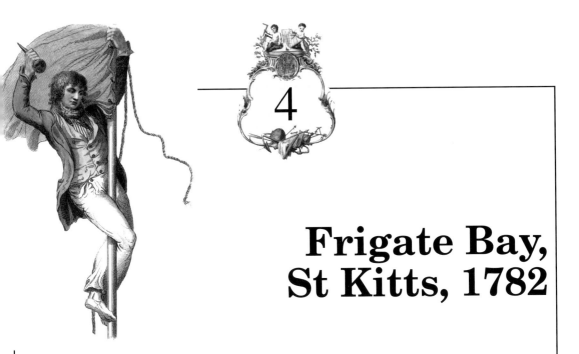

Frigate Bay, St Kitts, 1782

Eighteenth-century warfare could be seen, at a certain distance, as a very formalised, even ritualised business. The close-to reality was broken and battered bodies, smashed ships and a much greater degree of muddle, confusion and chaos than the tactical textbooks ever allowed for. Neat little arrows on the map, diagrams with little ship shapes, conceal a less organised, more happenstance, more human picture. However, there are occasional battles which can serve as textbook models of how an idealised battle might be fought. The battle fought in the West Indies in late January 1782 is a fine example of the kind. It also shows how a highly competent admiral with a well-trained fleet could use the tactics of fighting in line to worst a larger enemy fleet. Confusingly the battle has at least three titles — being known variously as the Battle of St Kitts, or of Frigate Bay, or as the Hood and de Grasse action.

A further source of confusion is that there is more than one Hood who is prominent in British naval history in this period, and two were on the same ship in this action. There is the Samuel Hood who fought this battle, who was Graves' second-in-command at the Chesapeake and Rodney's at the Saintes. He became the Lord Hood who was First Sea Lord at the outbreak of the French Revolution and then commanded the British Mediterranean fleet when it was invited to occupy Toulon by French Royalists. His younger brother

Alexander, later Lord Bridport, made a somewhat unsatisfactory commander of the Channel Fleet later in the French Revolutionary War. A pair of brothers, cousins of the two older Hoods, were also named Samuel and Alexander and served with distinction as captains in that war. We shall meet Samuel at the Battle of the Nile, where he commanded the *Zealous*, and he later became an admiral. His brother was killed in action the same year as the Nile (1798), but was already a captain in 1782, and was serving his cousin as the captain of his flagship, *Barfleur*, in the battle about to be described.

Our Samuel Hood was a somewhat contentious personality — pulled out of an administrative dockyard job to take up an active command. He has been described as very much a historian's admiral, leaving clear, articulate, written accounts on how he could always have done things better. For better or worse the conventional views of both the Chesapeake and of the Saintes are considerably coloured by Hood's account of what happened, and what might have happened. However, in the battle we are about to look at, Hood was in command and had nobody to blame or to sneer at if things did not go quite as he thought they ought.

Hood had been left in command of the British fleet in the West Indies by Admiral Rodney, who had temporarily returned to Britain for health reasons. He had 22 ships of the line, plus nine frigates at Antigua. The larger French fleet under de Grasse (24 ships of the line with another four expected from Martinique) was escorting a considerable force of troops in transports. The original French intention had been to invade the island of Barbados, but this was twice thwarted by contrary winds. In the end they made the best of a bad job by choosing to invade St Kitts instead. On 11 January they appeared off the island. The usual events of the invasion of a West Indian island at this time began to unroll. The small British garrison retired behind the fortifications of Brimstone Hill, the local inhabitants immediately declared their neutrality, and the French ships moored in Basse Terre Roads. The French general landed his men and began a siege of the garrison, which had already sent a message to Hood to warn him of the approach of the French.

Hood was certainly a thinking admiral, and he seems not only to have made a series of contingency plans, but also to have informed his captains of them. Certainly their actions in the next few days appear to indicate a well-trained and well-briefed team, used to working together. Initiative, mutual support and an appreciation of what their admiral wanted them to do with the minimum of signalling seems to have been a characteristic of the captains of this fleet, as it had been for Hawke's, and was to be for Nelson's.

St Kitts is separated from the neighbouring island of Nevis by a narrow channel, impassable to larger ships — and so the approach from Antigua is round the southern tip of Nevis (in French hands since 20 January). Even with this diversion the distance from Antigua to the anchorage where the French fleet was is no more than 60 miles. Hood sailed from Antigua late in the afternoon of 23 January, intending to arrive off the anchorage at daybreak the next morning, finding the French moored in no sort of formation and unprepared for an attack. He could then concentrate on a part of that fleet. This was an excellent plan but it was thwarted by the officer of the watch of the frigate *Nymphe*, who hove to that night in the path of the leading 74, *Alfred*, which was damaged in the consequent collision. Repairs were needed, and the British fleet did not round the point of Nevis until about 1pm.

De Grasse, not realising that Hood had an offensive purpose, seems to have feared that Hood was trying to put his smaller and weaker fleet (the French had, on average, bigger and more powerful vessels as well as more of them)

between the French fleet and the besieging army, though why he should put himself in such a dangerous position is not at all obvious. Perhaps this is just another example of the French doctrine of the overriding importance of the mission colouring their reactions. In any event the French admiral decided to take his fleet to sea, partly because he was expecting four ships of the line from Martinique, and he did not want Hood to get between him and his reinforcements. One of these ships did actually join him that day. The French fleet were out of the harbour and moving towards the British by sunset. Hood then turned to the southwards, apparently in flight, actually to lure de Grasse further away from the anchorage. The British tacked several times during the night to maintain their position to windward of the French, a position which meant that they retained the initiative.

Hood was now considering the possibility of moving into the anchorage that the French had left, and mooring in a defensible position. The French had been moored in no particular order off the town of Basse Terre. Hood was looking at the further, southern end of the bay, where the anchorage formed a ledge, which then dropped to very deep water. If a line of ships were anchored on the edge of this drop it would be difficult to anchor close to them, making a sustained attack on the line very hard to carry out.

The British fleet consisted mainly of 74s, 13 of them. The large Spanish prize *Princesa*, though rated as a 70-gun ship, was effectively another one of these larger two-deckers. It is significant that she wore the flag of the second-in-command, though presumably as much for her spaciousness as for her fighting power, rather than the second three-decker on the British side. The heaviest British ships were the two 98-gun three-deckers. Neither were in the same league as the French 110/112-gun *Ville de Paris*, a ship that marked the return of that navy to building three-deckers after a generation of relying on very large two-deckers (80s) as their largest ships. The remainder of the British line was formed from the seven 64-gun ships.

At dawn on 25 January both fleets were to the west of Nevis, with the French some miles downwind. It was at this time (about 5.30am) that Hood signalled his fleet to form line of battle on the starboard tack. The ships were to be a cable (600ft, or approximately three ships' lengths) apart. With these intervals, it will be seen that each fleet was spread out across several miles of sea. Even with this well-trained fleet it was not until 10am that the line was properly formed, with all the ships laid hove-to (stopped) in their correct positions in it. At 10.45am the line got under way under fighting sail, the triangular foresails and the topsails only. About an hour later the admiral prepared for the next stage in his plan by signalling his ships to prepare to anchor with lines (springs) attached to the cables so the ships could be swung whilst moored to direct their broadsides on to an approaching enemy. The French had been steering south on the starboard tack, but when the British got under way they came about on the other tack and then came slanting in towards the weaker fleet.

By noon the British were sailing along the coast of Nevis. They were so close that one of the frigates, sailing on the inside of the line, went aground and was wrecked (this was the 28-gun *Solebay*). The French were getting closer, but, because of the direction they were steering, falling behind. Their flagship, the huge *Ville de Paris,* was the first to get into range, and opened fire at the British rear. On de Grasse's left his leading ships were soon able to shoot at Hood's flagship, *Barfleur,* and the ships immediately behind. The danger here was that the last few ships in the British

line would be cut off unless they kept very close together, whilst they brushed across the front of the advancing French. If they did not do so the French could break through the line, 'double' them (attack on either side) and destroy them in detail; in other words they might share the fate of the French rear at Quiberon Bay. Hood had taken an enormous risk in this dash across the front of the French but resisted the temptation to turn back to help, which might well have proved disastrous. Instead he signalled his line to put on more sail to close the anchorage more quickly. He must have spent some anxious moments wondering whether his gamble

Below: A bird's-eye view of the action on 25 February 1782 at the stage when Hood has outmanoeuvred the French fleet (the one in the foreground in considerable disorder), got between it and its previous anchorage at St Kitts (the bay in the left background — the island in the centre background is Nevis), and is now filing past his opponent with both sides exchanging broadsides. The leading British ships, having passed the head of the French column, are peeling off towards the anchorage where they will anchor in a tight line; see the next picture, which is in the same series of prints. *NMM neg no: 1729*

Above: A print, probably made from an eye-witness sketch, showing a bird's-eye view of de Grasse's fleet unsuccessfully cannonading Hood's anchored line at Frigate Bay on 26 February 1782 after the English admiral had successfully lured the French out of the anchorage and then slipped in himself. The 'St Christopher's' in the caption is another version of the name 'St Kitts' — Kitt or Kit being an old-fashioned abbreviation for Christopher.
NMM neg no: 1728

would come off, but his captains did not let him down. This was all happening at about 2.30pm, and an hour later the leading ships began to turn and anchor one by one, head to stern, in a line going out in a westerly direction from the southern end of the anchorage. This was done under the cover of the centre and rear of the British fleet, which were now under heavy fire from the rapidly-approaching French, but replying in kind.

The crisis of this stage of the battle was now reached. The slow-sailing *Prudent*, third from last in the British line, was dropping astern. The French admiral was steering for this gap to cut off the last three British ships. He was prevented from doing so by the prompt action of William Cornwallis (later the most distinguished admiral commanding the blockade of Brest at the time of Trafalgar) in the *Canada*, next ahead of the *Prudent* who backed his sails and dropped back to fill the gap, straight into the path of the advancing French. The *Resolution* and *Bedford*, the ships immediately ahead of him in line, followed suit. This action was taken just barely in time. An officer in one of the ships that had already anchored said that he saw the bowsprit of the *Ville de Paris* appearing inside the British line,

but then disappearing again as she was forced to turn parallel to that line. The line of anchored ships was almost pointing in the opposite direction to the one they had come in, so they were in position to cover the last few ships of the British line as they came down to anchor, exchanging broadsides with the leading ships of the French line, and leading the French line, most of whom were too far astern to fire at them across the broadsides of their companions. The rear ships of the British line were anchoring in very deep water, on the edge of the shelf of the anchorage where it fell away. The *Canada* had to run out two cables end-to-end, and found herself anchored in 150 fathoms (900ft) of water. The depth of water meant that the last few ships anchored in such a position that their end of the anchored line bent backwards towards the north. The French ships, as they came up under the fire of the anchored head of the British line, could do little except pass along it, close to, firing and being fired at, with the anchored ships getting the better of the exchange. It was a very neat bit of mutual support with first the rear and then the head of the British line taking the brunt of the enemy attack and covering the other whilst it anchored. Hood had timed his move superbly. As one British captain put it: 'The taking possession of this road was well-judged, well conducted, and well executed, though, indeed, the French had an opportunity — which they missed — of bringing our rear to a very severe account. The van and centre divisions brought up to anchor under the fire of the rear, which was engaged with the enemy's centre: and then the centre, being at an anchor and properly placed, covered us while we anchored, making, I think, the most masterly manoeuvre I ever saw.' By 5.30pm it was all over and the thwarted French were standing away to the southwards.

Hood then set himself to reorganising his anchored line. Though he had put a local pilot in the leading ship with the aim of having her anchor close enough inshore to prevent the head of the line being turned by ships passing between it and the shore (which was what Nelson's fleet managed to do at the Nile, with disastrous consequences for the anchored French, as we will see in a later chapter), there was still too big a gap. So he moved up three ships from the rear, which had had to anchor in a higgledy-piggledy manner whilst under fire, to fill that gap.

In the end the lead ship was so carefully positioned that she was impossible for any enemy to reach in the prevailing wind, which would bring any attacking ship around the nearby point well outside of her. From her the line ran west-north-west to the 15th ship. This, the one at the outermost point of the line, was Hood's own flagship, *Barfleur*, one of his only two three-deckers and the most powerful ship he had. The last six ships carried the line back northwards, at an angle to the rest of the line,

Below: St Kitts 1782. A view of the action on 26 February by Maynard, as seen from the island of Nevis. The French fleet is standing into Frigate Bay, where the anchored line of British ships waits to repulse them. *NMM ref: BHC0437*

preventing any attempt to turn the end of the line.

The ships began to move to their allocated positions at daybreak on 26 January. At this stage the French were seven to eight miles away to the southward. At 7am they were seen to be approaching under full sail in line of battle. One British ship, *Canada*, was anchored in such deep water, as we have seen, that she had to cut her cable, and engaged under sail, but the rest of the British line was anchored snugly in position by the time the French were in range. The leading French ship, trying to head for the leading ship in the anchored line, was completely defeated by a shift in the wind, and was heading for the third at the stage when a concentrated fire was opened on her at just before 9am. The French were now experiencing the problem of attacking an unbreakable line. Their lead ship had to approach the line bow-on, completely unable to respond to the full broadsides of all the anchored ships which were in range, perhaps half a dozen or more. Turning would bring her own broadside to bear, but would carry her down the line to fresh adversaries ready to pour more fire into her, whilst the ships that followed her would be quite unable to support her, and would,

one-by-one, go through the same ordeal. The fire on the leading French ship was so intense 'that whole pieces of plank were seen flying from off her side'. As the French ships passed along the British line at varying distances, some, particularly the flagship, attempted to go as slowly as possible with backed sails. They were, however, suffering worse than their adversaries and had eventually to draw away. They managed to get up to launch another, more half-hearted, attack in the afternoon, but this merely confirmed the lesson of the morning that Hood was firmly in position and was giving his attackers a very hard time.

The French continued to cruise about, threatening attack, for the next few days. However, on 18 February the main reason for Hood's presence was removed as the British garrison on Brimstone Hill surrendered. The

Below: Map of St Kitts showing (1) and (2) the British fleet sailing into Frigate Bay and anchoring in the southern part, in succession in a bent line going west then north with the French just failing to catch the British, and then sailing along the anchored British line (3) and cannonading it (which they then repeated).

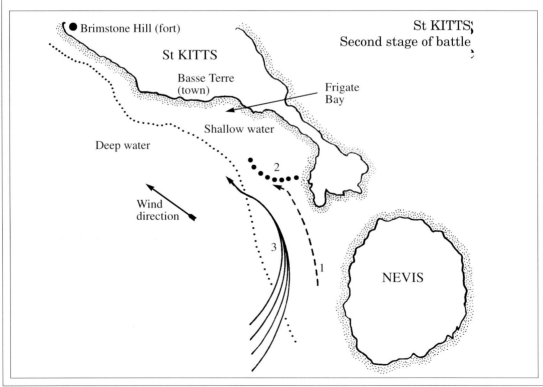

next day de Grasse withdrew to Nevis where he anchored to resupply his fleet from his storeships. This gave Hood the opportunity he required to depart. He called his captains on board, briefed them and synchronised watches. At 11pm the British ships swiftly and silently cut their cables, left decoy lights burning on the buoys and quietly decamped to Antigua, leaving de Grasse to wake the next morning to an empty anchorage. It was a very neat conclusion to a very neat series of manoeuvres, which remain a classic of their kind.

Apart from the wrecked British frigate neither side had lost a ship, though the French had probably suffered more damage. Casualties were 72 British and 107 French dead, 244 British and 207 French wounded.

British Ships at St Kitts

Three-decker 98-gun two
British: *Barfleur* (Flagship of Rear-Admiral Samuel Hood, Captain Alexander Hood [this is the cousin, not the brother]), *Prince George* (James Williams) — **two**

74-gun ships 13
British: *Alcide* (Charles Thompson), *Torbay* (John Lewis Gidoin), *Ajax* (Nicholas Charrington), *Shrewsbury* (John Knight), *Invincible* (Charles Saxton), *Monarch* (Francis Reynolds), *Centaur* (French prize — John Nicholas Inglefield), *Alfred* (William Bayne), *Russell* (Henry Edwyn Stanhope), *Resolution* (Lord Robert Manners), *Bedford* (Flag of Commodore Edward Affleck, Captain Thomas Graves [3rd]), *Montagu* (George Bowen), *Canada* (William Cornwallis) — **13**

70-gun ship one
British: *Princesa* (Spanish prize — Flag of Rear-Admiral Francis Samuel Drake; this ship was much larger than the old British 70s, which helps explain why she was being used as a flagship) — **one**

64-gun ships six
British: *Saint Albans* (Charles Inglis), *Intrepid* (Anthony Mulloy), *Prince William* (Spanish prize — George Wilkinson), *Belliquex* (Lord Cranstoun), *Prudent* (Andrew Barkley), *America* (Samuel Thompson) — **six**

Frigates etc nine
British: 40 *Fortunée* (French prize), 32 *Convert* (French prize), 28s *Pegasus, Lizard, Triton, Sibyl, Solebay* (wrecked during the battle), 24s *Eurydice, Champion* — **nine**

Right: Privateers were a continual threat to British trade in the West Indies throughout the era of the 'Nelsonic navy'. Here the British merchantman *Antelope* fights and captures the French privateer *Atalante* in 1793. Many of *Atalante's* crew were Americans. *NMM neg no: A785*

Above: The Battle of Chesme 1770 — a fireship attack by the Russians, whose fleet had come round from the Baltic to the Eastern Mediterranean, destroys the Turkish fleet. The flames and smoke of this destruction were probably very convenient for the artist, not only in enabling him to depict a dramatic scene, but in saving him from being too detailed about the appearance of the Turkish ships, on which he is unlikely to have had very much information. *NMM neg no: 2343*

Left: Sir (a Russian title) Samuel Greig 1735–1788, engraving of a portrait by Levitsky. A Scotsman, he originally served in the Royal Navy, was present at Quiberon Bay and the capture of Havana (1762), and was commissioned as a lieutenant in the same year. Just over a year later, after the end of the war, he went into Russian service and rapidly rose in rank. At the Battle of Chesme (1770) he commanded a division of the fleet under Count Orloff. He went on to command against the Swedes in 1788, winning the Battle of Hogland. He had also been governor of the Russian Baltic base at Kronstadt, and was Grand Admiral by the time of his death. His role in the building up of the Russian Navy was very important, and he brought many other Scotsmen in to serve with his adopted country. He is buried at Talinn (Reval) in what is now Estonia. His son also had a distinguished career as an admiral in the Russian service. *NMM neg no: 2986*

5

Oars and sails in the Baltic: Svenskund, 1790

Not all the naval battles fought between 1756 and 1816 were between the countries bordering on the North Atlantic; other navies besides the British, French, Spanish, Dutch and American fought in this period. The main reason behind these other wars, fought in the inland seas which border Europe to the east and south, was the expansion of Russia. To the south Russia fought the Turks in the Mediterranean and the Black Sea. In the north was the Baltic Sea, and there it was the Swedes who resisted Russian expansion. Sweden had had a seagoing sailing navy since the early 16th century, when she became a separate kingdom again. It was the westward advance of Russia that caused her to develop a different kind of navy altogether to match her eastern rival. Between St Petersburg at the easternmost end of the Gulf of Finland, westwards to where it opens out into the Baltic itself there is a scattering of rocky islands, large and small, and an indented coast where land merges with sea. This chain of islands carries across the Baltic to the Swedish coast, where again sea merges with land in a maze of what are called 'skerries' (small islands). Stockholm itself, the Swedish capital, is partly built on them. This is not an area suited to large seagoing ships. When Peter the Great of Russia began to build his capital on the Neva at the beginning of the 18th century and push westwards from it he built both a seagoing navy and a flotilla of Mediterranean-style galleys to operate amongst the islands. The Swedes were forced to respond in kind by building up their own 'skerries fleet' of rowing vessels. Thanks to expansion in the previous century they had owned large parts of the shoreline of the southern and eastern Baltic. These they had mostly lost by the late 18th century, but Finland was a different matter. Finland had been Swedish since the Middle Ages, and a series of wars were fought with Russia to protect it, and to keep it as an outer bulwark for the defence of Sweden herself. The chief base for the skerries fleet was on an island just off the Finnish capital Helsingfors (Helsinki) called Sveaborg (the Finns now call it Suomenlinna). One of the main focal points of the island chain to the east of this, slightly over half-way towards St Petersburg, was a stretch of water between islands and mainland, off where the modern city of Kotka has been built, an obvious place to bar the progress of an invader. The Swedish name for this was Svenskund (there is a modern Finnish name, but since no one who recorded the battle used it, it is best ignored).

In 1787 Turkey declared war on Russia and the energetic Swedish king Gustavus III (his later murder at a ball would provide Verdi with the plot for an opera) decided the time had come to fight Russia in a bid to recover the eastern parts of Finland, conquered earlier in the century. Although Russian resources were much greater than those of Sweden, Gustavus had one great advantage in the shape of the extremely clever man who had been building up his navy. Hendrik af Chapman (Henry Chapman) was, as his name suggests, the son of a Yorkshireman who had gone to Sweden to make his fortune. Chapman was a very important pioneer of naval architecture. He was also an inventive ship designer and an excellent organiser. He built up the main fleet base at Karlskrona, just as he enlarged the skerries fleet and its base at Sveaborg. He designed and built the first super-frigates (armed with 24-pounders) a little while before the Americans started building theirs. He also designed and built a whole series of innovative rowing and sailing vessels for the skerries fleet, some of them utilising what may well have been the first naval guns on rotating mountings ever developed. In these craft, the 'udemas', 'hemmemas', 'pojamas' and 'turumas', he tried to produce craft which were more suited to the conditions of skerry warfare, better able to cope with the combination of sails, oars and heavy guns necessary, than the versions of Mediterranean galleys hitherto used. The turuma was a sort of inshore corvette, rowed from the upper deck, with a battery of some 24 18-pounder guns on the lower deck, plus some three-pounders. The udema was quite extraordinary, with nine 12-pounder guns mounted on revolving mounts on the centre line, capable of firing on either broadside, but preventing the ship being rowed from benches on either side of the battery when they were in use. Two 18-pounders were mounted forward and two eight-pounders aft. The pojama was more like a galley with pairs of long guns mounted at either end, but none were left in service at the time we are considering. The hemmema was a later, less exciting and more sensible design; basically a shallow draft version of seagoing frigates or sloops, equipped to row with sweeps between the gunports. In many ways it was a larger version of the turuma. These craft were built to participate in the 1788–1790 war with Russia and carried 24 36-pounders and a couple of 12-pounders. All of these vessels (like the vessels built to fight on the American Great Lakes) could carry very much heavier armaments for their size than comparable seagoing vessels. Fascinating though these unusual craft are, none of them seem to have been a total success. Chapman's real triumph in designing craft for the skerries was in developing a range of smaller oared gun-boats. These were very successful, and very widely copied in Europe

and America. Versions of his gun-boat designs went on being used until steam supplanted the rowers in the middle of the 19th century. These skerries craft were intended to conduct amphibious campaigns along the coast, and included many troop transports. The crews were drawn from local peasant soldiers, a sort of naval militia, and the organisation of the fleet was totally different from that of the navy proper.

Whilst the Swedes had this well-established and well-provided skerries fleet, the Russians had a very small force indeed when war broke out and were forced to launch a huge emergency building programme at St Petersburg. This developed to such an extent that within two years they had equalled, if not surpassed, the Swedes in the size of their force. They built 'frigates' which seem to have been much the same as the Swedish hemmemas, chebecks (or xebecs, or shebecks) a variant of a Mediterranean design for a smaller vessel designed to sail and row. They copied the Swedish gun-boats, and also built a gun-boat-type vessel called a 'kaik' (perhaps a development from a Mediterranean caique?). They also had schooners and other craft, including their old standby, the galley.

The Russo-Swedish war of 1788–1790 produced a number of battles between both the deep-sea and the inshore fleets of the combatants. In both cases the advantage swayed backwards and forwards between the two sides. In the skerries chain Sweden lost a battle that had begun well when the king tried to hold his position too long at Svenskund in 1789. In early 1790 both the skerries fleet and the deep-sea one were at Viborg, in the eastern end of the Gulf of Finland, where the Russians contrived to trap the line of battle ships and destroyed or captured enough of them to ensure that the Swedes could no longer compete out at sea. However, the skerries fleet had escaped the trap, though with some difficulty and loss. The Russians fumbled the chance to capture the Swedish king on 4 July, and bad weather temporarily scattered a fleet which was not suited to it, different squadrons being driven to take shelter at various points along the coast. A day later, 5 July, the whole

Right: Svenskund, 1790, showing the Swedish larger craft in the centre with double lines of gunboats on either side, with blocking forces at the northern entrances to the harbour, also the main Russian attack on the western end of the Swedish line. There were actually even more rocks and small islets than shown.

force of the Swedish skerries fleet was concentrated in Svenskund, ready to stop the Russians exploiting their victory further to the westward. Its total loss had been seven galleys, 11 gun-boats and 30 transports. At the same time the Russian flotilla slowly got together for an advance. It was not until the 7th that the Russian commander, the Prince of Nassau-Siegen, was in a position to attack. He decided to do so at once, and by midnight of 9/10 July he had concentrated the entire Russian flotilla at the southern entrance of Svenskund harbour. He could not leave the Swedish force on the flank of his advance, but he had a reasonable chance of trapping and destroying it. However, the Swedes were in a very strong

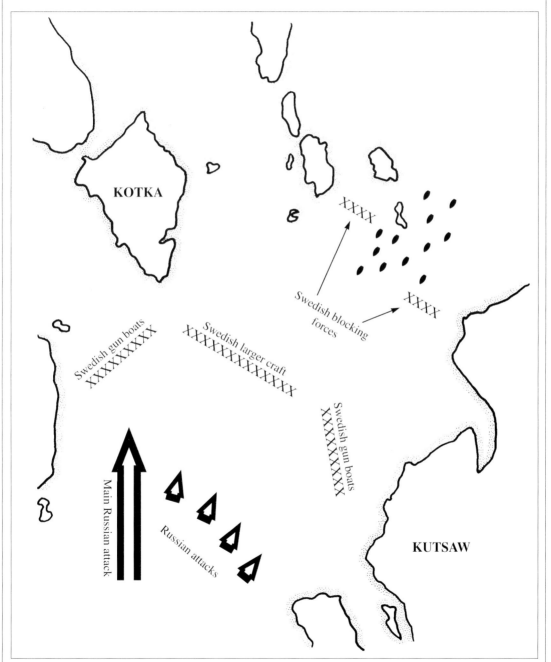

65

position with the chance to concentrate their fire on any vessels coming into the harbour to attack them.

The Swedish force was very considerable. Reinforcements more than made up for their losses, and their total available strength was as follows: five larger sailing and rowing vessels (two hemmemas, one turuma, two udemas); 18 galleys; 153 gun-boats (99 'sloops' with two big guns and 54 'yawls' with a single gun); 10 gun-vessels; eight bomb-vessels; one yacht (the king's command vessel). They therefore had 196 fighting ships, plus a transport force which was moored out of the way in a corner of the harbour, and carried about 1,200 guns between them.

The Russians had the following: 30 sailing and rowing vessels (eight 'frigates', eight chebecks, one hemmema — a prize taken from the enemy, eight schooners, three bomb-vessels, two 'half-prames'); 23 galleys; 77 gun-boats and 'kaiks'; three floating batteries; eight mortar boats. This made a total of 141 vessels, with about 1,500 guns. The Russians, although with fewer ships, had considerably more large vessels than their opponents. It is also possible that they had more men. So the imbalance in strength was not as great as it might seem.

The Swedish force occupied practically the same position as it had nearly a year before in August 1789 on the occasion of the first Battle of Svenskund. The northern approaches to the harbour were blocked, with a force of one turuma, one galley and 33 gun-boats protecting them. The main Swedish position formed a sort of funnel, with the wings sloping forward from the centre to the sides of the harbour entrance. The Swedish centre, containing most of the larger vessels, was positioned between two islets in the centre of the harbour. This consisted of two hemmemas, two udemas, one cutter, 17 galleys and 15 gun-boats. Stretching outwards from this came the Swedish right wing of 61 gun-boats, while on the left, behind a row of islets and rocks, was another force of 44 gun-boats. The eight bomb-vessels were not in the main fighting line. Three or four had been sent as scouts to the other side of Svenskund, and the rest were a reserve between the main line and the ships guarding the northern entrance.

Despite the strength of this position and its defenders, Nassau-Siegen attacked confidently enough. 9 July was the day of Czarina Catherine the Great's accession to the throne, and he chose that date as an auspicious day for the assault. He planned that his fleet should go in four columns. The left wing was to consist of 40 gun-boats and kaiks, with three floating batteries and three bomb-vessels, and was to go in first. Next was to come the right wing of 37 gun-boats and eight bombs. After these had softened up the defence, the two lines of the centre, the most powerful craft at his disposal — 23 galleys and the sailing vessels would deliver what he hoped would be the final push.

The morning of 9 July was not at all promising. There was a strengthening southwesterly breeze bearing heavy curtains of mist, but Nassau-Siegen did not stop his attack. At 8am the Russian fleet got under way, and at 9.30am the action began between the Russian left and the Swedish right. At first everything went well enough, but the wind and sea got up and the more exposed Russian gun-boats began to fall out of station. At about noon the sailing ships got into position, but at the same time the Russian left wing had to retreat. The gun-boats of the Swedish right wing were advancing steadily. Reinforced by 20 or more of the gun-boats from the other wing, this force was able to advance to a position where it flanked the ships of the Russian centre. Under constant fire from the side and ahead these soon fell into confusion. At about 2pm Nassau-Siegen got the gun-boats on his left into line again and renewed the attack, but after another two hours' fighting they again had to retreat. Meanwhile the gun-boats of the Swedish left wing had begun to advance to outflank the Russians. This caused the Russian gun-boats on this flank to retreat as well. This left the larger ships in the Russian centre exposed to fire from both flanks. Ships soon began to settle in the water, rowers and gun crews abandoned their duties to man the pumps and whilst some vessels sank, others ran ashore. Soon after 7pm Nassau-Siegen decided to retreat, but many of his sailing ships could not get away and were captured or burnt by the energetically advancing Swedes. Fighting ended at about 10pm that night but the Russians could not get far, and they were attacked at daybreak on the 10th and driven in confusion back along the coast, losing several ships on the way, some to the Swedes, some to previous damage and the effect of the bad weather.

The Swedes had won an impressive victory, and retrieved themselves from what might have been a disastrous situation. Their success in the skerries counterbalanced the losses of the battlefleet. Peace was signed shortly afterwards. The main reason for the success of the Swedes was their victory in the artillery battle. They had the advantage in number of guns and in position, and they made full use of both. In particular it was a victory for the aggressively handled and excellent Chapman gun-boats. Furthermore, the Russians were not helped by the bad weather which handicapped them far more than the snugly-ensconced defenders.

The Swedes suffered very little loss: one udema and three gun-boats were sunk, with 181 men killed and 123 wounded. The Russians, on the other hand, lost heavily. It is difficult to establish exact losses, but it is known that the Swedes captured three frigates, one chebeck, two floating batteries, seven galleys, two bombs, 10 kaiks, six gun-boats and four 'double sloops' (a variety of gun-boat). On top of these the Swedes also recaptured the hemmema which had been taken from them earlier. Ships sunk or otherwise destroyed are more difficult to establish, but probably include the following: two frigates, three chebecks, two half-prames, seven schooners, nine galleys, five bombs or mortar vessels, and an indefinite number of gun-boats. Out of 7,369 men lost about 6,500 were captured and therefore not much short of 850 were killed or drowned.

One of the biggest vessels lost in the action was the Russian frigate *St Nicholai* which sank in the entrance to the harbour. Her captain, named Mitchell, was one of the many Britons then serving with the Russian Navy. Like many fellow officers in that navy he had served in the Royal Navy. He was badly wounded in the leg and died of his wounds before the ship sank. Her hull, in the cold, nearly fresh waters of this harbour, is remarkably well preserved where it lies, a few feet below the surface.

It was discovered in the 1960s and a number of guns raised. In the 1980s the hull began to be properly excavated by Finnish archaeologists. As I happened to be lecturing in Kotka whilst excavations were going on I was lucky enough to be invited to dive on the wreck. It was a fascinating experience, the more so because of the extremely poor visibility. A river empties into the harbour and the water is very dark, partly because of silt, but even more because it is stained by peat. Your torch spreads a brownish glow about 2–3ft in front of you, otherwise you are shut in by the dark. You feel your way round the excavated forecastle compartments of the wreck, seeing the galley stove and structural items you have been briefed about. Above all you feel the wonder of diving on the remains of a ship which sank two centuries ago, and wonder what the dark, or the mud that the hull is sunk into, conceal of the men who died so suddenly and violently in that fierce encounter on a windy July day so long ago.

Right: Rowing and sailing gun-boats of the general type of this model served in all navies at this time for local defence and inshore work and for amphibious warfare. The type probably evolved in the Mediterranean — which is probably why the standard rig was lateen. Large numbers of similar vessels served in the Russo-Swedish conflict in the Baltic. This particular boat was of a type built for the Royal Navy in 1788, and for some years afterwards. There is some indication that the precise hull form derived from the specialised landing craft of the day ('flat-bottomed boats for the landing of men' — see the photo of a model of one of these in this book). The gun fired and recoiled on a 'slide' along the line of the keel. The only way of aiming it was to point the entire boat at the target, and much of the recoil was absorbed by the boat moving backwards through the water. When not actually in action the gun would be moved back along the slide towards the mast, so as to take the weight from out the bows and make the boat more seaworthy and easier to sail. *NMM neg no: B9627*

VICTORS OF THE NILE

SAUMAREZ   TROUBRIDGE   DARBY   LOUIS   PEYTON   BALL   HOOD

GOULD   FOLEY   WESTCOTT   THOMPSON   HALLOWELL   MILLER   BERRY

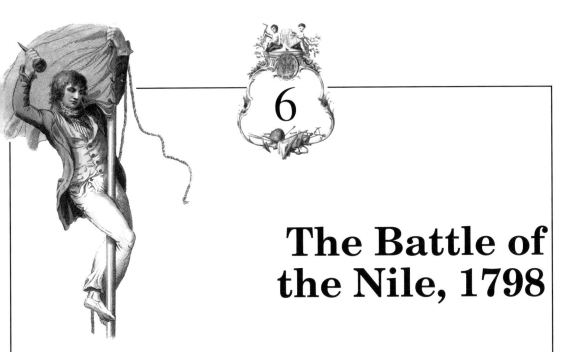

6

The Battle of the Nile, 1798

The battle variously known as 'the Nile' or 'Aboukir Bay' is the classic sea battle of annihilation. Having chased Napoleon Bonaparte's Egyptian Expedition across the Mediterranean, Nelson caught its escorting fleet at anchor and destroyed or took all but two of its ships of the line. As the two most recent French historians writing about the French Navy in this period put it: the defeat was crushing, absolute, and with no possibility for recovery. They also make clear that it marked the final defeat of French aspirations to win sea-supremacy over Britain. For Jean Meyer and Martine Acerra, Trafalgar was merely an epilogue, a battle in which the French and their allies were

Left: Heroes of the Nile, engraving — a group portrait of Nelson's 'band of brothers', his captains at the Nile. This was the period of immense enthusiasm for classical motifs — as the allegorical picture and the details of the surrounds of the portraits show, whilst an intense interest was growing in the civilisation of ancient Egypt. The scientists who accompanied Napoleon's expedition would begin to satisfy that interest. One of their discoveries was the Rosetta stone which, with its inscriptions in various scripts, proved the key to begin the unlocking of the hieroglyphs. A direct consequence of the victory of the Nile was that this stone was captured by the Royal Navy aboard a French ship — which is why it is now in the British Museum. *NMM neg no: 3563*

doomed from the start, and furthermore they knew it.

The story starts in early 1798, with the ambitious young General Bonaparte deciding to invade Egypt, then loosely subject to the Turkish sultan but actually ruled by an extraordinary group of self-perpetuating slave soldiers, the Mamelukes. Egypt would merely be the stepping stone to further conquests in the east. Napoleon hoped eventually to conquer Britain's recently acquired dominions in India. The path to Egypt had been left clear, for the British had been forced to abandon the Mediterranean over a year earlier when Spain entered the war against her. The French, with great speed, secrecy and efficiency, prepared an expedition at Toulon, which sailed from there on 19 May with 13 ships of the line, four frigates and some 23 smaller warships. There were also two old 64s and six frigates disarmed and turned into transports; what the French called armed *'en flûte'* (like a flute — with the empty gunports being like the holes in a flute) not to mention some 70 merchant ships requisitioned as troop transports and storeships. Despite this mass of shipping, troops and stores were loaded aboard the fighting ships as well, which would have handicapped them severely had they met the British fleet at sea. This armada was to rendezvous with other elements of the expedition at sea. A frigate, a corvette and about 55 transports came from Marseilles, a frigate and some 70 transports from Genoa, 22 small transports from Corsica and a frigate and 56 transports from Civitavecchia.

Even before the expedition sailed, however, the British had returned to the Mediterranean. On 9 May Rear-Admiral Nelson had sailed from Gibraltar with three 74s, two frigates and a 20-gun ship. He had been sent by John Jervis, Earl St Vincent, the formidable disciplinarian who commanded the Mediterranean fleet to find out what the French were doing. Rumours of the major expedition the French were preparing had reached London — but no firm information on its intended target. Nelson was off Toulon on 17 May, but two days later a strong wind got up which drove Nelson away from the land and then partially dismasted his flagship, *Vanguard*. She was saved from shipwreck and then refitted by the efforts of the squadron in an anchorage off the island of Sardinia. Unfortunately the same wind had taken the French fleet out of harbour and well on its way. Worse still for Nelson was that he lost his frigates through a misunderstanding — and therefore had lost the vessels best suited for reconnaissance. He returned to patrol off Toulon, where he was found by the brig *Mutine* which had been sent to tell him that he would be joined by nine battle ships detached from St Vincent's fleet. The admiral could spare these because he had been reinforced from Britain. The ships he sent were not, however, these reinforcements, tainted as he believed they were by the mutinies of the previous year. St Vincent sent his best ships that he had trained, with good commanders, epitomised by the captain who led the force to Nelson, Thomas Troubridge. On the way they had picked up reinforcements at Gibraltar: another 74-gun ship, and the small two-decker *Leander*. On 7 June they joined Nelson, who sailed southwards the next day.

Two days later (10 June) the French landed on Malta. The island was then under the control of the Knights of St John, the Hospitallers. These once-feared Christian corsairs had grown lax, and their control was resented by the native Maltese. There was little resistance when the French landed. On the 19th, leaving a garrison in the fortress-town of Valletta, they sailed, bound for Egypt, arriving off Alexandria on 1 July. Meanwhile Nelson had been chasing around the Mediterranean, desperately searching for his enemy on the basis of inadequate, and sometimes faulty, information. It was a desperate time for him. The French could have

been going anywhere in the Mediterranean — or towards the West Indies or Ireland. He was particularly handicapped by having no frigates to scout for him. This lack might well have been the reason for him missing the French fleet at a stage when subsequent comparison of the tracks taken showed that the fleets had been close to one another (22 to 24 June). On 22 June, Nelson, off Sicily, heard that the French had taken Malta and then sailed again. It seemed unlikely that the French were intending to invade Sicily, which had been very much a possibility. Nelson and his captains guessed that Egypt might be the destination and took the gamble of sailing there. Ironically their good seamanship and well-trained crews then ensured that the British fleet arrived off Alexandria on 28 July having overtaken the much slower French invasion convoy without seeing it. By the time the latter arrived, the British ships had departed to check the shores of Turkey and then sailed on to Sicily.

We are left wondering about one of the great 'what ifs' of history — what if Nelson had caught the French invasion fleet at sea, with Napoleon and his troops still aboard? The French fleet would have had severe problems with their decks cluttered by stores and soldiers, the invasion transports extremely vulnerable. The battle that did take place clearly demonstrates the much greater effectiveness of the British force, and the chances of the annihilation of both the French fleet and a high proportion of the transports seems quite likely. Napoleon's career could well have come to a premature end, both literally and metaphorically. Instead he won this particular game of maritime blind-man's buff, landed his troops and proceeded to conquer Egypt. The main advantage to the British of the prolonged period before the enemy was located, was that it gave Nelson and his group of captains plenty of time to get well acquainted, and for Nelson to discuss the various plans of action with his 'band of brothers'. Nelson was perfectly suited to the task of being the leader of an excellent and highly talented team. His magnetism, his ability to communicate, to make people love him, all worked to ensure that each captain knew what his admiral wanted him to do in a whole variety of circumstances, and to produce a situation where that task would be done willingly and effectively. This enthusiasm also communicated itself to the common sailors with whom the small, febrile admiral had an extraordinary rapport. This situation of co-operation, lifted to a very high level, and of

Above: This picture of the British fleet under Nelson at anchor in rigid formation in the Bay of Naples with Vesuvius in the background, by the local artist, G. Guardi, is supposed to show that fleet before the Battle of the Nile. Presumably this would be the visit of 17 June 1798 when Nelson was desperately searching for the fleet carrying Napoleon east, with no idea of his destination. At this stage Napoleon was still off Malta, consolidating his capture of the island. There is, however, a problem in this dating of the picture, which is the presence of what appears to be a British frigate moored by her own in front of the fleet. As we know, Nelson had no frigates with him, only the brig *Mutine*. Perhaps the British vessel in the picture was a privateer? She does not look like a merchantman. Perhaps, however, the picture was done at another time, or from memory, and is not quite as authentic a document as might be hoped. *NMM neg no: 2374*

Left: Engraving of Lemuel Abbott's self-portrait with his picture of Nelson in his hand. This artist committed suicide in 1803, but not before producing several of the best known portraits of Nelson. It is worth remembering that this was an era before photography had been invented, and we rely on the eyes and skills of men such as this for our view of the past and its inhabitants. *NMM neg no: 174*

informed, enthusiastic initiative and intelligent aggressiveness was the true 'Nelson touch', the very highest quality of leadership. It made an already very well-trained group of ships into a truly formidable force.

From Sicily, where he had provisioned and watered his ships, Nelson sailed for Cyprus as he thought the French might have landed in Syria. Off Greece, however, he heard that the enemy fleet had been sighted a month earlier on course for Egypt. He arrived off Alexandria just before midday on 1 August to find the harbour packed with French transports, but no sign of his chief target, Brueys' fleet. Disappointment was only temporary, however, as *Zealous* sighted the French warships moored in Aboukir Bay 15 miles along the coast to the east. Brueys had moved there because the channels into Alexandria harbour would have been very dangerous for his big ships. One of the transports had come to grief there as it was. This was the *Patriote* carrying much of the equipment of the scientists who accompanied the expedition. Her wreck has recently been discovered and excavated by underwater archaeologists. Aboukir Bay was reasonably sheltered and would give Brueys the chance to land the stores still aboard his ships whilst moored in a position which should be relatively easy to defend. The western end of this semicircular bay is marked by Aboukir Point and Aboukir Island to seaward of it, with a line of rocks and shoals connecting the two and extending beyond the island, narrowing the mouth of the bay. The western part of the bay is shallow, but it gets deeper to the east.

The island and the point were fortified and occupied by the French. Brueys' ships of the line were moored in a slightly bent line stretching south from the shallows just inside the island and in the westernmost part of the deeper water. The four frigates were anchored at intervals inside the line, and the smaller ships in shallower water further east. The French ships were anchored in the following order stretching from the *Guerrier* (74 guns — as are the others listed here apart from the 120 and the three 80s which are noted as such) moored nearest to the island, via *Conquérant, Spartiate, Aquilon, Peuple Souverain* (sometimes just called *Souverain*), *Franklin* (80), *Orient* (120, the flagship), *Tonnant* (another 80), *Heureux, Mercure, Guillaume Tell* (80), *Généreux* (80 — this concentration of the larger ships towards the rear of the line is interesting — another indication that Brueys thought that this would be the more likely end to be attacked) and *Timoléon*. This should have been a very strong

Above: Thomas Troubridge (1758–1807), an old shipmate and friend of Nelson. He had the misfortune of having a grandstand view of the Nile from his grounded ship. In the Admiralty from 1801 until 1804, he was then posted to the divided command of the East Indies Station. Coming back from this unfortunate experience his flagship was lost with all hands in a storm in the Indian Ocean.
NMM neg no: 6375

position, particularly as Brueys ordered ships to put springs to their cables. This means that each ship laid out anchors and put lines to them in such a way as the ship could be moved around at anchor by pulling in or letting out the cable. In turn this meant that they could get a much wider angle of fire for their broadsides. Furthermore, the prevailing wind blew along the line of the ships from the island end. Brueys believed that Nelson was likely to attack, if he attacked at all, from the southern end of the line, and the ships at the other end would be in a good position to come down to assist their comrades. An anchored line of ships was a formidable obstacle, if well placed, and there were several examples in the American War of Independence of an anchored line of ships deterring attack by a superior force, or, as at Frigate Bay, giving the attacker a very bloody nose. Brueys' line was, indeed, well positioned, but not enough care had been taken to ensure that the end ship was moored close enough to the shallows to prevent any of its opponents getting past. This was to prove a fatal flaw, because if there was sufficient room to pass, then the attacking ships could go down the line on either side of it, taking successive ships under attack from a ship on either side. This would be even more dangerous, as was the case here, if the defender was completely unprepared to fight both sides. He would be open to defeat in detail, presenting his enemy with the opportunity to knock out his ships one by one.

Having sighted Nelson, Brueys sent out two brigs to attempt to lure Nelson on to the shoals, and made preparations for battle. In mid-afternoon he seems to have briefly considered getting under way, but then to have decided that his enemy was unlikely to attack till the following morning; some of his crews were still ashore, as were much of his supplies. In the end he passively awaited the British onslaught, happy in the belief he was in a strong, nearly impregnable position. This would indeed have been the case had his ships possessed adequate seamanship to adhere to the closely serried defensive line he had planned, hard up against the shallows and impossible to break. Furthermore, he had every reason to expect that his opponent had insufficient time for a careful and safe approach before nightfall would put an end to any reasonable chance of battle until the next morning. Had he been up against a more cautious commander who had less reason to rely on the consummate seamanship of his fleet, Brueys would indeed have had the night to prepare for action. Nelson, however, had no intention of allowing the long-sought enemy to have any more time for preparation than it took him to get into position. This paid off handsomely — British eyewitnesses saw the decks of enemy ships still cluttered with crates and other stores as they opened fire, and these greatly hampered the efforts of the French gun crews. At 3pm Nelson signalled to prepare for action. An hour later he instructed his ships to prepare to anchor by the stern. This involved taking a cable and attaching it to the mizzen mast, lead it out of a stern port and carry it forward where it would be 'bent' (tied) to an anchor. When this anchor was let go it would therefore have two cables attached to it, one from the bow, the other from the stern. This would both prevent the ships weathercocking with the wind when they anchored and make it

Above: Miniature of Captain Alexander Ball (1757–1809). A thoughtful, sympathetic man and a fine commander, he assisted in saving Nelson's flagship, *Vanguard*, when she was dismasted, and then took part in the subsequent chase of Brueys and the Battle of the Nile as the captain of the *Alexander*. He then assisted in the siege of the French at Valletta, and made himself so well liked by the Maltese that they asked for and got him as their first British governor. He remained in this post till his death. *NMM neg no: 9168*

possible to move the ships round as desired (just like the French ships' springs). For ships with their armament pointing out of the sides with comparatively little sideways traverse, and whose bows and sterns were vulnerable to 'raking', this was particularly important.

By 5.30pm Nelson was abreast of the island and instructed his ships to form line of battle ahead and astern of the flagship as convenient. He then hailed Captain Samuel Hood of the *Zealous* to ask him if he thought the ships were far enough to the eastwards to clear the shoal. No one had a trustworthy chart of the bay (except, perhaps, Foley of the *Goliath*) but Hood offered to go in, sounding as he went, to act as a guide to the fleet. Ten years later his

Left: Admiral Lord James de Saumarez (1757–1836) as portrayed in an engraving of the Lane portrait. A very religious man, he was also a very distinguished naval officer with an impressive record of service. A lieutenant at the Dogger Bank action in 1781, he was captain of one of Rodney's ships at the victory of the Saintes the next year. In 1793 he was in command of the frigate *Crescent* when she took the *Réunion*. He played an important part in the victory of St Vincent (1797). The next year he was Nelson's senior captain in the chase to the Nile, having played a major part in saving his admiral when the *Vanguard* was dismasted. In 1801 he was in command of the squadron repulsed by the French at the Battle of Algeciras, but masterminded the rapid refitting of his ships which resulted in victory in the subsequent action in the Gut of Gibraltar. Probably his greatest service to his country, however, was his years as commander-in-chief of the British fleet in the Baltic from 1808 where he confronted major military problems and even more problematic diplomatic difficulties with superb judgement, patience and skill. Some of the quality of this grave, attractive and impressive man comes across in this picture.
NMM neg no: A4966

first lieutenant (Webley) remembered he had said in answer to the admiral's query as to whether he thought they could bear up for (turn towards) the enemy: 'I cannot say, we have 11 fathoms water, but if you will allow me the honour of leading you into battle, I will keep the lead going.' He [Nelson] answered, 'You have my leave and I wish you success', and then took off his hat. Captain Hood, in endeavouring to do the same, let his hat fall overboard and immediately said, 'Never mind, Webley! There it goes for luck! Put the helm up and make sail.' As he turned his ship towards the French fleet, however, the *Goliath* on the inside had a slight lead over him. According to one story, Thomas Foley, the captain of this ship, had a captured French chart which showed that there was water deep enough inside the *Guerrier*, the ship at the island end of the French line, for a ship of the line to squeeze past to the inside. Whether or not this is true, it is certain that Foley saw the opportunity to 'double' the French line, and he took it, just as his admiral wished him to. As Foley was moving into position Nelson hove to the *Vanguard*, to enable several ships to pass him, so that in the end he was near the middle of the British line — the most sensible position for the admiral if he wished to have some control over the battle as it developed. Nelson and Collingwood leading their respective lines into action at Trafalgar were very much the exception to this rule.

As the British fleet moved into action the sun was setting. It was going to be a night action, not a common event, but something which would give the better-trained fleet an even greater edge over their unprepared opponents. The British line was roughly as follows: *Goliath* leading, having just passed *Zealous*, then *Orion, Audacious, Theseus, Vanguard* the flagship, *Minotaur, Defence, Bellerophon, Majestic* and the little *Leander. Culloden* was somewhat to seaward, and behind her *Alexander* and *Swiftsure* were coming up under press of sail from Alexandria, which they had earlier been sent to reconnoitre. Despite the fact that Nelson was a junior Rear-Admiral 'of the blue', which was the colour of ensign his ships should have been flying, all his ships went into action flying that most distinctive of naval flags, the white ensign. This was probably simply because it would be more visible at night, though Nelson also allegedly had a preference for this flag. It was presumably this liking that helped to ensure that some half-century later, when a single flag was chosen for the Royal Navy, it should be the White that was selected, whilst the Red went to the Merchant Navy and the Blue ensign to the auxiliaries and other government vessels.

The actual number of true line of battle ships was the same on both sides — 13 — but this was the only respect in which the opposing forces were equal. The French had the only three-decker present, the massive *Orient* of 120 guns, originally known as the *Sans Culotte*, no longer a very politically correct name at this stage in the French Revolution, and which was changed in honour of the expedition. She was of slightly more than one and a half times the force of any of the ships in the British fleet. The French also had four 80-gun ships, larger and more powerful than any of their opponents. In general the French 74s were larger than their British equivalents. *Minotaur* was the largest British ship with 1,718 tons, whilst this compares to, for example, the *Spartiate* at 1,949 tons or the *Aquilon* at 1,869 tons. As a slight counter to this superiority in larger ships the British had one other vessel which could be, and indeed was, used to fight alongside the ships of the line. This was the *Leander*, a 50-gun ship. She was a small two-decker of a kind which had been regarded for a century as too small and weak to stand in the line of battle and was not much more powerful than the two bigger French frigates, 40-gun, 18-pounder-armed vessels. However, as we shall see, the *Leander* performed nobly in the battle. Nelson's

Left:
Vice-Admiral Brueys — an engraving showing the French commander defeated and killed at the Nile. His full name was François Paul Brueys d'Aiguilliers. Born in 1753, he served as a lieutenant during the American War of Independence, was kicked out of the navy under suspicion of being a royalist in 1793, reinstated in 1795 and promoted to rear-admiral. The gun in this picture is a puzzle, and one rather doubts if the artist had much idea what he was drawing. It is a carronade, with the usual hole for an elevating screw instead of a cascabel (rear end decoration) so that it can be mounted on a slide, with a quoin (wedge) for elevating. The odd draped object on the top of the gun is probably a lead cover on top of a gun-lock.
NMM ref: A3314

Above: Pocock's striking view of Aboukir Bay, looking east from just beyond and to the landward side of the French line. In the distance is the castle and town of Aboukir, and at the far end of the line, in the evening light, Foley's *Goliath* is coming round the end of that line in the move which sealed the fate of the French fleet. *NMM ref: BHC0513*

Below: Whitcombe's magnificent conception of the climactic moment of the Nile as *Goliath* heads in to turn the end of the French line, followed by the rest of the fleet, as seen looking west into the sunset from between the British and French lines.
NMM ref: BHC0515

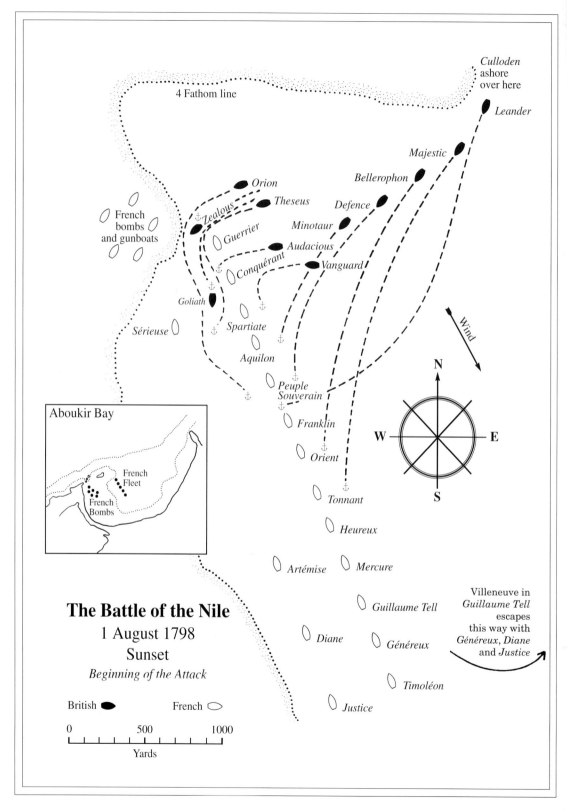

Culloden ashore over here

4 Fathom line

Leander

Majestic

Bellerophon

Orion

Theseus

Defence

Zealous

Minotaur

French bombs and gunboats

Guerrier

Audacious

Vanguard

Conquérant

Goliath

Sérieuse

Spartiate

Wind

Aquilon

N

Peuple Souverain

Franklin

W **E**

Orient

Tonnant

S

Aboukir Bay

French Fleet

French Bombs

Heureux

Artémise

Mercure

Villeneuve in *Guillaume Tell* escapes this way with *Généreux, Diane* and *Justice*

Guillaume Tell

The Battle of the Nile

1 August 1798

Sunset

Beginning of the Attack

Diane

Généreux

Timoléon

British ●   French ◯

Justice

0   500   1000

Yards

Left: The Battle of the Nile showing the position of both ships of both sides at sunset on 1 August with *Goliath* (inside *Conquérant*) and *Zealous* already anchored inside the upper end of the French line, and the subsequent paths of the other British ships to the positions where they let go their anchors. *Culloden*, with *Mutine* standing by her, is aground off the upper right hand of the map with *Swiftsure* and *Alexander* coming up fast to join in.

Above: This is Butterworth's picture of the dramatic moment at the Battle of the Nile as the *Goliath* rounds the head of the French line and fires a raking broadside into the bow of the *Guerrier*. Leading the British line (*Zealous* and the others are sailing close behind — on the left hand side of the picture), she is about to turn to the right down the line of anchored French ships. The massive shape of the three-decked *Orient* stands out, seventh down that line, taller than any other ship and with the tricolour flying from the top of the mainmast. *NMM neg no: A3822*

only other vessel, the brig sloop *Mutine*, commanded by the same Thomas Masterman Hardy who would captain *Victory* at Trafalgar, also gave sterling service.

In actual numbers of guns (1,138 to 1,084) the British had a slight superiority in the battle line, because of the numbers of carronades carried. These were not counted in the 'rated' armament of the ships — understandable enough if one knows that they were replacements for the old ½-pounder anti-personnel swivel guns which did not count in a vessel's stated armament, and because of their comparative lightness did not normally cause any reduction in the number of long guns. In weight of shot fired the French had an advantage, at least when long guns are counted; their larger ships carried 36-pounder guns on the lower deck as opposed to the 32s aboard British ships. Also, the French pound was heavier than the British one — which meant that a French 36-pounder ball was about the same weight as the British 42-pounder. However, this latter calibre of gun had become obsolete in the Royal Navy a quarter of a century before, as it was believed to be too heavy for easy handling and rapid firing on board ship. There is a further complication in that some of the French ships were in a very poor state and at least one, the *Conquérant*, could apparently only carry 18-pounders on her lower deck instead of the designed armament of 36s. What would matter in this battle, though, was less the number and calibre of guns than how they were brought into action and fought.

The first shots of the battle were fired at 6.20pm by *Conquérant*, *Guerrier* and the guns

Above: This splendidly vigorous Rowlandson engraving of the Nile, showing the 'Distressed situation of the French frigate LA SERIEUSE' is far from accurate, but rather fun. *NMM neg no: B5133*

on the island at the two leading British ships, *Goliath* and *Zealous* which were vying for first place. Captain Hood of the latter said to his First Lieutenant: 'I see Foley does not like to give up the lead; let him take it, he is very welcome to it; therefore shorten sail, and let him place himself, I suppose he will take the van [leading] ship.' Ten minutes later *Goliath* successfully swung past the bow of *Guerrier*, letting fly with a destructive raking broadside as she did so, and passed on her inner side. From this moment the French line was effectively doomed to piecemeal destruction. Captain Foley had intended to anchor alongside the *Guerrier*, but there was a slight delay in letting go the anchor, and instead he fetched up alongside the after part of the *Conquérant*. *Zealous*, following round the head of the French line, did manage to anchor abreast of the *Guerrier*, and fired with such effect that the French ship's foremast fell five minutes later, a most encouraging sight for the oncoming British line. Next round the head of the French column was the *Orion*, which fired a broadside into the *Sérieuse* frigate which left her in a shattered and sinking state. She had committed the error of firing into *Goliath* which had anchored just across from her. Captain Saumarez then anchored *Orion* a little more than abreast of the *Peuple Souverain*, but

slightly further away than he had intended, having been baulked by the unexpected appearance of *Theseus*. This vessel had actually contrived to pass between the first and second French ships, under *Guerrier's* stern and then coming to rest by the *Conquérant's* bow, something which should not have been possible had their captains followed Brueys' instructions to take lines to the next astern. Captain Miller of the *Theseus* had noticed that the French were firing high, so moved closer to their line, rightly presuming that their gun crews in the heat of the action would fail to lower the elevation of their guns. Thus far the seaward side of the French line was left unengaged — so Nelson took *Vanguard* along the outside of the French line and anchored alongside *Spartiate*. *Minotaur* and *Defence* followed suit, anchoring alongside *Aquilon* at 6.45pm and *Peuple Souverain* at 7pm respectively. The five leading French ships were between the fires of five British to port and three to starboard.

At this stage it was getting dark and another piece of Nelsonic forethought came into play as the ships hoisted four lights displayed horizontally at the mizzen peak. The sight of flames drifting closer indicated that

Below: A plan of the Battle of the Nile. This one was drawn up at Vienna, presumably at the time when Nelson was visiting the city on his triumphal return to England, accompanied by Lady Hamilton. An interesting note indicates that the map was drawn up with the involvement of that General Mack whose capitulation at Ulm was as great a victory for Napoleon as the near-simultaneous Battle of Trafalgar was a defeat. The Captain Capel who provided the details which make this plan more than usually accurate was the officer who succeeded Hardy in command of the *Mutine*. It shows the battle at the stage when all the British ships had come into action, bar the unfortunate *Culloden* [**D**] sitting on her shoal, with the *Mutine* [**F**] standing by her. The French rear can clearly be seen at the bottom end of the line of ships, anchored aloof from the struggle. *NMM neg no: A2339*

the French were attempting to use a fire raft against *Orion*, but she managed to fend this drifting menace off without taking any harm. It is not entirely clear whether this was a deliberate attempt to set ships on fire by the French, or just a mass of wreckage that happened to have caught fire accidentally. By this time *Bellerophon* was also coming into action and she, audaciously, chose to position herself outboard (on the outside of) the enormous three-decker, *Orient*. Shortly afterwards *Majestic* anchored in position next to the 80-gun *Tonnant*. *Culloden*, unfortunately for her, had passed too close to the shoals and grounded to the east of Aboukir Island. Poor unlucky Thomas Troubridge was destined to see a major battle take place without him as he tried to get his ship off a shoal. (His bad luck was not exhausted, for, returning from an unfortunate and argumentative command in the East Indies in 1807 his flagship, known for some time to be in a very poor state, disappeared without trace in

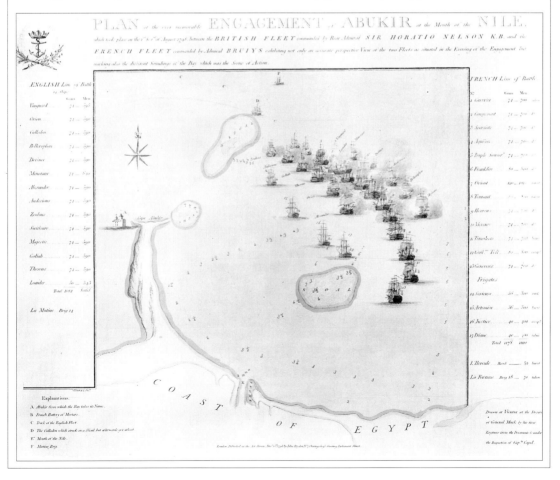

81

a tropical storm.) *Leander* had a brief look at *Culloden* to see if she could help, but Troubridge knew that there was even more useful work that ship could do and ordered her to carry on into the battle. Eventually the brig *Mutine* came up to assist, and at 2am the next morning *Culloden* got herself off, but at the expense of severe leaks and her rudder which had been bumped and battered off as she rocked on the shoal, so she could take no part in the battle.

At least *Culloden's* obvious distress and her signalled warnings meant that *Alexander* and *Swiftsure* could avoid the danger as they came up into action. Just after 8pm *Swiftsure* came across a dismasted ship drifting out of action. Fortunately she hailed before firing and found out that this was the disabled *Bellerophon* which had been engaging the French flagship in unequal conflict. Captain Hallowell of the *Swiftsure*, although uncertain where he was in the darkness and drifting smoke, realised this meant he was close to the French line, and he contrived to anchor in a position just alongside the gap between the *Franklin* and the *Orient*. The ship ahead of the *Franklin*, the *Peuple Souverain*, had parted her cable a little earlier and drifted out of the French line, creating a gap, which was brilliantly exploited by Captain Thompson of the *Leander* who contrived to anchor his ship in the gap, his port broadside raking the *Franklin*, his starboard the *Aquilon*, whilst being well out of the field of fire of either ship's broadside. This was a very sensible and effective position for the smallest and weakest ship in the British line.

Alexander, which had been forced to tack to get round the island, was the last British ship to get into action, which she did by taking advantage of the fact that *Tonnant* had let herself drift a little. This created a gap between that ship and the *Orient* which Captain Ball took his ship through and then anchored off the port quarter of the three-decker.

With the British ships all in position and engaging the enemy the French line was being 'rolled up' from the island end, with the unengaged French ships being able to do very little to help as the wind was blowing the British down their line whilst pinning them in position. The wretched *Guerrier* was rapidly dismasted, having been successively raked by *Orion, Theseus, Audacious* and *Goliath* as well as by the *Zealous* which remained battering her until she surrendered at 9pm after a gallant fight. Captain Hood observed: 'I could not get her commander to strike for three hours, though I hailed him twenty times, and

Right: Condy's version of the blazing *Orient* lighting up the surrounding battle scene. *NMM ref: BHC0511*

Below right: This atmospheric view of the Battle of the Nile by de Loutherbourg is set at a time just before the *Orient* explodes. Her fire illuminates the night battle. *NMM neg no: 6889*

seeing he was totally cut up and only firing a stern gun now and then at the *Goliath* and *Audacious*. At last being tired [of] firing and killing people in that way, I sent my boat on board her, and the lieutenant was allowed with the jolly-boat to hoist a light and haul it down to show his submission. From the time her foremast fell they had been driven from the upper decks by our canister [shot fired from cannon in the form of tin cases of musket balls which burst emerging from the muzzle and spread like blasts from a huge shotgun, the best way of killing large numbers of people at close range with cannon fire] and musketry [small arms fire]; and, I assure your Lordship [he was writing to his uncle, Lord Hood, the victor of St Kitts] from her bow to her larboard [port] gangway the ports on the main deck are [beaten] entirely into one, and her gunwale in that part entirely cut away, two of the main deck beams fallen on the guns in consequence. And is so much cut up that we cannot move her without great detention [delay] and expense, so I fancy the admiral will destroy her.' This was the sort of damage that could be done by heavy gunfire at close range.

The combined powers of *Goliath* and *Audacious* completely disabled the *Conquérant* and caused her to strike her flag in about 12min. *Spartiate* was the main target for *Vanguard* and, briefly *Theseus*, whilst also receiving some fire from *Minotaur* and, later, *Audacious* as well. Completely dismasted, she too surrendered just after 9pm. Her opponents later commented on the effectiveness of her gunfire, apparently of much higher quality than that of her neighbours. Her determined resistance certainly caused comparatively high casualties to the ships which had fought her. Her next astern, *Aquilon*, had used her springs to fire into *Vanguard*, but then had to cope with the powerful fire of *Minotaur*, which had a heavy, though short-ranged, upper battery of 32-pounder carronades. *Theseus* also fired upon *Aquilon*, another ship which had lost all her masts and suffered heavily before her surrender at 9.25pm. As we have already seen *Peuple Souverain* was attacked by *Defence* and

Orion, and with her cable either broken or shot away, had drifted out of action. She came to anchor, no longer firing, abreast of the *Orient*.

At first the *Franklin* had escaped without a direct opponent, though under distant fire from some guns of the *Orion*. However, *Leander* then put herself in a raking position, *Swiftsure* started using some of her after guns to fire on the French 80, and then *Defence* and *Minotaur*, having dealt with *Aquilon*, joined in the party by attacking her starboard bow and beam respectively. She would eventually surrender, her main and mizzen masts brought down, shortly before midnight. This was after the most spectacular, tragic and awful event of the battle, the immolation of the French flagship.

The first ship to engage the *Orient* was given very short shrift — *Bellerophon* lost two masts in short order and then her third when she attempted to set a sail on it. It was the sprit sail set on her bowsprit which got her away from her huge antagonist, though she did not escape being fired into by the *Tonnant* for a while. *Orient* was soon under attack again, this time from *Alexander* and *Swiftsure*. At about 9pm Captain Hallowell saw that fire had broken out aboard his huge antagonist, and he concentrated *Swiftsure's* shots on the area round the fire. Whether the fire would have spread without this is a moot point, but whatever the case, spread it did, and around 10pm it reached the magazines. Certainly the ship was already in a bad way. Admiral Brueys, already twice wounded, was almost cut in two by a cannonball. Mortally wounded, he still refused to be taken below, saying 'A French admiral ought to die on his own quarterdeck.' He was dead before the fire broke out. His death was rapidly followed by the mortal wounding of Captain de Casa Bianca, his flag captain (the other captain of the ship, Ganteaume, was one of the less than 100 people who survived from her crew; he managed to swim to another French ship, to fight the British again as an admiral at a later date). Casa Bianca's young son was aboard and refused to leave his father. This very sad event

Below: This Le Breton engraving shows the *Tonnant* at the Battle of the Nile, with her gallant Captain Dupetit-Thouars being placed in the bran tub from which he continued to command his vessel despite his dreadful wounds. Despite the fact that it was produced some 50 years after the battle, this probably gives a good idea of the scene on the quarterdeck of a ship in battle with the gun crews hard at work. Above and abaft it, on the poop, the small arms men are in action, with the tricolour nailed to the stump of the mizzen mast. The French artist has depicted the British ship in the background as rather larger than she actually would have been — the *Tonnant* was, in fact, larger than any British ship which took part in the Battle of the Nile. *NMM neg no: B9284*

was the inspiration of Mrs Hemans' much-parroted and much-parodied 'The boy stood on the burning deck/whence all but he had fled'. Those who escaped did so by swimming — for example 14 of them swam to the *Orion*. Some of those who were picked up from the water had lost everything but their lives; the log of the *Alexander* records the issue of clothing to naked French survivors.

As the fire gained and started to consume the rigging, nearby ships stopped firing and began to take precautions. Those who could moved away, sails were wetted, ports and hatches closed. Cartridges were removed from upper decks and bucket brigades organised to fight any consequent fires. When the *Orient* did finally blow up, however, it seems to have been an even greater shock than anyone had expected. The blast was appalling, as was the sheer volume of sound which temporarily deafened most of the spectators. Blazing bits of the ship fell all around, causing havoc. *Alexander* and *Franklin* were both set on fire by flaming debris, but fortunately both ships managed to put out the fire, the former by turning her stern into the wind so that the fire on the bow blew away from the ship and could be put out by the 'fire engine' (force pump carried by all larger ships) and bucket brigades organised from the crew. *Swiftsure* was hit by a large chunk of mast, which Captain Hallowell later had made into a coffin which he presented to his friend, Nelson. Temporarily there was no firing; everyone seems to have been too shocked and stunned to do much for a little while. Then *Franklin* resumed firing for a time with the three guns left in action before she surrendered with two thirds of her crew dead or wounded. The battle began to pick up again, though at a lesser tempo. The British crews had been fighting for six hours or more and were very tired. *Tonnant* was now the focus of attack. She had disabled the *Majestic* by bringing down her main and mizzen mast, and withstood more distant fire from *Swiftsure* and *Alexander*. Having been totally dismasted herself she managed to withdraw from action by letting out her cable, having fought hard and long. Her crew's bravery and stubbornness owed much to the heroic example set by their captain, Dupetit-Thouars, who had first one arm then the other shot off, and finally one of his legs. He insisted on staying on deck, put into a bran tub in an attempt to staunch his bleeding and continued to issue orders till he became unconscious from loss of blood, then died.

Majestic, having been disabled by *Tonnant*, drifted down the French line to catch her jib-boom (the outer end of her bowsprit) in the rigging of *Heureux* whose fire caused more damage and loss. She finally came to anchor between *Tonnant* and *Mercure* both of which, by then, had shifted from their original positions. By now men were getting very tired indeed, after a night of intense activity, clouds of smoke, shattering noise and great danger. Captain Miller of the *Theseus* wrote to his wife: 'My people were also so extremely jaded, that as soon as they had hove our sheet-anchor up they dropped under the capstan-bars, and were asleep in a moment in every sort of posture, having been then working at their fullest exertion, or fighting, for near twelve hours...'

At this late stage of the night those ships still in French hands had all moved away downwind towards the eastern end of the bay, though being, as yet, hardly damaged apart from the shattered *Tonnant*. As dawn broke at about 4am on 2 July some of these ships engaged the two nearest British ones, the *Alexander* and the much-battered *Majestic*. The firing attracted *Theseus* and *Goliath*. The former came to anchor not far away from the French frigate *Artémise* which fired into her and then surrendered. The *Artémise's* crew then set fire to their ship (apparently after surrendering their ship — not conventionally approved behaviour at that time) and escaped by rowing to the shore. For the second time in this battle a ship blew up. Meanwhile the remaining French ships moved away from their attackers into the recesses of the bay. In this process both *Heureux* and *Mercure* contrived to run themselves aground. These two surrendered after a brief exchange of shots with *Goliath*, *Theseus*, *Alexander* and *Leander*. The French frigate *Justice* had briefly tried to approach the *Bellerophon,* still a dismasted wreck and therefore in some danger of capture even by a lighter ship. *Zealous,* sent by signal from Nelson, soon scared the frigate off.

Whilst this was going on, at about 6am, the remaining French ships were left with no British ships in their immediate vicinity. The shattered *Tonnant* was in no condition to move, and the *Timoléon* ran herself aground whilst trying to tack. This left Rear-Admiral Villeneuve with his own *Guillaume Tell* and the *Généreux*, the frigates *Diane* and the rejoined *Justice* and a clear escape route to the open sea, which he took. The *Zealous*, justifying her name by her lonely attack, tried to cut off the escape of the four undamaged French ships. Her fire forced the *Guillaume Tell* to turn away, but Nelson recalled her before she could lay herself alongside the

Above: This is Dodd's impression of the scene in Aboukir Bay after the Battle of the Nile. The wrecked frigate in the left foreground is presumably intended to be the *Sérieuse* and the blazing two-decker perhaps the *Timoléon*. However, this is more likely to be a generalised artist's impression than an attempt at an accurately researched representation of what had happened. *NMM neg no: 1092*

Généreux or cut off the stern frigate. The British ships had all been damaged in their rigging, though, apart from *Bellerophon* and *Majestic*, not particularly seriously, but for the moment there was no prospect of supporting Captain Hood. In the exchange of fire between the lone British ship and the four French, the former had her rigging badly cut up, but the main damage on deck was only the smashing of a 'pipe' (barrel) of wine.

Rear-Admiral Villeneuve was much criticised for failing to support the head of the French line and for fleeing the battlefield. However, as he wrote when explaining his actions, Brueys in his orders '...had foreseen the case where he could call the van [head of the line] to the support of the centre or rear if these were attacked, but he had put down no article which would take the ships of the rear to the help of the vanguard, because the thing was impossible, and he would have divided his squadron without being able to take any advantage from it... I have talked about this business with several of the captains of the van. All are agreed... that in the moment when they were most heavily attacked by the enemy, they had never hoped for support from the ships of the rear; and that the loss of the squadron had

been decided at the moment when the English ships had been able to double the head of the line. Aboard the ships of the rearguard the thought of up-anchoring and making for the centre of the combat did not occur to anyone because it was impracticable.' One can set against this the suggestion made by a contemporary British chronicler: 'Had [the French rear at the beginning of the action] got under way and stood out, they would have found full employment for the five or six British ships that had not got into action. They would have undoubtedly have captured the *Culloden*, and prevented the *Alexander* and *Swiftsure* from entering the bay...' Maybe the ships and men that had attacked his fleet might have been able to do something under these circumstances; it is, however, unfair to blame

Villeneuve with his less well trained crews and the evidence he had of the high efficiency and fighting spirit of his enemy for saving what he could from the overwhelming disaster that had struck his fleet, just as it is unfair to saddle him with the blame for the failure of the French Navy to match the skill and fighting power of the Royal Navy the next time he confronted the victor of the Nile, seven years later at the Battle of Trafalgar. Certainly Brueys was at fault in failing to check that the head of his line was close enough to the shoals to prevent the doubling of his line, but he was not really expecting the Nelsonic lightning-stroke that hit him, the pell-mell attack that pushed the French fleet off balance and kept it there. Given the initial flaw in the French position, and the quality of their opponents, there could really be little doubt of the outcome of the battle. Superb captains were matched by highly trained crews with high morale, the whole led by a man who came near to the ideal leader for such a team, someone who excelled in communicating his intentions and encouraging and enthusing his excellent subordinates. The 'Nelson touch' reached its apogee on that hot summer evening and night off the Egyptian coast.

Nelson himself was out of action for some time. He was wounded early in the action by a splinter which hit him above his blind eye, cutting a strip of flesh which temporarily blinded him. The combination of this and shock had briefly made him think he was done for, but fortunately this was far from the case, and he could return to his quarterdeck with the wound sewn up in time to oversee the later stages of the battle, though still fairly groggy from shock and concussion. Captain Westcott of the *Majestic* had been killed by a musket shot from the *Tonnant* (which finally surrendered to *Theseus* and *Leander* on the morning of the 3rd). The British altogether lost 218 men killed and 617 wounded. The heaviest casualties were, as one might expect, aboard *Bellerophon* (49 dead, 148 wounded) and *Majestic* (50 and

Below: Nelson is pictured coming back on to the quarterdeck of the *Vanguard* after his head wound has been dressed. The flames of the burning *Orient* illuminate this dramatic scene from the Battle of the Nile which became one of the most famous set-pieces of the dramatic story of the admiral's life, in part due to popular prints like this. The men in the foreground pulling on a rope are hoisting out a boat, directed by the boatswain who can be seen just below and to the right of the stern of the boat blowing on his 'call' (whistle). *NMM neg no: A8887*

Above: This print was done long after the action it represents: the gallant struggle between the 50-gun *Leander*, carrying the dispatches reporting the Battle of the Nile, and the much larger and more powerful *Généreux* of 80 guns on 17 August 1798. This picture by Seaforth shows the smaller vessel succeeding in raking her larger antagonist before the long-delayed but inevitable surrender. *NMM neg no: B9407*

143 respectively). The bitter and effective defence of the *Spartiate* was responsible for most of the 30 dead and 76 wounded aboard *Vanguard*, the next biggest casualty list. It is interesting that the losses of the ships which attacked the outside of the French line were much greater than those of the others which passed through that line and engaged from the inside. This is a clear indication of the fact that the French had discounted any possibility of attack from the shoreward side, and had made no preparation for it.

The French loss was, inevitably, much greater than the British, particularly because of the total loss of their flagship. Besides Brueys, Casa Bianca and Dupetit-Thouars, the captain of *Aquilon* was also killed whilst Captain Dalbarade of the *Conquérant* never recovered from his wounds. The total of dead and wounded is not known for certain, estimates varying between 2,000 and 5,000. It is probable that about 1,600 dead and 1,500 wounded are figures that give the right idea of the scale of human suffering involved. One British seaman described the scene of battle revealed by sunrise: 'An awful sight it was, the whole bay was covered with dead bodies, mangled, wounded and scorched, not a bit of clothes on them but their trousers.'

On 2 and 3 August the British fleet cleared up after the action, seeing to wounded men and ships. *Timoléon* was set on fire by her crew and blew up on the afternoon of the 3rd when *Theseus* and *Leander* approached. *Tonnant* was finally forced to surrender to these two British ships earlier that same day. The British also landed on Aboukir Island and captured the guns and mortars of its battery. Nelson's report on the battle was given to Captain Berry, who was put aboard the *Leander* and sent off to carry the news of this smashing victory to Gibraltar and beyond. However, this 50-gun ship fell in with that 80-gun escapee from the battle, the *Généreux*. *Leander* was in an impossible situation, chased by a ship both faster than her and very much more powerful. She turned to fight and kept the unequal battle going for an astonishing four hours before

Above: A drawing made of the *Canopus,* the 80-gun ship taken from the French, as the *Franklin,* at the Nile in 1798 which went on to have a very distinguished career in the Royal Navy (and to have her lines copied for building a class of similar vesels). The date on this picture is 1866, four years after she was hulked. So it was probably done from memory by the artist — who was a Commander Horner — and shows her off Malta, accompanied by a 10-gun sloop, and with a cutter in the foreground. *NMM neg no: A8172*

finally having to surrender. *Généreux* towed her shattered and dismasted hulk to Corfu, then in French hands. On the way they were sighted by the *Mutine* which was carrying a duplicate set of dispatches (a practice which this event showed to be thoroughly sensible!). Later Corfu was captured by a joint Turkish-Russian force, and the Russians returned *Leander* to the Royal Navy.

Of the prizes taken in the battle, *Guerrier* (as predicted), *Heureux* and *Mercure* were considered too damaged to save and were destroyed. *Conquérant* was never fitted for sea by the Royal Navy. As we have seen, she was already considered weak and in a bad state, and she had suffered more damage in the fight. The same occurred to *Aquilon,* renamed *Aboukir* in honour of the battle. *Peuple Souverain* (an ideologically unsuitable name for the British) renamed *Guerrier* by the Royal Navy, was taken no further than Gibraltar where she became a hulk. *Spartiate* and *Tonnant* had active careers in British service, the former finally becoming a sheer hulk (used for hoisting masts in and out of ships by the huge pair of sheer legs placed on board — a sort of floating crane for harbour use) in 1842 at Plymouth, and was finally broken up in 1857. The latter was broken up in 1821. *Franklin,* renamed *Canopus,* remained one of the favourite ships of the Royal Navy for nearly half a century. Her longevity owed much to two major rebuilds, but also to her reputation as a fast sailer. In a series of sailing trials of ships of the line in the 1830s she beat all-comers. This may have owed even more to her crack captain than to her original design, but certainly her story has been used as a major argument in the continuing debate about whether French warship design was 'better' than English. Her design was used as a basis for a class of large two-deckers of 84 guns, nine of which were built in the years after the end of the Napoleonic War (between 1815 and 1831), providing a large and powerful part of the active British battlefleet of the next quarter-century.

All four French ships that had escaped from Aboukir Bay fell into British hands later.

Left: Lady Hamilton as Britannia with bust of Nelson, showing him as the hero of the Nile (which is the battle going on in the background), so presumably done before the Battle of Copenhagen in 1801. This totally 'over the top' picture shows how much Aboukir established Nelson as a national, and indeed international, hero. *NMM neg no: 8847*

Généreux was taken on 18 February 1800 trying to carry supplies to Valletta, then besieged by the British and Maltese. She was pursued by a British force and the frigate *Success* hung on her heels, causing enough damage and delay — the frigate's fire mortally wounded the French captain — for the *Foudroyant,* closely followed by the *Northumberland,* to overhaul the French ship and make her surrender. It was then *Guillaume Tell's* turn. She tried escaping from Valletta, but again the gallant and skilful tactics of smaller British ships — this time the 64 gun *Lion* and the frigate *Penelope* — assisted the *Foudroyant* to take her. This was a very hard-fought action, and the French ship inflicted considerable damage on her assailants before surrendering. She was renamed *Malta* in British service, converted to a reserve depot ship at Plymouth in 1831 and broken up in 1840. *Généreux* saw active service only for a couple of years; she was laid up in 1802 at the time of the Peace of Amiens, and remained in that state till broken up in 1816. The two frigates *Diane* and *Justice* were both at Malta during the siege, and attempted to get away at the same time. The latter succeeded, for a while, finally being taken in Alexandria harbour when that port fell to the British on 2 September 1801 (she was handed over to the Turks). *Diane,* however, was caught by the British frigate *Success,* which was leading the pursuit. She became the British *Niobe,* serving throughout the Napoleonic War, to be converted to a troopship in 1814 and broken up in 1816. So Britain not only deprived her adversary of the use of a number of ships, but also got good service out of a number of them as well.

There is a final footnote before we leave the ships that fought in this battle. Apparently a few years ago a group of Egyptian and French divers discovered and worked on the remains of the *Orient* in Aboukir Bay. This, alas, seems to have been a treasure hunt with little archaeological content — at least there has so far apparently been no attempt to publish any of the findings of this expedition.

The results of the battle were striking. The most obvious one was that Bonaparte was isolated in Egypt with his army. They had already won the Battle of the Pyramids and gone on to conquer the entire country. Now, however, they were cut off from home. A thrust towards Syria was foiled before the walls of Acre, where 'Sir' Sidney Smith (his knighthood was from the King of Sweden, and not very highly regarded by his brother officers), that posturing, self-promoting but brilliant officer, assisted the Turkish garrison in its defence. Napoleon himself managed to escape from Egypt in a frigate and returned to France and his destiny. His army remained trapped in Egypt, despite a couple of attempts by the French fleet to resupply it. Eventually, in 1801, the British landed an army at Alexandria in a brilliant amphibious operation, launched from Britain. The landing was opposed, but the Navy's fire support enabled the Army to sweep ashore and defeat the French. This was the first real military victory obtained by the British against the French in that war. The French army surrendered on terms, though the news of the victory arrived too late to affect the signing of the Peace of Amiens.

Back in 1798 Nelson's spectacular victory established him as an international hero and heartened all opponents of Revolutionary France. Turkey and Naples came into the war at the side of Britain. Malta would fall into British hands with Captain Alexander Ball, who had endeared himself to the native Maltese during the siege of the French garrison in Valetta, becoming the first British governor of the island. The battle became a popular subject for artists, with the spectacular loss of the *Orient* as the favourite scene. As Nelson himself observed: 'Victory is not a name strong enough for such a scene.'

Perhaps most important of all, the Battle of the Nile confirmed the moral ascendancy of the British Royal Navy over its chief rival. It also set a new standard in naval victories — of absolute victory with the loser deprived of nearly all his ships. No other battle between fleets of approximately equal size in the age of fighting sail was quite so strikingly complete, not even Trafalgar. The performance of the British fleet was of the highest quality. The consistent impression is of smooth teamwork combined with the maximum of intelligent initiative; of a powerful, well-oiled machine swinging into action. It was doing so against an enemy who did not lack gallantry, but who were nowhere near as well trained, organised or led. Most of all it was the achievement, not just of Nelson, but of his 'band of brothers' as well.

The fleets at Aboukir Bay

* = taken

Three-decker 120-gun nil/one
British: **nil**
French: *Orient* (Flagship — blew up — Vice Admiral F. P. Brueys, Captains H. Ganteaume and L. de Casa Bianca) — **one**

Two-deckers 80-gun nil/four
British: **nil**
French: **Franklin* (Flag of Rear-Admiral A. S. M. Blanquet du Chayla, Captain M. Gilet), **Tonnant* (A. A. Dupetit-Thouars), *Généreux* (Le Joille), *Guillaume Tell* (Flag of Rear-Admiral P. C. J. B. S. Villeneuve, Captain Saulnier) — **four**

Two-deckers 74-gun 13/eight
British: *Vanguard* (Flag of Rear-Admiral Horatio Nelson, Captain Edward Berry), *Orion* (Sir James Saumarez), *Culloden* (Thomas Troubridge), *Bellerophon* (Henry d'Esterre Darby), *Minotaur* (Thomas Louis), *Defence* (John Peyton), *Alexander* (Alexander John Ball), *Zealous* (Samuel Hood), *Audacious* (Davidge Gould), *Goliath* (Thomas Foley), *Majestic* (George Blagden Westcott), *Swiftsure* (Benjamin Hallowell), *Theseus* (Ralph Willett Miller) — **13**
French: **Heureux* (J. P. Etienne), **Spartiate* (M. J. Emeriau), **Aquilon* (H. A. Thévenard), **Mercure* (Cambon), **Guerrier* (J. F. T. Trullet [the first]), **Peuple Souverain* (P. P.Raccord), **Conquérant* (S. Dalbarade), *Timoléon* (burnt — J. F. T. Trullet [the second]) — **eight**

Small two-decker 50-gun one/nil
British: *Leander* (Thomas Boulden Thompson) — **one**
French: no equivalent

Frigates nil/four
British: **none**
French: *Sérieuse* (12-pounder — sunk), *Artémise* (12-pounder — burnt), *Diane* (18-pounder — flag of Rear-Admiral D. Decrès), *Justice* (ex-*Courageuse* — 18-pounder) — **four**

Small craft
British: *Mutine* (brig — [Thomas Masterman Hardy])
French: *Railleur, Alerte* (brigs), three bomb-vessels, one of which was sunk, and several gun-boats

Above left: This cartoon of Nelson destroying revolutionary crocodiles was produced to celebrate the Battle of the Nile. *NMM neg no: A3255*

Above: This painting by J. M. W. Turner shows the dramatic shipwreck of the *Minotaur* in 1810, several years after her involvement in the Battle of the Nile. *NMM neg no: 2705*

Below: Originally published a year after the Battle of the Nile this picture by William Elmes is inscribed 'Admiral Nelson's Victory over the French Fleet near the Mouth of the Nile'. The ship shown broadside in the centre probably represents *L'Orient* on fire before she blew up. *NMM neg no: C784*

Above: Mortella Tower, Corsica, put up such stiff resistance to British attack in 1794 that it was made the prototype for the 'Martello' towers built to defend the English coast. *NMM neg no: C1083*

Below: The *Baileys*, an armed cutter, off the Eddystone lighthouse in 1795. This type of vessel was used by the navy although in this instance is probably a privateer. *NMM neg no: X72*

Defence against invasion by the Boulogne Flotilla

Stopping foreign invasions coming by sea has always been one of the main purposes of a navy. Throughout our period it was a major duty for the Royal Navy. There were two main types of threat, which might be found separately or together. In the first instance there was the prospect of a longer range invasion by troops carried in transports, merchant ships or warships, supported by a battlefleet. An example of this was the invasion force that the French were gathering in the Morbihan in 1759, which was, as we have seen, foiled by the British victory at Quiberon Bay. At the same time the French were gathering the second type of invasion force at Le Havre, a short-range invasion, to be carried aboard specially built landing craft — flat-bottomed barges with just enough seaworthiness to get across the Channel on a calm day. The craft gathered together for that force were subjected to a very heavy bombardment by bomb-vessels under Rodney's command. The high angle mortars with their explosive shells were the best weapon to use against such a target. They had comparatively long range and could fire from outside the range of ordinary cannon, though their accuracy left much to be desired. In 20th century terms this was an area weapon rather than a precision munition. Many shells had to be fired to produce a satisfactory result. Rodney's bomb-vessels fired so much that they cracked most of the mortars which did not actually explode, and even their stout construction was inadequate to absorb the repeated shocks of firing. None of them actually sank from their leaks, but all had to be nursed back to Portsmouth and then given major rebuilds before they could be used again.

During the American War of Independence the real danger of successful invasion was greater than at any other time in the entire period from the beginning of the 18th century to the Battle of Waterloo (1815). This was because the combined fleets of France and Spain were close to establishing control of the Channel. They outnumbered the British Channel Fleet, which itself was riven by politics after the indecisive Battle of Ushant against the French fleet the previous year and its disastrous legacy of quarrel and court martial. No invasion force was sent, the British fleet evaded action and the combined fleet, and was plagued first by delay and then by a real plague. 'Ship fever' (what we would now call typhus) ravaged the crews, killing far more than ever died in battle. No such combination was tried again in that war, and the British government breathed again. It had been very lucky, for the French had plans to seize Portsmouth, and with the combined fleet controlling the channel could have landed a large force wherever they chose. The invasion schemes of the French Revolution and of Napoleon were never as seriously threatening. They either hoped for a surprise landing by a landing flotilla without fleet support, an

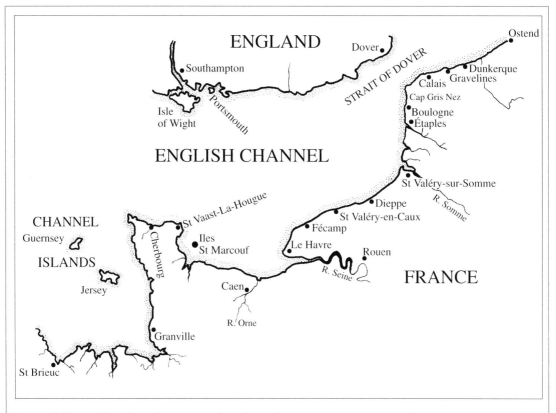

ENGLAND

Dover

Ostend

Southampton

STRAIT OF DOVER

Dunkerque
Calais Gravelines
Cap Gris Nez
Boulogne
Étaples

Isle
of Wight

Portsmouth

ENGLISH CHANNEL

St Valéry-sur-Somme
R. Somme

CHANNEL

St Vaast-La-Hougue

Dieppe
St Valéry-en-Caux
Fécamp

Guernsey

Cherbourg

Iles
St Marcouf

Le Havre

Rouen

ISLANDS

R. Seine

FRANCE

Jersey

Caen

R. Orne

Granville

St Brieuc

Above: Map of the English Channel during the Napoleonic War.

impossibility with a force large enough to have a chance of defeating the defenders' land forces; or they were attempting complex combinations of fleets from various ports with elaborate timetables and diversionary moves. The latter was the case with Napoleon's plan which led to the Trafalgar campaign, an over-elaborate landsman's plan which had no chance of succeeding against the realities of wind, weather, inadequately trained crews and a competent, experienced enemy high command. We will look at the failure to bring a French fleet into the Channel to support the landing craft of the invasion flotilla in the later chapter on Trafalgar. Here we will look at the first line of defence against the Napoleonic flotilla and its Revolutionary predecessor in the period between 1797 and 1805.

This first line of defence, the small ships serving in the Channel, has never been given its due. A recent book by a military historian on the defence of Britain against Napoleonic invasion does not even begin to consider it. The historian in question spends some time on the British battlefleet; he then discusses the land defences in great detail, from the Martello towers and the Royal Military Canal to the Militia and the Fencibles. As a discussion of

the military second line of defence, it is excellent. But if the French had tried crossing the Channel it would have been the frigates, sloops and gun-brigs of the Royal Navy and the gun-boats of the Sea Fencibles (not a force that is mentioned at all in the aforesaid book) which would have met them. It is very unlikely indeed that many would have managed to fight through to the beaches of the English coast. From 1794 the Royal Navy had been building specialised shallow draft vessels (originally called gun-boats, later gun-brigs) for coastal defence and offence. These supplemented more conventional warships in patrolling off the enemy bases. We will see frigates, sloops, cutters and schooners employed in attacking the invasion flotilla whenever it showed itself. The force specifically intended for use against that flotilla was based on the Downs, the anchorage between the Goodwin Sands and the coast of the county of Kent. Just north and east of Dover, this is where the distance between England and France is at its least, and where the Channel merges with the North Sea.

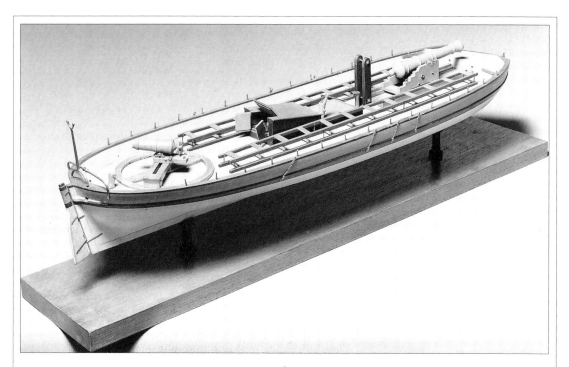

Above: Some 50 boats like this model were built for inshore work by the Royal Navy in the years after Trafalgar. There is clear influence here from the designs of the Swedish pioneer naval architect Chapman, which were copied or imitated throughout the western world. In this particular design the long gun forward had a small degree of traverse on a pivoted slide, whilst the carronade aft was on a rotating mounting, so could fire in any direction. The rig was the usual (for a gun-boat) lateen.
NMM neg no: C535

Eventually, when the formidable Admiral Lord Keith took command of the force, he would establish his headquarters ashore in a mansion on the cliffs of the North Foreland, from which he could see and signal to his forces in the Downs. On a clear day he would also have been able to see the French coast. Under his command also came the local defence craft manned by the Sea Fencibles. These were a maritime militia, fishermen and watermen (not to mention smugglers and wreckers) who were exempt from the press gang, and who would man gun-boats, some specially built, some converted from barges, Dutch hoys and the like as well as shore batteries and, in some cases, Martello Towers. They were never put to the test, but it is likely that, in waters they knew well and fighting to preserve their homes and families, they would have proved formidable adversaries to the laden landing craft. The invasion, probably fortunately for the French army, was never attempted, but there were a number of battles, large and small, mostly caused by the British determination to disrupt invasion preparations. We will now look at a selection of these, in which the Royal Navy's traditional attitude that the proper limits of its activity were the sea-coasts of the enemy was taken as far as it could go.

The serious threat of invasion began in 1797, inspired by Napoleon. From the autumn of 1797, all the harbours along the coast, from Antwerp to Cherbourg, began rapidly filling with gun-vessels and flat-bottomed boats for the invasion of England. The creation and maintenance of this flotilla was the business of the *Commission des Côtes de La Manche.* The Commission consisted of General Andréossi (director-general), M. Forfait, director, and Rear-Admiral La Crosse, inspector-general; and local inspectors, under La Crosse, including captains Ganteaume, Dumanoir Le Pelley, and de Casa Bianca — a group of considerable talent. The flat-bottomed landing boats, which were built in hundreds for the Commission, were popularly known as 'Muskein boats' after the Antwerper who had produced their plans. However, it seems likely that he was copying the designs of that great Swedish designer, Chapman. As these boats, and the seamen and soldiers who

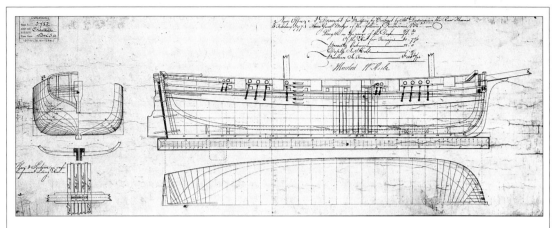

Above: The Admiralty design plan for the *Acute* class gun-brigs of 1797. This particular plan was sent to the Dudman shipyard at Deptford on the Thames for building three vessels by contract: the *Blazer*, *Clinker* and *Cracker*. (The odd names are explained by the fact that all these anti-invasion gun-boats were given names usually given to foxhounds, allegedly specifically the names of the First Lord of the Admiralty's hounds. This is the first instance of the Royal Navy taking a common theme for the naming of the ships of a particular class.) Another 12 of the class were launched by other builders. This represents the second stage in the evolution of the design of these anti-invasion craft. The original *Conquest* class of 1794 were flat-bottomed and shallow draft, slightly more so than the design shown here. They had gun ports low in the bow to take two long 24-pounder 'chase' guns, which would have been difficult to work or fire in anything except a flat calm. The ports for these guns, as we can see from the plan, were moved up in the 1797 design. The rest of the armament was six 18-pounder carronades a side. After completion some of the 1794 vessels were fitted with 'sliding keels' (dagger boards) to give them extra keel area to improve their sailing abilities without compromising their shallow draft. These were built into the 1797 design from the start; they are shown by dotted lines in their extended position below the keel in the plan, which also depicts the structural arrangements made round the slots in the keel. The later classes built in numbers in 1800 and 1804 abandoned the big bow chasers for an armament of carronades, later supplemented by a couple of six-pounder long guns as bow chasers. They also abandoned the flat bottom and shallow draft to become, in effect, smaller versions of the brig sloops of the period.
NMM neg no: ADM 3782

Right: The hull plan of the gun-boat *William* shows a small coaster converted for coastal defence during the invasion scares of the 1790s. This was the sort of vessel which would be manned by the Sea Fencibles, a sort of maritime Home Guard or Militia. The really interesting point about this particular conversion is the mounting of the long gun forward.

This is on a rotating mount, a forerunner of the turret, mounted on a 'ball race' of cannon balls. This vessel was converted to a gun-boat at Plymouth in 1795, under the supervision of Sir Sidney Smith, who was probably remembering the mountings he had seen on gun-boats designed by Chapman when he was serving with the Swedish navy.
NMM neg no: ADM 6501

were intended to man them, gathered in the ports, it occurred to someone that they might be used to clear up a local annoyance, whilst obtaining experience and a small taste of action.

There was a British garrison on the two small islands of St Marcou. They are three or four miles distant from the shore of the Cotentin peninsula, just off St Vaast La Hogue, and near the route of coasters sailing between Le Havre and Cherbourg. As he considered they would form a good base for harassing French coastal trade, and the French had no forces on them, the enterprising Captain Sir William Sidney Smith took them over in July 1795. By 1797 they were held by a force of about 500 seamen and Marines, under the orders of Lieutenant Price, of the *Badger,* a four-gun gun-boat converted from a Dutch hoy which had been purchased and armed for the service. The French decided to use part of their invasion force to attempt the recapture of these islands. On 5 April, the 38-gun frigates *Diamond* and *Hydra* found 33 flat-bottomed boats in Caen roads, escorted by a few gun-brigs and commanded by Muskein himself. They were on their way from Le Havre to attack St Marcou. The British frigates attacked but *Diamond* grounded and they were unable to do anything effective that night. On the following morning the flotilla carried on westward, but, upon the appearance offshore of

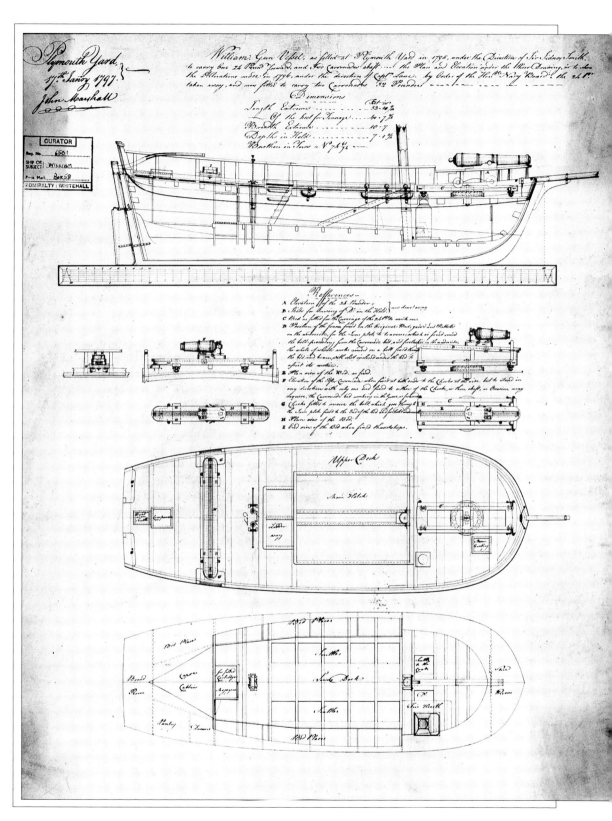

99

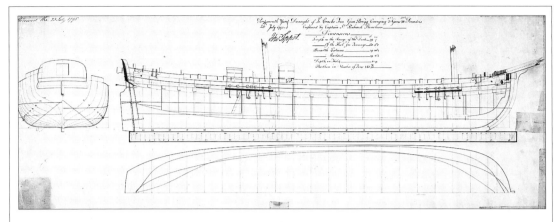

Above: Hull plan of the French invasion gun-boat *Crache Feu*, typical of the craft prepared by the French Republic for a possible invasion of Britain in the 1790s, and much like the landing craft built for Napoleon. This boat was captured by the Royal Navy and these plans were 'taken off' her hull.
NMM neg no: ADM 6361

a British 50, it turned back east, pursued by the frigates, and took shelter in the mouth of the River Orne. There it was later joined by about 40 more landing craft and armed fishing boats and seven gun-brigs from Cherbourg. Captain Muskein, with his increased force, managed to reach La Hogue undetected, where he lay, awaiting calm weather, in order to attack Lieutenant Price.

His opportunity came on the night of 6 May. The British had warning of his approach, but there was a dead calm and the *Adamant*, 50, *Eurydice*, 24, and the sloop *Orestes*, the only warships in the area, could not get near the islands to help in their defence. In the darkness, the French, with 52 craft carrying 5,000–6,000 men, placed themselves to attack at dawn. At daybreak on the 7th the French brigs were seen at about 350yd from the British fortifications. The 17 guns which would bear on them opened fire. The French replied vigorously, and their landing craft advanced with great determination to land their men, but the effect of the sinking of six or seven of these laden boats caused the others to change their minds and withdraw. The loss of the attackers was probably upwards of 1,200 killed, drowned and wounded. On the British side, but one man was killed, and only four were wounded, in spite of the fact that the defence had been fired on by 80 guns or more. As the enemy drew off, the three British warships managed to get within range, but the calm prevented them from cutting off the retreat of the flotilla. As a recent French book has put it, this gives a fair idea of the probable result had the invasion of Britain been attempted at this time, even in the unlikely event of the mass of the flotilla evading attack from warships in mid-channel.

Not all British scuffles with the invasion craft were equally successful. In the spring of 1798 it became known that many small craft were fitting out for troops at Flushing (Vlissingen) and were about to be conveyed, by way of the Bruges Canal, to Ostend and thence to Dunkirk. It was decided to try to bring this plan to naught by destroying the lock gates and sluices at Ostend, and so rendering the canal useless. Captain Home Riggs Popham, who had made himself into a great expert on combined operations (he was an inventive and enterprising officer who also devised the code of flag signals that was adopted by the Royal Navy) was the naval officer given this job, in collaboration with troops under Major-General Sir Eyre Coote.

The expedition assembled off Margate, sailing on 14 May, and anchored off Ostend just after midnight on 19 May. Although the weather was bad, nearly all the troops were at once landed to the northeast of the town. The landing was unopposed. At about 4.15am the Ostend batteries opened fire upon the nearest British vessels, the *Wolverine*, *Asp* and *Biter*, and by about 8.30am had so badly damaged the first two that Popham signalled to them to up-anchor and move further out. The bomb-vessels *Hecla* and *Tartarus* had already begun to shell the town and harbour, and, upon the withdrawal of the *Wolverine* and *Asp*, the *Dart*, *Kite* and *Harpy* moved as near to their old places as was possible at low tide.

The lock gates and sluices, together with several gun-boats, were apparently destroyed (though the French accounts state that the

Above: At a pinch soldiers could be landed in ordinary ships' boats, but the Royal Navy, at least, had specialised landing craft as well. These were the 'flat-bottomed boats for the landing of men' depicted by this contemporary model. There were several versions of differing lengths, some with round and some with square sterns. They were built in considerable numbers, very often in prefabricated kit form, to be assembled close to the landing point. This was certainly the case with the Havana expedition of 1762 (see the picture of that landing over the page which shows large numbers of boats of this type taking soldiers ashore from the transports). A double row of soldiers sat in the centre of the thwarts (benches), with the sailors who rowed the boat on either side of them. They often mounted a small swivel gun (half-pounder, placed in a swivel which rotated on a timber post in the bows) as a fire-support weapon. Some boats of this kind would be converted to take a bigger gun in the bows and act as gun-boats. Quite a few types of purpose-built gun-boat were evolved from this design. *NMM neg no: A926*

locks survived) by the troops at 10.20am, but at noon, when it was decided to re-embark, the weather was so bad that the attempt was totally hopeless. The British troops were stuck on shore. The French attacked in force on the 20th and, after they had lost 65 killed and wounded, the landing force had to surrender.

With the defeat of the Dutch fleet at Camperdown, and the approach of winter, the threat of invasion diminished towards the end of 1797. In 1798 Napoleon turned his attention to Egypt, and it was not until 1801 that he contemplated breathing new life into the invasion threat. In what nowadays would be called a 'PR move' Nelson, just returned from his victory at Copenhagen, was appointed to command the defences of the coast from Orford Ness to Beachy Head, the most threatened corner of the English coast from beyond the north side of the Thames Estuary to Brighton. He hoisted his flag in the 32-gun frigate *Medusa,* at anchor in the Downs, and on 3 August, obeying instructions from the Admiralty, crossed to Boulogne to endeavour to destroy the flotilla which was assembled under the guns of the lately strengthened fortifications of the place. He had with him 30 vessels, mostly gun-brigs and bomb-vessels. On the 4th the latter shelled the part of the French flotilla which was within range of their mortars. There are conflicting claims, but it seems that the fire was too inaccurate to do serious damage, the two gun-boats which had been damaged were easily repaired and that no French were either killed or wounded. On the British side three persons were wounded. The bombs had fired more than 900 shells to little effect. Nelson, therefore, determined to try the effect of a 'cutting out expedition' (we would probably call it a commando raid using boats) on a large scale.

He organised the armed boats of the squadron into four divisions and, on the night of 15 August, sent them in accompanied by a division of boats armed with howitzers (short guns firing shells) to provide fire support. The boats assembled round the *Medusa* and started off from her at about 11.30pm. Owing to the darkness, the tide and the currents, the divisions soon became separated and could not co-operate as had been planned. The boats of one division, driven far to the eastward, had to split up and proceed independently. Just before dawn on the 16th, some of these succeeded in reaching and attacking a brig which lay close to the pier-head, but, though they carried her, they were forced to abandon her as she was secured by a chain which they could not sever, and was swept by the fire of four craft moored quite close to her. As daylight broke, they retreated, with heavy losses.

The second group of boats was less affected by the current and, at about 12.30am, some ran alongside the brig *Etna*. But boarding nets arranged to prevent easy access to the deck and a heavy fire forced the men back. Other boats captured a lugger, but were repulsed by the brig *Volcan* and the two sub-divisions retired with a loss of 21 killed and 42 wounded. The third division was also driven back after it had fought most gallantly and had lost five

Above: One of the classic night-time 'cutting out' operations is shown here. The ship in the centre of the picture is the extraordinary experimental vessel *Dart* (see the plan of this ship for more information). Here she is capturing and sailing out of an enemy harbour (which is what 'cutting out' means) the frigate *Désirée*.

This 1800 scene set in Dunkirk Roads may make some think of the fictitious Jack Aubrey's exploit in the *Polychrest* cutting out the *Fanciulla*. However, in the actual event *Dart* got away to fight another day — in the Battle of Copenhagen, for example, whilst her attack was on a total of four moored French frigates and was supported by two gun-brigs and (as can be seen) fireships. *NMM neg no: A4305*

Above right: Plan of bombardment of Boulogne 1800, showing the position of Nelson's ships and the defensive dispositions of Rear-Admiral La Touche. The semi-pictorial plan of the action is supplemented by a map showing the location of Boulogne in this contemporary French print. *NMM neg no: A3259*

Right: The artist Serres painted a magnificent sequence of pictures showing the progress of the Havana expedition of 1762 which was a model of how to organise and carry out an amphibious operation, and captured Cuba for Britain. The original paintings are held by the National Maritime Museum. This is a print of one of them showing the actual assault landing. On the right are the supporting warships, whilst between them and the shore the hired merchant transports put the troops into the flat-bottomed landing craft which are rowing them to the shore. *NMM neg no: 4355*

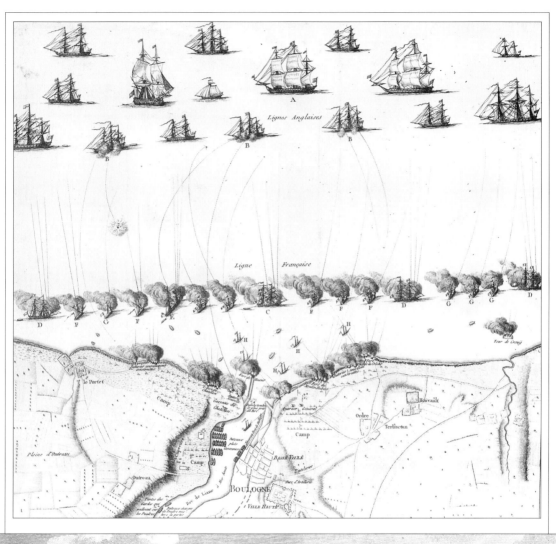

killed and 29 wounded. The fourth division, unable to get near the enemy before day broke, came back without loss.

The French, who had been reinforced since 4 August, claimed to have run down eight British boats and to have taken four, and to have lost only 10 killed and 30 wounded. The total British loss was 44 killed and 126 wounded. Nelson never seems to have been particularly successful in attacks of this kind, and this one must count as a defeat.

No other large scale attack was made against the invasion flotilla, but on the night of 20 August, the boats of a small squadron attacked six French flats which lay covered by five field-guns and a party of infantry between St Valery and Etaples. Three were taken and brought off, and the other three were scuttled by their crews. The British losses were only one killed and four wounded. The signing of the Peace of Amiens then temporarily ended the threat from the invasion flotilla.

In 1803 war was renewed and Napoleon revived the threat with greater resources than ever before. He began to collect gun-boats and other craft for the purpose in various ports from Ostend to Granville. British cruisers were stationed before all these ports, and not only did the enemy seldom venture out without being attacked, but also he was frequently attacked when still lying at his moorings in supposed safety.

On the morning of 14 June, the four-gun French gun-vessels *Inabordable* and *Commode* were chased on shore under batteries near Cap Blanc-Nez by the 36-gun frigate *Immortalité*, 36, and the 18-gun brig sloops *Cruiser* and *Jalouse*. When the tide permitted, the *Cruiser* and *Jalouse* stood in, and, anchoring with springs on their cables so that they could move their broadsides round as desired, took on and silenced the batteries. This having been done, the boats of the squadron boarded and brought off both vessels, losing only one man wounded.

On 1 August, the 38-gun frigate *Hydra* prevented a French armed lugger, the *Favori*, four, from entering Le Havre. She was forced to haul close to the beach near the mouth of the River Touque. Captain George Mundy sent his boats to cut her out or destroy her. As they approached, her crew abandoned ship and then joined some troops behind the sandbanks to open fire with small arms on the attackers. Despite their fire, the *Favori* was carried off at the cost of one man killed.

On 14 September, at 8am, the 36-gun frigate *Immortalité* accompanied the bomb-vessels *Perseus* and *Explosion* on a mission to bombard the Dieppe batteries and 17 vessels, building or fitting out in that port. They continued the fire until about 11.30am, setting fire to the town in three places. They then went along the coast to St Valery-en-Caux, where six other vessels were constructing. At 3pm they began an hour-long bombardment. It is doubtful whether very much damage was done, but the loss was only one missing and five wounded.

On the evening of 13 September, the *Cerberus*, a 32-gun frigate flying the flag of Rear-Admiral Sir James Saumarez, with the sloops *Cherwell* and *Kite*, the schooner *Eling* and the cutter *Carteret* anchored quite close in front of the town of Granville to await the arrival of the bombs *Sulphur* and *Terror,* for an attack on the numerous gun-boats lying within the pier, and to damage the port. The *Terror* appeared towards midnight, but, as she grounded in the darkness at low water, she was not able to get into her intended position until 2am on the 14th. She then shelled the gun-vessels and batteries for over three hours, but was recalled towards daybreak and re-anchored out of gunshot, with a loss of two men slightly wounded. Soon afterwards the *Sulphur* finally appeared, but little could be done that evening, as the tide prevented even the small craft from getting sufficiently close. On the morning of the 15th, however, all the ships were able to position themselves effectively and from 5am to 10.30am they fired away as fast as they could, though it is not certain that they produced very much effect. The falling tide then forced a withdrawal. They had been opposed by 22 gun-vessels, besides the batteries on shore, but suffered no loss and very little damage. In withdrawing, the *Cerberus* grounded on a shoal. Nine gun-boats emerged from port and began to fire on her but they were eventually compelled to retire and at the end of three hours the *Cerberus* was refloated.

On the night of 27 September a division of small craft, under the control of the sloop *Autumn*, bombarded Calais for several hours, apparently inflicting some damage, but receiving none. The British vessels were then driven off by a gale. On the following day, taking advantage of their absence, numerous French gun-boats left Calais for Boulogne and made their destination safely although chased and fired at by the frigate *Leda*. On 29 September, 25 other gun-boats attempted to follow. The *Leda* drove two ashore, where they were wrecked, but the rest reached their destination, making, with those already there, a flotilla of 55 in all. On 31 October, near Etaples, Captain Honyman of the *Leda*, who had with

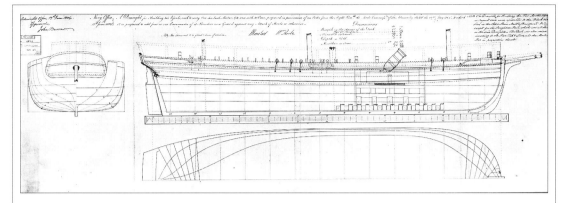

Above: This Admiralty plan was the design for building two mortar boats on the Thames, for providing high-angle shell fire from the 10in mortar which can be seen on its reinforced mounting a third of the way along the hull from the bow. They were intended for use against the invasion flotilla in its bases. The plan also shows two different positions for two masts. The original rig was intended to be that of a brig with the masts being of equal length and set forward and amidships (in the middle), whilst the rig adopted was that of a ketch with a large mast amidships and a small one in the stern, both of which are vertical rather than raked backwards, as are the masts for the original brig rig. The design was intended for rowing (notice the thole pins for the oars along the gunwale) as well as sailing, but does not seem to have been a success. *Convulsion* and *Destruction* were built in 1804, but were sold in 1806, a service life of not much over a year.
NMM neg no: ADM 6852

him the sloops *Lark* and *Harpy*, saw a gun-brig and six schooners and sloops coming out of port and making for Boulogne. He ordered the *Lark* and *Harpy* to chase, but the hired cutter *Admiral Mitchell*, which was already off Boulogne, attacked to such good effect that although she had to fight with a land battery at Le Portel as well, she succeeded, after two hours and a half, in driving ashore the gun-brig and one of the sloops. The *Admiral Mitchell* suffered in her rigging, had a carronade dismounted, but only five men wounded.

Actions of this kind continued as the invasion preparations gathered impetus in 1804. On 15 May, a squadron under Commodore Sidney Smith was watching the coast between Flushing and Ostend. He flew his flag in the 50-gun ship *Antelope*. One inshore group consisted of the *Cruiser,* 18, and *Rattler,* 16, off Ostend. Another British force was cruising off Calais and a line of four gun-brigs was stationed between the two groups to pass signals. On the evening of this day 23 gun-vessels were seen to emerge from Ostend

harbour and to anchor near the lighthouse. The captain of *Cruiser*, Hancock, recalled the four gun-brigs to his assistance and sent the hired armed cutter *Stag* to the commodore with news of what was happening. As darkness came on, Hancock got under way with his two sloops and anchored within long range of the pier batteries. In this position he hoped to prevent the escape of the enemy. On the morning of the 16th, it was perceived that the four gun-brigs had either not seen or not understood the signal of recall, and the signal was again hoisted. At 9.30am the *Rattler,* which lay somewhat to the eastward of the *Cruiser,* signalled, first five sail, and then a fleet, to the east-south-east. The strangers were a Franco-Dutch flotilla which, under Rear-Admiral Ver Huell, had sailed from the Inner Wieling early that morning in order to reach Ostend. They consisted of the two ship-rigged 12-gun 'pramees', *Ville d'Anvers* and *Ville d'Aix,* 19 schooners, and 38 'schuyts' (Dutch single-masted coastal craft), mounting between them a total of more than 100 long guns, besides carronades and mortars, and having on board about 4,000 troops. At 10am the two sloops, as soon as it was possible to take advantage of the tide, up-anchored and began to work towards the enemy. An hour later, the wind shifted to the southwest, which was favourable to the sloops. This caused Ver Huell to turn back towards Flushing. At much the same time Sir Sidney Smith received the news of the enemy and set off from Schoneveld with the *Antelope*, and the frigates *Penelope* and *Aimable*. At about noon he sighted the two sloops. But their captains, instead of waiting for him, pressed on and at 1.30pm the *Cruiser* overhauled one of the rearmost schuyts which surrendered. The Dutch commander turned back towards Ostend with all his force but eight of the schuyts. The two British sloops were exposed to fire from his flotilla and also from the shore batteries at Blankenberghe. Despite this the sloops managed to drive Ver Huell's flagship *Ville d'Anvers* and four schooners aground.

At 3.45pm the *Aimable* was the first of the larger British ships to get into action and by about 4.30pm the other two had succeeded in getting into range as well. At 7.45pm they ceased firing and withdrew as the tide was on the ebb and they were in danger of going aground. By then a large proportion of Ver Huell's flotilla had been driven ashore, and the retreat of the survivors was covered by the Ostend gun-boats which had come out of harbour the previous evening. Despite two later attempts by the British to destroy her, the *Ville d'Anvers* and five out of eight grounded schooners and schuyts were refloated and taken into the basin at Ostend.

At this time Le Havre was the assembly point for the vessels of the invasion flotilla that had been fitted out in the Seine and its tributaries before they could be sent on to Boulogne. On 23 July, and again on 1 August, a force of sloops, bombs and small craft, controlled by the frigate *Melpomene*, bombarded and fired the town, but it does not appear that the French preparations were much delayed.

The British blockading divisions, though often driven off or otherwise hampered by bad weather, were occasionally helped by it. On 19 July, for example, a strong wind and heavy sea threatened the French flotilla moored off Boulogne and in the evening forced some of the vessels to leeward to up-anchor and make to windward. Others ran for Etaples. Forty-five brigs and 45 luggers remained in the road (anchorage). About 24 miles to the westward lay the frigates *Immortalité* (Captain Owen) and *Leda,* with several small craft. Owen ordered the sloop *Harpy,* 18, along with the brigs *Bloodhound* and *Archer*, to run in and open fire upon the vessels attempting to claw off the land. They were presently joined by the *Autumn* and for several hours the flotilla was under attack. By daylight on the 20th, only 19 brigs and eight luggers remained in the road. The bad weather continuing, these soon began to slip and to run for Etaples or St Valery-sur-Somme. The *Autumn* and her consorts were too far to leeward to intercept them, but as soon as the tide had risen enough, the two frigates stood in close to the town. How far the British fire had contributed to the result is not known, but it could be seen from the frigates that a brig, a lugger and several large boats were stranded westward of the harbour, that three other brigs and a lugger were total wrecks on the rocks

near Le Portel, and that a brig and two luggers, anchored close to the rocks had signals of distress flying and were in clear danger. More than 400 Frenchmen are known to have died. Napoleon himself was present to see this disaster.

In August 1804, a British squadron of nearly 20 vessels cruised off Boulogne under Rear-Admiral Thomas Louis in the 50-gun *Leopard* (it seems the 50s were still considered very useful for the purpose of acting as flagships for anti-invasion task groups — presumably their combination of two gun decks, comparatively light draft and reasonable seaworthiness contributed to their suitability). Its main concentration usually lay about 10 miles to the northwest, while a division, under Captain Owen, kept just out of shell-range of the shore batteries. On 25 August, a division of gun-boats, under Captain Julien Le Ray, forming part of the 146 vessels of the class then in the road, up-anchored and began moving out towards Pointe Bombe, off which lay the British gun-brig *Bruiser*. She opened fire upon them, and the firing attracted the *Immortalité* which, at 2.30pm, began to engage both the gun-vessels and the batteries. She soon found, however, that she was too close inshore and eventually moved out to a distance of about three miles. Early on the following morning the brigs *Bloodhound* and *Archer* were in distant action with some luggers which were rounding Cap Gris-Nez very near the shore, and later in the day another division of gun-boats, together with some mortar vessels which had come from the Elbe, weighed and joined Captain Le Ray, who was manoeuvring between Ambleteuse and Vimereux. The united force then numbered 60 brigs and more than half as many luggers. It would appear that Bruix had ordered it out in hope of causing some of the British cruisers either to run aground while in chase or to venture into positions where they could be destroyed by the batteries. At 4pm the *Immortalité*, with the *Harpy*, the gun-brig *Adder* and the hired armed cutter *Constitution*, eventually joined by the *Bruiser*, approached the flotilla, and began to engage it at 4.15pm, standing close-in after the enemy. The batteries opened heavy fire and most of the craft remaining in the roads weighed and proceeded to the assistance of their friends. At about 5pm the *Constitution* was sunk by a 13in shell which, falling on her deck, passed through her bottom. Her crew were all saved by the boats of the squadron. A big shell also fell in the *Harpy*, but stuck in a beam and failed to burst. The *Immortalité* was twice hit, but the total British casualties were only one killed and four wounded. The batteries were clearly still able to protect their friends and, after having forced one or two gun-boats to beach themselves in order to avoid sinking, Captain Owen drew off. There was some desultory firing on the 27th and 28th, but no serious damage was inflicted on either side.

The problem of attacking the invasion flotilla in its bases led in the autumn of the year 1804 to the adoption and employment of a new weapon known as a 'catamaran'. It was an invention of the American Robert Fulton, who had already tried to sell Napoleon a submarine he had invented. Napoleon had provided insufficient support, interest or money, so Fulton was now offering the products of his fertile mind to the British. The catamaran was in effect a floating bomb. It consisted of a lead-lined chest, measuring about 21ft long by 3ft 3in broad, and having a flat top and bottom and wedge-shaped ends. Within were about 40 barrels of powder and various incendiaries, clockwork machinery and enough ballast to bring the deck of the device to water level. The outside of the whole was waterproofed by being covered with canvas, and well tarred. The complete machine weighed about two tons. Upon the withdrawal of a peg, the clockwork, after running for a given time, which might be 6–10min, would fire a pistol and explode the charge. The catamaran, which was supplied with a floating grappling iron, designed to hook the machine on to an enemy's anchor cable, had to be towed to its destination.

The new weapon was first tried in October 1804, when the presence of about 150 French craft, moored in double line outside Boulogne Pier, seemed to promise a favourable opportunity for attack by catamarans and fireships. On the morning of 1 October, Admiral Lord Keith in the *Monarch*, 74, with three 64s, two 50s and a number of frigates, sloops, bombs, brigs and cutters, anchored about five miles from the flotilla. Later in the day, the flagship, three frigates and some smaller vessels weighed and re-anchored just beyond gunshot of the enemy who, under Rear-Admiral La Crosse, in the prame *Ville de Mayence*, expected and was fully prepared for an attack, his boats rowing guard and his shore batteries being all alert. On the following day, at about 9.15pm, the fireships *Amity, Devonshire, Peggy* and *Providence*, towed by armed launches, set out to attack, with a strong tide and fine breeze carrying them in. The French opened fire as they approached. Some gun-boats came out and started to fight the British launches. Having

Above: Robert Fulton (1765–1815), the American inventor who, having failed to sell Napoleon his submarine, went to Britain and developed his 'catamaran'. He sold this explosive device to the British government for use against the invasion flotilla. Returning to the USA he built the first commercially successful steamboat. At the time of his death he was building the first steam warship for use against the British blockade. *NMM neg no: 586*

made ready and cast off their vessels, the launches withdrew, leaving the fireships to drift. The French tried in vain to sink them. At 10.15pm the *Providence* blew up between two of the enemy's gun-boats but did no harm beyond wounding a couple of men. At 10.35pm the *Peggy* exploded after having passed through the French line. She wounded three persons. The *Devonshire* did not blow until about 1am on 3 October. Like the *Providence,* she wounded two men only. As for the *Amity,* she blew up doing no damage at all. At the same time four or five catamarans were employed, the last exploding at about 3.30am. Only one seems to have done any damage, and that owing to an accident. Some French soldiers and seamen, while chasing British boats in a 'péniche' (No 267), ran foul of one of the infernal machines and were blown to pieces, losing their commander and 13 men. The attack, although it cost no British lives, must be regarded as a complete failure, seeing that the expenditure of four fireships and four or five catamarans caused a comparatively small loss of life and did no serious damage to

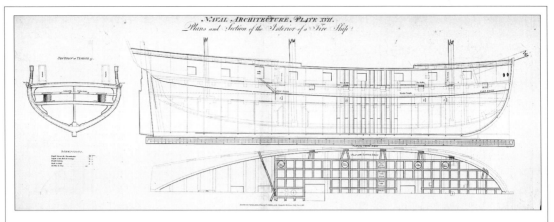

NAVAL ARCHITECTURE. PLATE XVII.
Plans and Section of the Interior of a Fire Ship.

the flotilla at all. The French, besides complaining bitterly about uncivilised forms of warfare, took the warning and protected their flotilla from similar attempts by partially surrounding it with a very elaborately constructed arrangement of booms and chains.

On 8 October, the look-outs in Jersey having detected a number of French lugger-rigged gun-vessels going northward close under the Normandy coast, the sloop *Albacore* went in search of the enemy. Towards evening, she forced five of the gun-vessels to anchor under a battery. The sloop lay off until 10am on the 9th, when, with a favourable tide, he stood in under a heavy fire, anchored with springs on his cables near the gun-vessels and only just outside the edge of the surf. He then cannonaded the enemy until all five luggers drove ashore with the waves breaking over them. The *Albacore* dragged her anchor, and was obliged to slip her anchor and go out to sea before she could complete the work of destruction. She was somewhat damaged, but none of her men were hit.

At 4pm on 23 October, a division of two prames and 18 armed schuyts left Ostend for the westward, and was chased by our old friend the *Cruiser*, 18, the gun-brigs *Blazer*, *Conflict*, *Tigress* and *Escort*, and the hired armed cutters *Admiral Mitchell* and *Griffin*. At 5.18pm the leading prame was brought to action and at 6.35pm she stopped firing. As the tide was falling and darkness was increasing, the vessels were in very shallow water and unfamiliar with both shoals and currents, the *Cruiser* moved out to sea and anchored. The *Conflict*, however, had grounded and could not get off. She was abandoned. An attempt to refloat her was afterwards made by the *Admiral Mitchell* and *Griffin*, but by that time she was high and dry and in possession of the enemy, who were supported by field guns and howitzers on shore.

Above: Steele's printed version of an Admiralty plan of a fireship. Notice the extra 'fire deck' underneath the gun deck, divided into a grid by channels along which fuses are run, with barrels of combustibles placed inside the subdivisions of the grid. The fire ports in the sides of this deck are hinged at the bottom, so that when retaining ropes burn through, they fall open causing a draught to fan the flames which will then emerge through the ports, as will fireballs from the roman-candle-like fireworks mounted just inside. Everything was designed for spreading the fire as quickly and as fiercely as possible. The ship shown in this plan was purpose built, belonging to the last class of fireships built, and was very fine-lined, so that it could keep up with the fleet. *NMM neg no: B4019/17*

The British had to retire leaving the *Conflict* a prize of the enemy.

On 8 December, an attempt was made, under the direction of Captain Popham (who we have already met at Ostend) of the *Antelope*, to destroy Fort Rouge. This was a battery built on piles at the mouth of Calais harbour. He used the fire-vessel *Susannah* and a couple of catamarans. The *Susannah* exploded, but did little harm; one of the catamarans drifted clear of the fort, the other failed to blow up. This was the last time anybody tried to do anything with the catamaran.

As 1805 began, Napoleon was making his last preparations for invasion. The part of the Franco-Dutch flotilla we saw being driven into Ostend the previous year had managed to move as far as Dunkirk. Here it was awaiting an opportunity for stealing piecemeal along the coast to its new base at Ambleteuse, a few miles north of Boulogne.

At 9pm on 23 April, a dark night with a strong wind blowing, a division of 33 gun-vessels and 19 transports got under way from Dunkirk road. It safely passed Gravelines and

Calais without detection but, just before dawn on the 24th, it was thrown into some confusion by the wind shifting and by the change of tide. The greater number of the craft made for an anchorage between Caps Blanc-Nez and Gris-Nez, although eight armed schuyts were too far to leeward to be able to follow. At the break of day the enemy was discovered by a British squadron at anchor off Boulogne. This consisted of the *Leda*, the sloops *Harpy* and *Railleur*, the bomb *Fury*, and the gun-brigs *Bruiser, Archer, Locust, Tickler, Firm, Monkey, Gallant* and *Watchful*, the latter two being on guard off Ambleteuse. They were the first to get into action at 8am with the schuyts, which were aided by some of the gun-brigs and by the shore batteries. The *Gallant*, hit between wind and water, had to leave off to stop her leaks, but the *Watchful* captured one schuyt, and the *Railleur*, with the *Locust* and the *Starling* soon catching up, took six more. On the following morning the *Archer* captured another schuyt which had drifted out to sea. The British only lost one seaman wounded. The rest of the enemy's flotilla reached Ambleteuse, assisted by armed launches sent out from Boulogne by Rear-Admiral La Crosse, who now commanded the naval force on the coast.

A somewhat similar attempt to move craft from the west to Boulogne began a little later. On 10 June a French division, consisting of the sloops *Foudre* and *Audacieuse*, 15 gun-vessels and 14 transports sailed from Le Havre for Fécamp. They were chased by the frigate *Chiffonne*, the sloop *Falcon*, the gun-brig *Clinker*, and the hired armed cutter *Francis*. The French ships were caught but, with the French vessels gradually edging in under the protection of the shore batteries, the British began to get the worst of the exchange of fire, though some of the enemy craft were aground by then. The division ultimately got under the protection of the forts of Fécamp.

On 15 July the gun-brigs *Plumper*, commanded by Lieutenant James Henry Garrety, and *Teazer* were becalmed, and to avoid being carried into danger by the tide, anchored at some little distance from one another near the Chausey Isles, off Granville. They were observed from there and during the following night seven gun-vessels, each mounting three long 24-pounders and an 8in howitzer, and full of men, were sent out to attack them. They approached under oars and at 2.30am on the 16th they opened fire on the *Plumper*. She was not able to make any adequate resistance and at length, after her captain had lost his arm, she surrendered. At 8.45am the French boats,

reinforced by their new prize attacked the *Teazer*, which set all sail and tried to escape, but was soon surrounded and captured.

Practically all of the Ostend division of the invasion flotilla which still had not got to its destination was assembled by the end of May at Dunkirk under Ver Huell, now Vice-Admiral, who was anxiously awaiting an opportunity to carry it on to Ambleteuse. Unfavourable winds were the main reason for it not putting to sea until 17 July, when most of it went out at 6pm and began to make its way down the coast. Some small craft remained behind, with instructions to follow if a British attack happened. Ver Huell had with him the four French prames, *Ville d'Aix, Ville d'Anvers, Ville de Génève*, and *Ville de Mayence*, and 32 large schooner-rigged gun-vessels. He formed his vessels into two lines, with the openings in the outermost column covered by the ships of the innermost one. At about 6.30pm they were spotted by a British squadron lying off Gravelines and which consisted of the 20-gun *Ariadne*, three or four sloops and bombs, and less than half a dozen gun-brigs. As soon as Captain King of the *Ariadne* saw how the enemy was heading, he cut his cables and made sail towards Ver Huell. He opened fire at about 9.15pm. The attack drove ashore or disabled 11 of the gun-vessels and damaged the *Ville de Génève* in spite of the very heavy fire kept up both by the flotilla and by the batteries. Between 11pm and midnight, the rest of the division succeeded in anchoring off Calais. The noise of the firing brought the 50-gun *Trusty* from the Downs, with the 28-gun frigate *Vestal*, and three sloops. The *Vestal* outsailed the rest and joined King at 4am on the 18th. Another attack was made on the flotilla, but the Dutch were too well protected by the forts and, after a two-hour cannonade, the British sailed away to participate in another engagement.

Rear-Admiral La Crosse, at Boulogne, knowing of Ver Huell's movements, had organised a diversion in favour of his colleague, and had ordered several divisions of gun-vessels to get under way as if to attack the British squadron off the port. This squadron, which included the frigates *Immortalité* and *Hebe*, and the 20-gun *Arab*, got under way to meet the French, 113 craft in all, and ultimately drove them to take shelter under the batteries near Wimereux. *Trusty* and her consorts came up to join in this fight. Ver Huell wanted to continue his passage, and, as all the coast between Calais and Ambleteuse had been provided with many very powerful batteries, he weighed from Calais road at 3pm on 18 July, taking Marshal

Davout with him in his schooner, the *Bantam,* and accompanied by three out of his four prames, and 21 out of his 32 gun-vessels. He made for Cap Blanc-Nez, off which lay the *Trusty, Vestal, Ariadne* and about a dozen smaller craft. At 4pm the French batteries on the heights opened up in order to drive off the British vessels. They did this to such good effect that Ver Huell was able to proceed, without serious problems, until he was off the village of Wissant. There the shore batteries could not give as much protection and the attack was renewed. The *Arab,* 20, the sloops *Calypso* and *Flèche,* and some of the gun-brigs had succeeded by 7pm in driving six of the gun-vessels ashore. They had to draw away when off Cap Gris-Nez. The *Arab* had been damaged. The frigates, drawing too much water to get within effective range of the smaller Batavian vessels, confined their attention chiefly to the prames, and, though they were later joined by the 36-gun frigate *Renommée,* they managed only to drive ashore two schooner gun-vessels. Soon after 7pm, the rest of the flotilla anchored in safety under the forts of Ambleteuse and Andresselles. The frigates were forced to move off to repair damages and, while they were away, the whole of the Franco-Dutch flotilla seems to have found its way to Boulogne. Shortly afterwards the total of landing craft assembled there had risen to 1,104.

The division under Captain Hamelin, which had reached Fécamp from Le Havre in June, put to sea again early on the morning of 23 July in order to continue along the coast to the northeast. There were around 30 craft in this group. They were attacked by the 22-gun *Champion* with the gun-brigs *Clinker* and *Cracker,* plus the hired armed cutter *Frances.* By 10.30am many of the smaller of the French craft had been forced ashore under the batteries of Seuneville, while all the rest of the flotilla were sheltering under the batteries of St Valery-en-Caux. The British ships lost only two killed and three wounded, but were so damaged that they had to go to the Downs to refit. This left, literally, the coast clear for Captain Hamelin to make the rest of his way to Boulogne without hindrance.

In July 1805 the invasion flotilla comprised 1,339 armed and 954 unarmed vessels, intended to carry 163,645 men and 9,059 horses, and was made up of six grand divisions along the coast from Etaples, via Boulogne, Wimereux and Ambleteuse to Calais. The last two ports were for the Dutch and Italian troops respectively. Twice, on 3 August, Napoleon experimented with embarking the entire army. On the second

Right: Contemporary view from the *Naval Chronicle* of the harbour and castle at Dartmouth. *NMM neg no: 5061*

occasion the whole operation was accomplished in 90min. The problem, however, was less that of getting the troops aboard the transports than getting the transports out of their harbours, a feat which would require at least two tides. This would be a difficult enough operation in the most favourable of conditions. A persistent flat calm was possible. What was quite impossible, given the constant vigilance of the British ships, was avoiding enemy interference with the process. This was why Napoleon dreamed up the elaborate plan which led to Trafalgar: he needed to decoy or destroy the British main fleets, and have his own fleet in the Channel to protect the crossing. It was unlikely in the extreme that this scheme would work. Even if it had, the combined fleets would have had a difficult, probably impossible, job in beating off the clouds of smaller craft which would have made determined and skilful attacks on the vulnerable transports. The actions we have been describing show clearly enough that the invasion craft were not capable of defending themselves adequately even when not carrying troops. Casualties would have been horrendous, probably disastrous. There would be later actions involving the flotilla as the years went by, one of them in front of Napoleon's eyes as he watched the ubiquitous British small craft administering yet another check to his vessels, but the verdict was already clear: 'I do not say the French cannot come, I do say they cannot come by sea' — Lord St Vincent had it right.

In the event, of course, it was the more distant battlefleets of Cornwallis, Calder, Collingwood, Nelson and others that prevented any attempt to launch an invasion; just as over a century later Fighter Command did the same. What is, however, not usually noticed, is that in both cases it was the anti-invasion forces of the Royal Navy in the narrow seas which deterred attack, would have destroyed any actual attempt at invasion, and created the conditions in which the only way in which invasion could conceivably happen was if first Villeneuve and then Goering had succeeded.

Right: Brig-sloop *Penguin,* captured in 1795 from the Dutch. Typical of the small ships forming the defence against invasion she was described at the time as 'a very beautiful vessel of her rate and sails remarkably fast'. *NMM neg no: 3398*

W Hodges R A del

Wells sculp

Above: The French *Formidable*, shown here in an earlier action in 1801 against the British off Cadiz, was captured at the Battle of Trafalgar and renamed *Brave*. NMM neg no: B9280

Below: The British frigate *Loire* shown attacking El Muros fort in June 1805. The print is 'Dedicated by Permission of his Lordship (Nelson) previous to his going to attack the Combined Fleets.' *NMM ref no: C670*

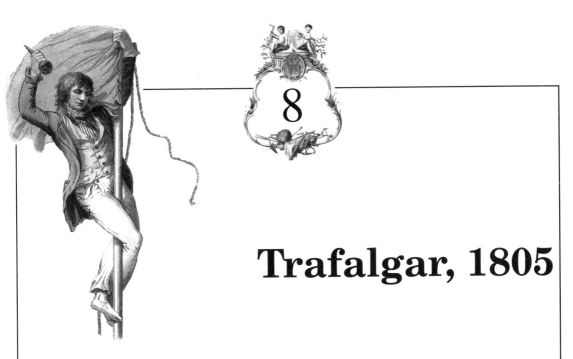

8

Trafalgar, 1805

Trafalgar is the last major fleet battle to have been fought under sail at sea. During the final decade of the Napoleonic War the Royal Navy never quite managed to force action on to a French fleet. Navarino (1827) was fought against a materially inferior enemy who were at anchor in harbour.

The long build-up to Trafalgar is basically the story of Napoleon's plans for an invasion of Britain which involved the decoying away of the British fleet and the eventual arrival of his own to hold the Channel narrows long enough for the *Grande Armée* to be transported to Kent. The plan foundered — as it was bound to do — on the unlikelihood of decoying enough of the Royal Navy away from home waters to leave them defenceless, and on the unco-operativeness of winds and weather. The French commander, Admiral Villeneuve, had been given a virtually impossible task from the start.

In March 1805 Villeneuve sailed from Toulon with the French Mediterranean fleet. Nelson, in command of the British Mediterranean fleet, as always too short of scouting frigates, failed to intercept him and started off what was to prove to be a long pursuit. The French passed through the Strait of Gibraltar and set out for the West Indies. Aware that Nelson was close behind him, Villeneuve did not intend to stay in the Caribbean. His voyage there was merely intended to decoy Nelson away from Europe

and it worked. Nelson still thought of the West Indies as a major source of British power and the experience of the American War of Independence lingered in a feeling that the area was one where great sea battles happened between large fleets. French strategists, however, no longer thought in these terms and were wholly concentrating on their invasion plans. Lingering there only long enough to take HMS *Diamond Rock*, an island off Martinique commissioned as a British warship, and a thorn in the side of the local French, Villeneuve then set off eastwards. He hoped to combine with the Brest fleet and then proceed up-Channel. Nelson, who had missed him through faulty information in the West Indies, resumed his pursuit.

The elderly naval administrator who had been recalled to become First Lord of the Admiralty, Charles Middleton, Lord Barham, was equal to the ensuing crisis. A concentration of British warships was organised off Ushant; the Brest fleet continued to be firmly bottled up by the blockading fleet under Cornwallis. On 22 July Villeneuve was intercepted by the well-positioned force of Rear-Admiral Calder off Cape Finisterre. Calder had 15 ships, Villeneuve 20, and the weather was very foggy. The resultant action was rather confused, but Calder contrived to capture two Spanish ships and his casualties were less than a third of those suffered by the Franco-Spanish fleet. He had, moreover, made

certain that Villeneuve would not make any further attempt to carry out the original plan, but instead decided to take refuge in first Ferrol and then Cadiz, taking counsel from his fears and abandoning the possibility of invasion at the first sign of opposition. It seems somewhat unfair that Calder should have been the butt of a popular agitation suggesting that he should have captured more than two ships, and should have been recalled for court martial. On the other hand, like Villeneuve, and with less cause, he had been taking too much counsel of his fears, being too cautious and not aggressive enough.

Nelson arrived back in European waters too late to catch Villeneuve but took his fleet to Gibraltar. He then left Collingwood keeping an eye on Villeneuve in Cadiz whilst he went home for some leave.

There matters should have remained. The French had, unsurprisingly, been foiled in their attempt to decoy the Royal Navy away from its defence of the western approaches to the channel. Napoleon's plan looked good on paper, but relied too much on precise timing, failed to take account of the weather and the practicalities of operating and co-ordinating sailing fleets over long distances, and above all discounted the skill, knowledge and sense of priorities of the enemy. Ships had manoeuvred over great distances to very little effect, and the French and Spanish fleets were back being blockaded at their bases. Napoleon was working on a scheme to move the ships at Cadiz into the Mediterranean — to return to Toulon, possibly doing damage to the British on the way.

This was the stage at which Villeneuve 'jumped the gun' and precipitated battle by

Above: One of Pocock's carefully annotated sketches of the Battle of Trafalgar, prepared as the basis for a later painting. *NMM neg no: 8605*

Right: One of the souvenir prints rushed out to commemorate Trafalgar, complete with misleading plans of the battle, copies of the relevant gazette letters and listings of ships involved, casualties, etc. *NMM neg no: A560*

taking his fleet and that of his Spanish allies to sea. Napoleon had been predictably angry with him; accusations of lack of nerve, even cowardice, were uttered. Worse still, news reached Cadiz that a replacement for him was on his way to take over command. With some hope of attaining victory over the numerically inferior British fleet he took his own ships and those of his Spanish allies to sea. Thus he gave Nelson, now back from leave, the opportunity he had been longing for to smash an enemy fleet. Villeneuve was no fool. He predicted fairly clearly what Nelson's plan of attack would be — an attempt to concentrate on the rear of his fleet, double it and deal with the ships he had isolated before the rest of the cumbersome Allied fleet could come back to rectify the balance. He was, however, expecting defeat even if he was hoping for a victory. He and the men of his fleet were at a psychological disadvantage as well as not being as well-trained or as well-integrated as their adversaries. The Royal Navy's 'habit of victory' and Nelson's prestige were a potent force in their own favour. So, also, the superior training of the men and quality of the officers gave the British fleet a greater strength than their actual numbers would indicate.

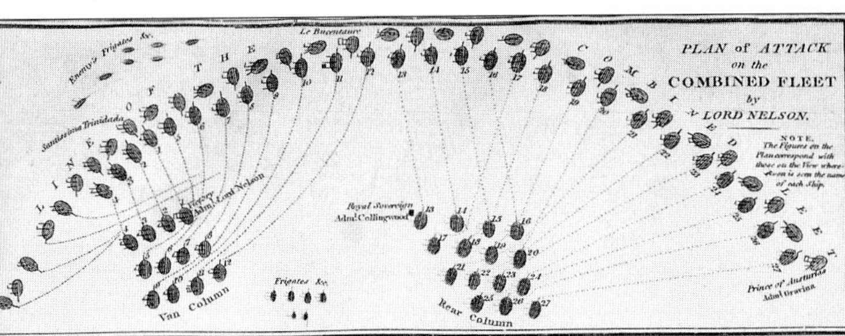
PLAN of ATTACK
on the
COMBINED FLEET
by
LORD NELSON.
NOTE. The Figures on the Plan correspond with those on the View where-ever is seen the name of each Ship.
Royal Sovereign
Adml. Collingwood
Van Column
Rear Column
Frigates &c.
Prince of Asturias
Adml. Gravina
Le Bucentaure
Santissima Trinidada
Enemy's Frigates &c.
Victory
Adml. Lord Nelson

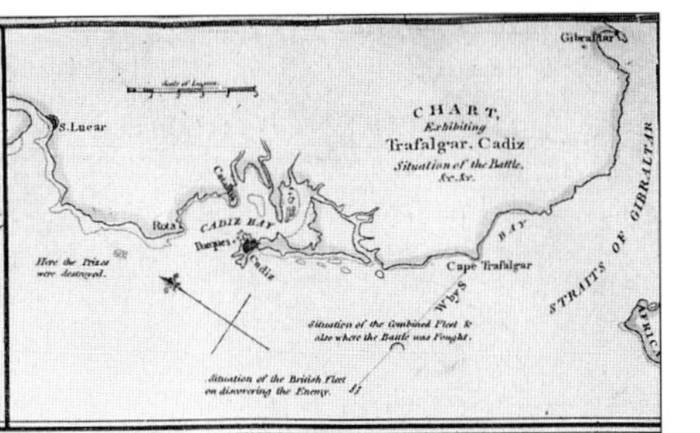
CHART,
Exhibiting
Trafalgar, Cadiz
Situation of the Battle,
&c. &c.
Gibraltar
S. Lucar
CADIZ BAY
Rota
Cadiz
Cape Trafalgar
BAY
STRAITS OF GIBRALTAR
Here the Prizes were destroyed.
Situation of the Combined Fleet & also where the Battle was Fought.
Situation of the British Fleet on discovering the Enemy.

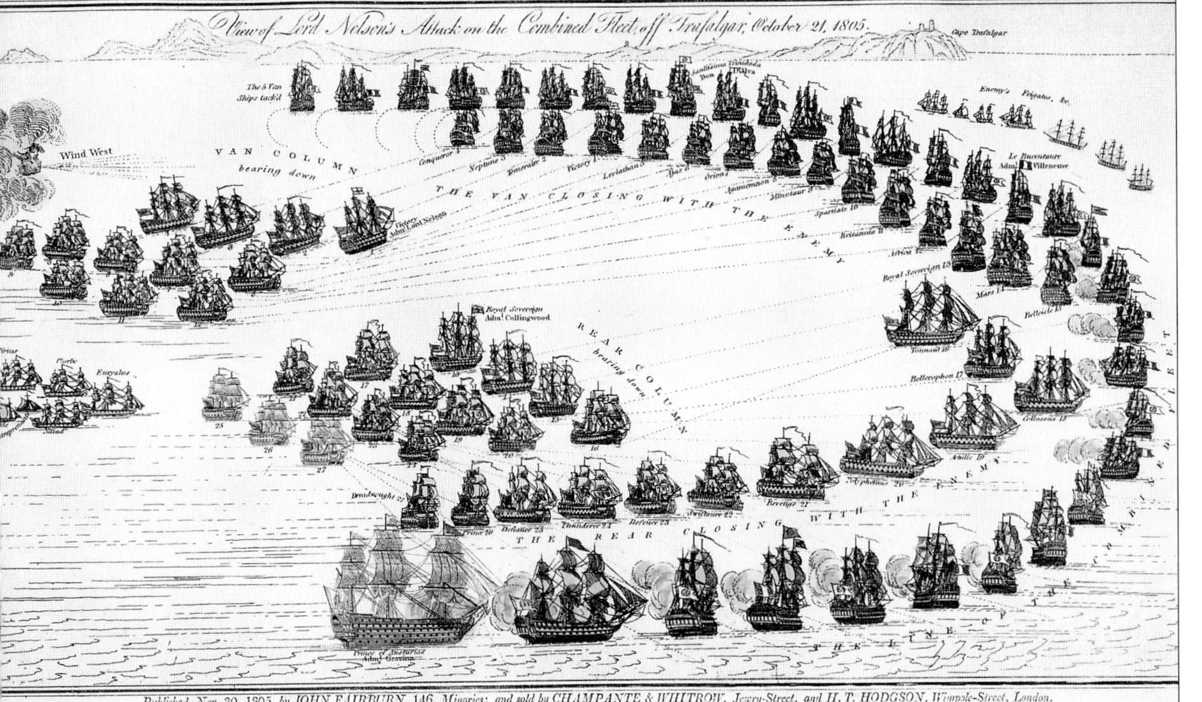
View of Lord Nelson's Attack on the Combined Fleet, off Trafalgar, October 21, 1805.
Cape Trafalgar
The 5 Van Ships tack'd
Wind West
VAN COLUMN bearing down
THE VAN CLOSING WITH THE ENEMY
REAR COLUMN bearing down
THE REAR CLOSING WITH THE ENEMY
THE LINE OF THE COMBINED FLEET
Enemy's Frigates, &c.
Le Bucentaure
Adml. Villeneuve
Santissima Trinidada
Victory
Adml. Lord Nelson
Royal Sovereign
Adml. Collingwood
Euryalus
Prince of Asturias
Adml. Gravina

Published, Nov. 30, 1805, by JOHN FAIRBURN, 146, Minories; and sold by CHAMPANTE & WHITROW, Jewry-Street, and H. T. HODGSON, Wimpole-Street, London.

FAIRBURN's PLAN OF LORD NELSON's VICTORY OVER THE COMBINED FLEET, OFF TRAFALGAR, OCTOBER 21, 1805.

From the LONDON GAZETTE EXTRAORDINARY, Nov. 6, 1805.

EURYALUS, *off Cape Trafalgar, October 22, 1805.*

SIR,

THE ever to be lamented Death of Vice-Admiral Lord Viscount Nelson, who, in the late conflict with the enemy, fell in the hour of Victory, leaves to me the duty of informing my Lords Commissioners of the Admiralty, that on the 19th Instant, it was communicated to the Commander in Chief from the ships watching the motions of the enemy in Cadiz, that the Combined Fleet had put to sea; as they sailed with light winds westerly, his Lordship concluded their destination was the Mediterranean, and immediately made all sail for the Streights' entrance, with the British squadron, consisting of twenty-seven ships, three of them sixty-fours, where his Lordship was informed by Captain Blackwood, (whose vigilance in watching, and giving notice of the enemy's movements, has been highly meritorious,) that they had not yet passed the Streights.

On Monday the 21st Instant, at daylight, when Cape Trafalgar bore E. by S. about seven leagues, the enemy was discovered six or seven miles to the Eastward, the wind about West, and very light, the Commander in Cheif immediately made the signal for the Fleet to bear up in two columns, as they are formed in order of sailing; a mode of attack his Lordship had previously directed, to avoid the inconvenience and delay in forming a Line of Battle in the usual manner. The Enemy's Line consisted of thirty-three ships, (of which eighteen were French and fifteen Spanish,) commanded in Chief by Admiral Villeneuve; the Spaniards, under the direction of Gravina, wore, with their heads to the Northward, and formed their Line of Battle with great closeness and correctness; but as the mode of attack was unusual, so the structure of their Line was new;—it formed a crescent convexing to leeward—so that, in leading down to their Centre, I had both their Van, and Rear, abaft the beam;—before the fire opened, every alternate ship was about a cable's length to Windward of her second a-head, and a-stern, forming a kind of double line, and appeared, when on their Beam, to leave a very little interval between them; and this without crowding their ships. Admiral Villeneuve was in the Bucentaure in the centre, and the Prince of Asturias bore Gravina's flag in the rear; but the French and Spanish ships were mixed without any apparent regard to order of national squadron.

As the mode of our attack had been previously determined on, and communicated to the Flag-Officers and Captains, few signals were necessary, and none were made, except to direct close order as the lines bore down.

The Commander in Chief in the Victory led the weather column, and the Royal Sovereign, which bore my flag, the lee.

The action began at twelve o'clock, by the leading ships of the columns breaking through the Enemy's line, the Commander in Chief about the tenth ship from the van, the second in command about the twelfth from the rear, leaving the van of the Enemy unoccupied; the succeeding ships breaking through, in all parts, astern of their leaders, and engaging the Enemy at the muzzles of their guns; the conflict was severe; the Enemy's ships were fought with a gallantry highly honourable to their officers, but the attack on them was irresistible, and it pleased the Almighty disposer of all events, to grant his Majesty's arms a complete and glorious victory; about three P. M. many of the Enemy's ships having struck their colours, their line gave way; Admiral Gravina, with ten ships joining their Frigates to Leeward stood towards Cadiz. The five headmost ships in their van tacked, and standing to the southward, to windward of the British line, were engaged, and the sternmost of them take; the others went off, leaving to his Majesty's squadron Nineteen ships of the line, (of which two are first rates, the Santissima Trainidada and the Santa Anna,) with three flag Officers, viz. Admiral Villeneuve, the Commander in chief, Don Ignatio Maria D'Aliva, Vice-Admiral, and the Spanish Rear-Admiral Don Baltazar Hidalgo Cisneros.

After such a victory it may appear unnecessary to enter into encomiums on the particular parts taken by the several commanders; the conclusion says more on the subject than I have language to express; the spirit which animated all was the same: when all exert themselves zealously in their Country's service, all deserve that their high merits should stand recorded; and never was high merit more conspicuous than in the battle I have described.

The Achille (a French 74,) after having surrendered, by some mismanagement of the Frenchmen took fire and blew up; two hundred of her men were saved by the tenders.

A circumstance occurred during the action, which so strongly marks the invincible spirit of British Seamen when engaging the Enemies of their Country, that I cannot resist the pleasure I have in making it known to their Lordships: the Temeraire was boarded by accident, or design, by a French ship on one side, and a Spaniard on the other; the contest was vigorous, but, in the end, the combined ensigns were torn from the poop, and the British hoisted in their places.

Such a battle could not be fought without sustaining a great loss of men. I have not only to lament, in common with the British navy, and the British nation in the fall of the commander in chief, the loss of a Hero, whose name will be immortal, and his memory ever dear to his Country; but my heart is rent with the most poignant grief for the death of a friend, to whom, by many years' intimacy, and a perfect knowledge of the virtues of his mind, which inspired ideas superior to the common race of Men, I was bound by the strongest ties of affection; a grief to which even the glorious occasion in which he fell, does not bring the concolation which perhaps it ought; his Lordship received a musket ball in his left breast, about the middle of the action, and sent an Officer to me immediately with his last farewell; and soon after expired.

I have also to lament the loss of those excellent Officers Captains Duff of the Mars, and Cooke of the Bellerophon; I have yet heard of none others. The Royal Sovereign having lost all her masts, except the tottering foremast, I called the Euryalus to me, while the action continued, which ship lying within hail, made my signals, a service Captain Blackwood performed with great attention; after the action, I shifted my flag to her, that I might more easily communicate my orders to, and collect the ships, and towed the Royal Sovereign out to seaward. The whole fleet were now in a very perilous situation, many dismasted; all shattered in thirteen fathom water, off the shoals of Trafalgar, and when I made the signal to prepare to anchor, few of the ships had an anchor to let go, their cables being shot; but the same good providence which aided us through such a day, preserved us in the night, by the wind shifting a few points, and drifting the ships off the land, except four of the captured dismasted ships, which are now at anchor off Trafalgar, and I hope will ride safe until those gales are over.

Having thus detailed the proceedings of the fleet on this occasion, I beg to congratulate their Lordships on a victory, which, I hope will add a Ray to the Glory of his Majesty's Crown, and be attended with public benefit to our Country.

I am, &c.

(Signed) C. COLLINGWOOD.

William Marsden, Esq.

SIR, *Euryalus, off Cadiz, Oct. 24, 1805.*

IN my letter of the 22d I detailed to you, for the information of my Lords Commissioners of the Admiralty, the proceedings of His Majesty's squadron on the day of the action, and that preceeding it, since which I have had a continued series of misfortunes, but they are of a kind that human prudence could not possibly provide against, or my skill prevent. On the 22d in the morning a strong southerly wind blew, with squally weather, which however did not prevent the activity of the Officers and seamen of such ships as were manageable from getting hold of many of the prizes (thirteen or fourteen) and towing them off to the Westward, where I ordered them to rendezvous round the Royal Sovereign, in tow by the Neptune: but on the 23d, the gale increased, and the sea ran so high, that many of them broke the tow rope, and drifted far to Leeward, before they were got hold of again, and some of them taking advantage in the dark and boisterous night, got before the wind, and have perhaps drifted upon the shore and sunk; on the afternoon of that day the remnant of the combined fleet, ten sail of ships, who had not been much engaged, stood up to Leeward of my shattered and straggled charge, as if meaning to attack them, which obliged me to collect a force out of the least injured ships, and form to Leeward for their defence; all this retarded the progress of the hulks, and the bad weather continuing, determined me to destroy all the Leeward most that could be cleared of the men, considering that keeping possession of the ships was a matter of little consequence compared with the chance of their falling again into the hands of the enemy; but even this was an arduous task in the high sea which was running. The Captains of the Prince and Neptune cleared the Trinidad and sunk her. Captains Hope, Bayntun, and Malcolm, who joined the fleet this moment from Gibraltar, had the charge of destroying four others. The Santa Anna had her side almost beat in; and such is the shattered condition of the whole of them, that unless the weather moderates I doubt whether I shall be able to carry a ship of them into port. I have taken Admiral Villeneuve into this ship. Whenever the temper of the weather will permit, and I can spare a frigate, I shall collect the other Flag Officers, and send them to England, with their flags, (if they do not all go to the bottom,) to be laid at His Majesty's feet. There were four thousand troops embarked, under the command of General Contamin, who was taken with Admiral Villeneuve in the Bacentaure.

I am, Sir, &c.

William Marsden, Esq. (Signed) C. COLLINGWOOD.

SIR, *Euryalus, off Cadiz, Oct. 28, 1805.*

SINCE my letter to you of the 24th, stating the proceeding of His Majesty's squadron, our situation has been the most criticle, and our employment the most arduous that ever a fleet was engaged in. On the 24th and 25th it blew a most violent gale of wind, which completely dispersed the ships, and drove the captured hulls in all directions. I have since been employed in collecting and destroying them, where they are at anchor upon the coast between Cadiz and six leagues Westward of San Lucar, without the prospect of saving one to bring into port. I mentioned in my former letter the joining of the Donegal and Melpomene, after the action; I cannot sufficiently praise the activity of their Commanders, in giving assistance to the squadron in destroying the enemy's ships. The Defiance, after having stuck to the Aigle, as long as it was possible, in hope of saving her from wreck, which separated her for some time from the squadron, was obliged to abandon her to her fate, and she went on shore. Capt. Durham's exertions have been very great. I hope I shall get them all destroyed by to-morrow, if the weather keeps moderate. In the gale the Royal Sovereign and Mars lost their foremasts, and are now rigging anew, where the body of the squadron is at anchor to the N. W. of San Lucar. I find that on the return of Gravina to Cadiz, he was immediately ordered to sea again, and came out, which made it necessary for me to form a line, to cover the disabled hulls——that night it blew hard, and his ship, the Prince of Asturias, was dismasted, and returned into port; the Rayo was also dismasted, and fell into our hands; Don Enrigue M. Douel, had his broad Pendant in the Rayo, and from him I find the Santa Anna was driven near Cadiz, and towed in by a frigate.

I am, Sir, &c.

William Marsden, Esq. (Signed) C. COLLINGWOOD.

SIR, *Queen, off Cape Trafalgar, Nov. 4, 1805.*

ON the 28th ultimo I informed you of the proceedings of the squadron to that time. The weather continuing very bad, the wind blowing from the S. W. the squadron not in a situation of safety, and seeing little prospect of getting the captured ships off the land, and great risk of some of them getting into port, I determined no longer to delay the destroying them, and to get the squadron out of the deep bay. The extraordinary exertion of Capt. Capel, however, saved the French ship Swiftsure; and his ship, the Phœbe, together with the Donegal, Capt. Malcolm, afterwards brought out the Bahama. Indeed, nothing can exceed the perseverance of all the officers employed in this service. Capt Hope rigged and succeeded in bringing out the Ildefonso; all of which will, I hope, have arrived safe at Gibraltar. For the rest, Sir, I enclose you a list of all the enemy's fleet, which were in the action, and how they are disposed of, which, I believe, is perfectly carrect. I informed you, in my letter of the 28th, that the remnant of the enemy's fleet came out a second time, to endeavour, in the bad weather, to cut off some of the hulks, when the Rayo was dismasted, and fell into our hands; she afterwards parted her cable, went on shore, and was wrecked. The Indomptable, one of the same squadron, was also driven on shore, wrecked, and her crew perished. The Santa Anna and Algeziras being driven near the shore of Cadiz, got such assistance as has enabled them to get in: but the ruin of their fleet is as complete as could be expected, under the circumstances of fighting them close to their own shore. Had the battle been in the ocean, still fewer would have escaped. Twenty sail of the line are taken or destroyed; and of those which got in, not more than three are in a repairable state for a length of time.

In clearing the captured ships of prisoners, I found so many wounded men, that to alleviate human misery as much as was in my power, I sent to the Marquis de Solana, Governor-General of Andalusia, to offer him the wounded to the care of their country, on receipts being given: a proposal which was received with the greatest thankfulness, not only by the Governor, but the whole country resounds with expressions of gratitude. Two French frigates were sent out to receive them, with a proper Officer to give receipts, bringing with them all the English who had been wrecked in several of the ships, and an offer from the Marquis de Solana of the use of their hospitals for our wounded, pledging the honour of Spain for their being carefully attended. I have ordered most of the Spanish prisoners to be released; the Officers on parole; the men for receipts given, and a condition, that they do not serve in war, by sea or land, until exchanged. By my correspondence with the Marquis, I found, that Vice Admiral D'Aliva was not dead, but dangerously wounded, and I wrote to him a letter, claiming him as a prisoner of war.

I am, &c.

William Marsden, Esq. C. COLLINGWOOD.

Total of *Guns* in the British Line of Battle - - 2148
Total of *Guns* in the Line of the Combined Fleet 2648—Majority 500!

J. Hartnell, Printer, Bermondsey-Street, Southwark.

LIST of the BRITISH FLEET.

VAN COLUMN.		REAR COLUMN.	
1. *Victory*, Admiral Lord Nelson, -	100	13. *Royal Sovereign*, Ad. Collingwood,	100
2. *Temeraire*, E. Harvey, - - - -	98	14. *Mars*, G. Duff, - - - - - -	74
3. *Neptune*, T. F. Freemantle - -	98	15. *Belleisle*, W. Hargood - - -	74
4. *Conqueror*, J. Pellew, - - - -	74	16. *Tonnant*, C. Tyler - - - -	80
5. *Leviathan*, H. W. Bayntun, - -	74	17. *Bellerophon*, J. Cooke, - - -	74
6. *Ajax*, *J. Pilfold, - - - - -	74	18. *Colossus*, J. N. Morris - - -	74
7. *Orion*, E. Codrington, - - -	74	19. *Achille*, R. King, - - - - - -	74
8. *Agamemnon*, Sir E. Berry, -	64	20. *Polyphemus*, R. Redmill, - -	64
9. *Minotaur*, C. J. M. Mansfield, -	74	21. *Revenge*, R. Moorsom, - - -	74
10. *Spartiate*, Sir F. Laforey, - -	74	22. *Swiftsure*, W. G. Rutherford, -	74
11. *Britannia*, Rear Admiral Northesk	100	23. *Defence*, G. Hope, - - - - -	74
12. *Africa*, H. Digby, - - - - - -	64	24. *Thunderer*, *J. Stockham, - -	74
Euryalus, Hon. J. Blackwood, -	36	25. *Defiance*, P. C. Durham, - -	74
Sirius, W. Prowse, - - - - -	36	26. *Prince*, R. Grindall, - - - -	98
Phœbe, T. B. Capel, - - - -	36	27. *Dreadnought*, J. Conn, - - -	98
Naiad, T. Dundas, - - - - -	38	* Senior Lieutenants commanding for Capts. Brown & Lechmere, called home to give evidence on the trial of Sir R. Calder.	
Pickle, J. R. Lapenotiere, - -	10		
Entreprenante, J. Puver, - -	10		

LIST of the COMBINED FLEET, and HOW DISPOSED OF.

IN POSSESSION OF THE BRITISH.

1. *San Ildefonso*, 74 Guns, (Spanish)
2. *San Juan Nepomuceno*, 74 Guns, (Spanish)
3. *Bahama*, 74 Guns, (Spanish)
4. *Swiftsure*, 74 Guns, (French)

WRECKED AFTER THE BATTLE.

5. *Monarca*, 74 Guns, (Spanish) *wrecked* off San Lucar.
6. *Fougeux*, 74 Guns, French) *wrecked* off Trafalgar, all perished, & 30 Temeraire's men.
7. *Indomptable*, 84 Guns, (French) *wrecked* off Rota, all perished.
8. *Bucentaur*, 80 Guns, (French) Admiral Villeneuve, Commander in Chief, taken, *wrecked* on the Porques, some of the crew saved.
9. *San Francisco de Asis*, 74 Guns, (Spanish) *wrecked* near Rota.
10. *El Rayo*, 100 Guns, (Spanish) *wrecked* near San Lucar.
11. *Neptuno*, 84 Guns (Spanish) *wrecked* between Rota and Catolina.
12. *Argonaute*, 74 Guns, (French) on Shore in the Port of Cadiz.
13. *Berwick*, 74 Guns, (French) *wrecked* to the Northward of San Lucar.
14. *Aigle*, 74 Guns, (French) *wrecked* near Rota.

BURNT.

15. *Achille*, 74 Guns, (French) *burnt* during the Action.
16. *Intrepide*, 74 Guns, (French) *burnt* by the Britannia.
17. *San Agustin*, 74 Guns, (Spanish) *burnt* by the Leviathan.

SUNK.

18. *Santissima Trinidad*, 140 Guns, (Spanish) Rear-Admiral Don Baltazar, H. Cisneros, *sunk* by the Prince, Neptune, &c.
19. *Redoutable*, 74 Guns, (French) *sunk* astern of the Swiftsure.
20. *Argonauta*, 80 Guns, (Spanish) *sunk* by the Ajax.

RETURNED TO CADIZ, CHIEFLY WRECKS.

21. *Santa Anna*, 112 Guns, (Spanish) Vice-Admiral Don Ignacio D'Aliva; wounded severely in the head, taken, but got into Cadiz in the Gale, *dismasted*.
22. *Algeziras*, 74 Guns, (French) Rr. Ad. Magon killed; got into Cadiz *dismasted*.
23. *Pluton*, 74 Guns, (French) returned to Cadiz in a sinking state.
24. *San Juste*, 74 Guns, (Spanish) returned to Cadiz, has a *Foremast only*.
25. *San Leandro*, 64 Guns, (Spanish) returnd to Cadiz *dismasted*.
26. *Neptune*, 84 Guns, (French) returned to Cadiz, and *perfect*.
27. *Heros*, 74 Guns, (French) returned to Cadiz, with *lower Masts in*.
28. *Principe de Asturias*, 112 Guns, (Spanish) Admiral Don Federico Gravina; wounded in the Arm, returned to Cadiz, *dismasted*
29. *Montanez*, 74 Guns, (Spanish) returned to Cadiz.

ESCAPED, AFTERWARDS CAPTURED BY SIR R. STRACHAN, NOV. 4.

30. *Formidable*, 80 Guns, (French) Rear-Ad. Dumanoir; hauled to southward & *escaped*.
31. *Mont Blanc*, 74 Guns, (French) hauled to the southward, and *escaped*.
32. *Scipion*, 74 Guns, (French) hauled to the southward and escaped.
33. *Duguay Trouin*, 74 Guns, (French) hauled to the southward, and *escaped*.

LIST of KILLED and WOUNDED.

	Kill.	*Woun.*	*Total.*		*Kill.*	*Woun.*	*Total.*
Victory - - - - - -	57	75	132	Brought forward	298	693	991
Royal Sovereign - -	47	94	141	Ajax - - - - - -	2	9	11
Britannia - - - - -	10	42	52	Orion - - - - - -	1	23	24
Temeraire - - - - -	47	76	123	Agamemnon - - -	2	7	9
Prince - - - - - -	none	none	—	Spartiate - - - -	3	20	23
Neptune - - - - - -	10	34	44	Africa - - - - - -	18	44	62
Dreadnought - - - -	7	26	33	Belleisle - - - - -	33	93	126
Tonnant - - - - -	26	50	76	Colossus - - - - -	40	160	200
Mars - - - - - - -	29	69	98	Achille - - - - - -	13	59	72
Bellerophon - - - -	27	123	150	Polyphemus - - -	2	4	6
Minotaur - - - - -	3	22	25	Swiftsure - - - -	9	8	17
Revenge - - - - - -	28	51	79	Defence - - - - -	7	29	36
Conqueror - - - - -	3	9	12	Thunderer - - - -	4	12	16
Leviathan - - - - -	4	22	26	Defiance - - - - -	17	53	70
Carried forward	298	693	991	Total	449	1214	1663

Above: A portrait of Charles Middleton, Lord Barham (1726–1813). He was an opinionated, hard-working naval administrator, who spent most of his very long working life at the Navy Board and then the Admiralty. From 1778 to 1790 he was the most important member of the Navy Board which, nominally subject to Admiralty control, ran most of the day-to-day business of the navy. He was on the Admiralty Board in the early years of the war of the French Revolution. In 1805 he was recalled from retirement to act as First Lord after Melville had been impeached. His strategic handling of the campaign which led to the Battle of Trafalgar was masterly. *NMM neg no: 2412*

The Allied fleet got under way at Cadiz on 19 October, and were reported by British frigates to Nelson. On the 20th the Allied fleet sighted the British fleet. Just before dawn on the 21st, the day of the battle, Villeneuve discovered that the British were to windward and not, as he had expected, to leeward of him. He also discovered that Nelson had with him a larger force than had been expected. The commander-in-chief of the Allies, therefore, instead of, as he intended, restricting his own line of battle to 21 ships, with a separate reserve 'squadron of observation', allowed his ships to form a line of battle on the starboard tack upon the squadron of observation, led by the Spanish admiral, Gravina. This improvised and somewhat disorganised proceeding helps to explain the mixture of ships from the *Principe de Asturias* then occupying the head position in the van to the *Neptuno* bringing up the rear and the unevenness of the line thus formed. Day broke with the hostile fleets about 11 miles apart. The British were about 21 miles north by west from Cape Trafalgar at this stage. At 6.40am Nelson signalled for the British fleet to form into two columns and prepare for battle. About 10min later he turned the two columns eastwards towards the enemy and began to close under full sail. The Allies had been sailing northwest, but, seeing that action was imminent, Villeneuve signalled to turn on to the other tack and head back towards Cadiz. The wind was already falling, though a heavy swell was running, and the Allied line took a considerable time to bear round. This meant that not only had it reversed its direction, but it was in considerable disorder. Even when the evolution had been completed, the Allied line was very ill-formed and crowded up, some ships being to leeward and some to windward, and some ahead and some astern of their proper stations, much of the column being two and even three ships deep, and part of its centre sagging away to leeward.

At this stage the Allies were heading roughly northward. The British were slowly approaching at about three knots. Both columns were headed by flagships. This was unusual; admirals usually controlled their fleets from the middle of the line and, as we have already seen, Nelson himself had let other ships replace his in the lead of the column bearing down on the French line at the Nile. The lead ship in a column would take the brunt of enemy fire from several ships as she approached his line head on and with no opportunity to retaliate until she broke through, which is a good explanation of why the two biggest, heaviest and least vulnerable British ships, *Victory* and *Royal Sovereign*, were in that position. However, not only would these ships be at considerable risk, they would be the first to be sucked into the immediate concerns of fighting their direct adversaries, taking their admirals into a position where they could do little to change plans or redirect ships. However, probably both Nelson and Collingwood were happy with both the plan of attack and the quality of the initiative of their immediate subordinates, and were concerned

Left: William Carnegie, 7th Earl of Northesk (1758–1831), was the third in command of the British fleet at Trafalgar, but is remembered for little else, apart from being briefly imprisoned by the Nore Mutineers in 1797. This sketch is by Hibbert. *NMM neg no: 1906*

Above: This detail from an engraving shows Admiral Gravina, the distinguished, competent and brave commander of the Spanish fleet at Trafalgar, who was mortally wounded during the battle, though he managed to preserve his ship and retreat to Cadiz with what was left of the Allied rear. *NMM neg no: 2025*

above all to provide an example of leadership rather than of direction. The event seems to have proved them right.

Whilst they were slowly nearing the enemy, Nelson was asked if he would permit the 98-gun three-decker *Temeraire,* which was then close astern, to pass the *Victory*. 'Oh, yes; let her go ahead,' said he. The permission was passed on, but it would appear that Nelson was having his little bit of fun. He put on more sail in an attempt to prevent overtaking, and when this seemed to be failing, hailed *Temeraire* with: 'I'll thank you, Captain Harvey, to keep in your proper station, which is astern of the *Victory*.'

In order to make sure that his communications remained good, Nelson kept the captains of his frigates aboard *Victory* till she was under enemy fire. Captain Blackwood of the *Euryalus,* that observant and useful frigate commander, wrote an account of his commander on the brink of battle which bears quotation: 'He seemed very much to regret, and with reason, that the enemy tacked to the northward, and formed their line on the larboard instead of the starboard tack, which latter line of bearing would have kept the Strait's mouth open. Instead of which, by

forming to the northward, they brought the shoals of Trafalgar and St Pedro under our lee; and also, with the existing wind, kept open the port of Cadiz, which was of infinite consequence to them. This movement was in a great degree the cause of Nelson's making the signal to prepare to anchor, the necessity of which was impressed on his mind to the last moment of his life. He frequently asked me what I should consider as a victory — the certainty of which he never for an instant seemed to doubt, although, from the situation of the land, he questioned the possibility of the subsequent preservation of the prizes. My answer was that "considering the handsome way in which battle was offered by the enemy, their apparent determination for a fair trial of strength, and the proximity of the land, I thought, if 14 ships were captured, it would be a glorious result", to which he always replied: "I shall not, Blackwood, be satisfied with

Above: This drawing of the old Second Rate three-decker *Temeraire*, originally built as a 98-gun ship but later reclassed as 104 guns, in the early stages of being broken up (the old phrase 'taken to pieces' is perhaps more appropriate) at John Beatson's yard at Rotherhithe in September 1838 was made by William Beatson. When this ship was being towed up the Thames from Sheerness to this destination, she was seen by the painter Turner who proceeded to paint perhaps the best known of all his pictures 'The fighting *Temeraire* being towed to her last berth', with its gorgeous sunset and suitably symbolic black steam tug. *NMM neg no: A1805*

Left: Abbott's portrait of Eliab Harvey (1758–1830). The artist killed himself in 1803 so the picture shows Harvey a little before he commanded *Temeraire* at Trafalgar, where she was second in the column behind *Victory* and thoroughly distinguished herself. Harvey, as a rear-admiral, became thoroughly embroiled in the messy aftermath of Cochrane's fireship attack in the Basque Roads (1809) — approving neither of his commander, Admiral Gambier, nor Cochrane. He was dismissed and, although reinstated later, never had a seagoing command again. He was known as a reckless gambler. *NMM ref: BHC2752*

anything short of 20." About 10 o'clock his Lordship's anxiety to close with the enemy became very apparent. He frequently remarked to me that they put a good face upon it; but always quickly added, "I'll give them such a dressing as they never had before." Admiral Villeneuve assured me that, on seeing the novel mode of attack intended to be made on the combined fleets, and which at that moment, he confessed, he could not in any way prevent, he called the officers of his ship around him, and, pointing out the manner in which the first and second in command of the British fleet were each leading his column, exclaimed: "Nothing but victory can attend such gallant conduct." As we were standing on the front of the poop, I took his hand, and said, "I trust, my Lord, that on my return to the *Victory* I shall find your Lordship well, and in possession of twenty prizes", on which he made this reply: "God bless you, Blackwood; I shall never speak to you again."' It was also to Blackwood that Nelson, having signalled to Collingwood: 'I intend to pass through the van of the enemy's line to prevent him from getting into Cadiz', turned and said 'I'll now amuse the fleet with a signal.' Out of the subsequent conversation with John Pasco, *Victory*'s signal lieutenant, came the famous message 'England expects that every man will do his duty'. This seems to have been generally well received, though Collingwood was tetchy about it. Aboard *Bellerophon* it was received with three cheers and a general shout of 'No fear of that!'. Blackwood, back aboard the *Euryalus*, continued to enhance his reputation as one of the best of frigate captains by the part his ship played in repeating signals, watching the progress of the battle, and after its end, in devoted assistance to the crippled ships left to the mercy of a gathering storm.

The two fleets slowly coming together were somewhat different in both numbers and types of ship.

The Spaniards had three very big three-deckers, larger than anything that the British had, particularly in the case of the magnificent *Santisima Trinidad*. Sources vary as to whether she had 140 or 130 guns at this time, and experts argue as to whether she should be described as a four-decker. What is certain is that she was the largest ship present and, at that time, the largest in the world. On the other hand the British had more three-deckers, the three 100-gun flagships and four of the smaller 98s. We have already seen that *Temeraire* appears to have been a reasonable sailer, capable of taking on the renowned

Above: Sir Henry Blackwood (1770–1832), though later a distinguished admiral, made his name as a frigate captain. As captain of the *Penelope*, his harrying of the French 80, *Généreux*, was a major factor in her capture. He is most famous for his role as captain of the *Euryalus* at Trafalgar. *NMM neg no: 1263*

Victory, but the other three 98s appear to have been considered sluggish and unmanoeuvrable though invaluable in battle, and actually had instructions from Nelson not to try and stay in formation, but to be sailed as best suited their individual peculiarities, so as to arrive in action at the earliest possible moment. If the British had seven three-deckers to the three enemy ones, they only had 20 two-deckers to the enemy's 30. Furthermore, the British only had one 80-gun ship (the captured *Tonnant* which we have already met on the other side at Aboukir Bay) against six French ones, whilst there were three of the elderly, weak and nearly obsolescent 64s in their fleet against only one Spanish ship of this type. The largest parts of both fleets consisted, as usual, of the ubiquitous 74-gun ships, of which the British had 16 against the 23 of their opponents. The numbers of smaller vessels were more

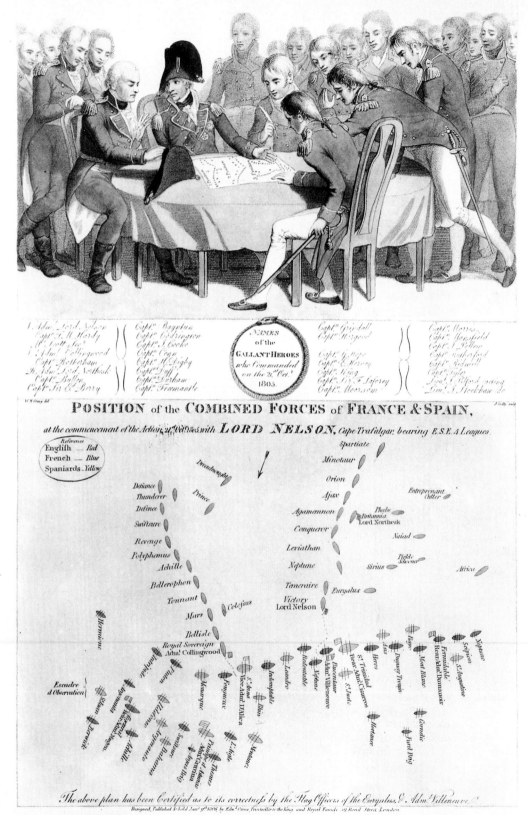

Left: One of the many plans of the Battle of Trafalgar rushed out after the battle, made a more attractive purchase by a somewhat imaginative rendition of Nelson discussing his plans with his captains. The plan itself is 'certified as to its exactness by the Flag Officers [presumably signal officers?] of the *Euryalus* [as the "repeating frigate" — passing on the admiral's signals in the best position to have a general idea of what was going on] & Adm. Villeneuve'. *NMM neg no: 1846*

approximately even, with the French having one more frigate than the British.

This battle is so often seen as a backcloth to the drama of the death of Nelson, with a perspective solely obtained from the *Victory's* quarterdeck, that it probably makes more sense to follow Collingwood's column into action first. After all, it was this column that was in the lead and the one which went into action first. The story of the battle once the columns approached the line turns into the experience of the individual ships in the order in which they arrived in the fray, and their experience in the murderous mêlée which developed in clouds of gunpowder smoke. It was, of course, Nelson's intention to bring on just such a mêlée, where the better gunnery and the quality of the individual commanders would tell against their equally gallant but less well organised foes. It was for that reason that the signal 'engage the enemy more closely' was kept flying from *Victory* as she sailed into action.

The first shots were fired, around noon, by the *Fougueux*, ranging on the *Royal Sovereign* which was steering for the ship next ahead of that French vessel, the Spanish three-decker *Santa Ana*. The next few minutes were crucial. If Spanish and French gunnery was good enough, the concentration of the broadsides of several ships on each of the leading British ships should be adequate to damage them enough either to stop them, or leave them in no fit state to take advantage of their position once they reached the Allied line. Each successive British ship could be given the same reception, raked from bow to stern when they were approaching on a course which gave them no chance to retaliate to the concentrated fire of their opponents. The British were gambling on not receiving critical damage during this approach phase, because if they contrived to pass through this danger zone without critical damage, they would then be in a position to return the battering they had received with interest. Passing through the enemy line they would be in a position to fire raking broadsides

into the bows and sterns of their opponents. All the following ships would be arriving in one part of the enemy line, so that the odds would rapidly swing in favour of the column.

The advantage would then be with the ships that could fire their guns at the faster rate, and this, as the battles of the last century had proved one after the other, was the British forte.

The gamble paid off with both British columns, and *Royal Sovereign* proceeded to provide a fearful example of just how raking fire worked. She had received no serious damage in her approach, and at 12.10pm slowly passed through the enemy's line between the *Santa Ana*, the flagship of Vice-Admiral de Alava, and the *Fougueux*, firing her port guns double-shotted into the stern of the former at very close range and the starboard guns into the bow of the latter, apparently killing and wounding by that one broadside alone nearly 400 people. The range was so close that Collingwood, who had been munching an apple, threw the core after the broadside into the Spanish ship's shattered stern. She then ranged close along the starboard broadside, and subsequently on the bow, of the *Santa Ana* with which she began a furious point-blank range battle. The *Fougueux*, came up to rake Collingwood's flagship from astern, while the *San Leandro* raked her from ahead and the *Indomptable* on her starboard quarter and *San Justo* on her starboard bow poured in shot from under 300yd. However, this unco-ordinated concentration of fire soon came to an end as the other ships realised they were doing as much harm to each other as they were to the British vessel — and Collingwood was left alone to fight it out with de Alava. *Royal Sovereign* had fought unsupported for a quarter of an hour, providing a splendid example of the fighting value of a three-decker with a well-trained crew, but now help was on its way. *Belleisle* was next to arrive. This 74 had suffered from the fire of the Allied rear and was only able to retaliate with a few shots fired at the *Monarca*. Now, however, she fired into the already battered *Santa Ana's* lee quarter, then turned round to attempt to rake the *Indomptable* which, however, managed to turn away in time.

Already the Allied rear was becoming jumbled and confused, some of the ships pressing forward to support the centre and others hesitating, their sails shivering or aback. The whole rear, moreover, was soon clouded by the smoke which rolled slowly downwind from the guns of the British lee column as, ship by ship, it drew near enough to

Above: 'England expects' a mid-Victorian 'history painting' of the hoisting of Nelson's famous signal. The legend is well under way in this picture where, despite all the careful research, everything looks a little bit too glossy and perfect for real life: hagiography rather than history. *NMM neg no: A752*

reply and then cut through the grouped mass of French and Spanish ships ahead and astern of the *Santa Ana*. That ship, having been battered by the *Royal Sovereign* to the extent of losing all her masts and the ability to resist further, surrendered to her nearly equally crippled opponent.

Belleisle, the next British ship in action, having made the *Indomptable* turn away, began a distant duel with the *San Juan Nepomuceno*, until the *Fougueux* ran her bow into the side of the British ship. After 20min the *Mars* began to fire at the French vessel which then withdrew to the northward, but left *Belleisle* a wreck. Soon afterwards the French *Achille* took up the task of punishing the dismasted British ship, which could make little reply because of the mass of wreckage covering her engaged side. Meanwhile one other French ship (*Aigle*) and two Spaniards also fired at her. Her next trial was at 2.30pm when the French *Neptune* put herself in a raking position on the bow. Fortunately by 3.15pm the *Polyphemus* came up on her bow, at 3.20pm the *Defiance* took on the *Aigle* and, most

heartening of all, at 3.25pm the British *Swiftsure* fired her first, devastating broadside into the stern of the French *Achille*. Despite her battered state the *Belleisle* had still one further task to undertake. She had one boat still capable of floating and sent it across to take the surrender of the *Argonauta* which had drifted close.

Next astern of her in the British line was the *Mars*, which had difficulty in finding a gap to break through the Allied line. Already being fired at by the *Pluton* from astern she had to turn head to wind to avoid ramming the *Santa Ana*. In this awkward position she was turning her stern towards *Monarca* and *Algésiras*, but fortunately the arrival of the *Tonnant* then

TRAFALGAR

21 October 1805

POSITION AT ABOUT NOON

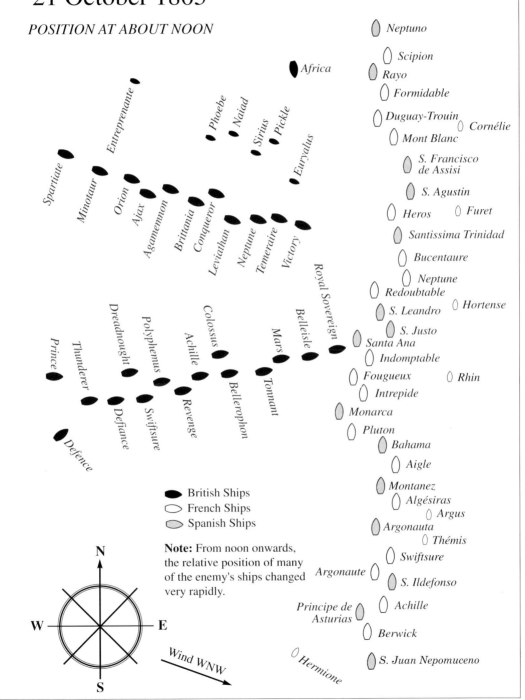

Neptuno

Scipion

Rayo

Formidable

Africa

Duguay-Trouin

Cornélie

Mont Blanc

Entreprenante

Phoebe

Naiad

Sirius

Pickle

Euryalus

S. Francisco de Assisi

S. Agustin

Spartiate

Minotaur

Orion

Ajax

Agamemnon

Brittania

Conqueror

Leviathan

Neptune

Temeraire

Victory

Heros

Furet

Santissima Trinidad

Bucentaure

Neptune

Royal Sovereign

Redoubtable

S. Leandro

Hortense

S. Justo

Dreadnought

Polyphemus

Colossus

Achille

Belleisle

Mars

Santa Ana

Indomptable

Prince

Thunderer

Fougueux

Rhin

Intrepide

Bellerophon

Tonnant

Monarca

Revenge

Swiftsure

Defiance

Pluton

Bahama

Defence

Aigle

Montanez

Algésiras

Argus

British Ships

French Ships

Spanish Ships

Argonauta

Thémis

Swiftsure

Note: From noon onwards, the relative position of many of the enemy's ships changed very rapidly.

Argonaute

S. Ildefonso

Principe de Asturias

Achille

N

Berwick

W

E

Hermione

S. Juan Nepomuceno

Wind WNW

S

Above left: Just after midday the *Belleisle* broke through the Allied line, as shown here, to become heavily engaged with a number of French and Spanish ships. This was painted by someone serving aboard her at the time — Lt Nicholas of the Royal Marines — and is one of a sequence of paintings by him showing his ship at various stages of the battle. *NMM neg no: 1532*

Below left: This painting of HMS *Belleisle* as she was at 1pm during the Battle of Trafalgar is another painting by Lt Nicholas, Royal Marines, who was aboard. This one shows her at the stage when she was in the midst of foes and her masts began to fall. *NMM neg no: 1531*

Above: Portrait by Raeburn of Captain George Duff (1764–1805), killed at Trafalgar in command of the *Mars. NMM ref: BHC2666*

diverted attention from the now unmanageable *Mars* which was then further battered by shot from *Fougueux* and, again, *Pluton*. Captain Duff's head was taken off by a shot from the latter. The arrival of further British ships finally drove off her assailants, but the fate of the *Mars* is an awful warning of what could have happened to the British columns had their enemies been better gunners, or just luckier.

Tonnant, the big, ex-French, 80-gun ship was next into action. She had initially aimed to cut the Franco-Spanish line just in front of the bow of the *Algésiras*, but that ship backed away from the danger and instead *Tonnant* cut the enemy's line astern of the *Monarca,* which she first raked and then came up yard-arm to yard-arm. The Spanish ship soon dropped astern and apparently struck her colours, though she subsequently rehoisted them. The British ship was diverted by the *Algésiras* trying to cross her stern. The helm was put hard a-port, and Captain Tyler succeeded in running on board his opponent and tangling up with her port bow. The two ships fired furiously into each other and the Frenchman made a very determined attempt to board. After this failed she surrendered at about 2.15pm. About quarter of an hour later the *San Juan Nepomuceno*, which had for some time been the target for the fire of the *Tonnant's* foremost port guns, also surrendered. The boat sent to board her, however, sank. The Spaniard then appears to have rehoisted her colours, but was then fired on by the *Dreadnought* and surrendered again.

The *Bellerophon* broke through the Allied line about a quarter of an hour after the *Tonnant* had done so, passing under the *Monarca's* stern. That ship had rehoisted her colours so the British ship was turning to come into action on her broadside, but fouled the *Aigle,* which was to leeward. So from about 12.15pm the *Bellerophon* was closely engaged on both sides, to port with the *Monarca* and to starboard with the *Aigle.* Soon afterwards another Spanish ship fired into her port quarter. The French *Swiftsure*, from a somewhat greater distance, was firing into her starboard quarter. Meanwhile the *Bahama* could and did rake her with a few forward guns from nearly astern. The result of all this was that soon after 1pm the *Bellerophon* lost her main and mizzen top-masts. The fallen rigging caught fire from the flashes from her own guns. About 10min later her captain was killed. However, the *Colossus* began to engage the French *Swiftsure* and the *Bahama.* The other Spanish vessel which had been annoying her (probably the *Montañez)* dropped astern. The *Bellerophon* was still in grave difficulties; the *Aigle,* after having made more than one fruitless attempt to board, broke away and dropped astern also, being raked as she went, first by the *Bellerophon* and afterwards by the *Revenge.* The *Bellerophon* was then entirely

Above: The storm after Trafalgar, with *Victory* (in the centre of the picture, seen from astern) at anchor. For some reason, the suffering of the damaged and dismasted survivors of the battle in this storm was a popular subject for artists and print-sellers.
NMM neg no: X1899

disabled but still capable of making the *Monarca* surrender at last. She also sent parties to take the surrender of the *Bahama*, which had been reduced to submission by the *Colossus.*

This latter ship as she neared the enemy was going to pass astern of the French *Swiftsure* which, to avoid being raked, turned towards her so the *Colossus* ran past her starboard side, firing as she went and soon was locked alongside the *Argonaute* which lay to leeward. The British ship's starboard battery had nearly silenced the Frenchman's port one within 10min and the *Argonaute* looked nearly ready to surrender, but the ships drifted apart, though not before the French ship was well raked. Throughout this engagement the *Colossus* had also been fighting the French *Swiftsure,* which lay on her port quarter, and the *Bahama*, which was nearly abreast of her to port. Just before 3pm the French *Swiftsure*, which had by that time moved so far ahead that she both got in the way of the fire of the *Bahama* and received the full broadside of the *Colossus,* dropped astern, practically beaten, and once more exposed the *Bahama* to the *Colossus's* fire which quickly obliged the Spaniard to surrender. In the meanwhile the

French *Swiftsure* made a last effort, endeavouring to turn in order to rake the *Colossus's* stern, but Morris turned quickly enough to escape most of the shots intended to rake him, and replied with his starboard broadside. Almost simultaneously the *Orion* shot another broadside into the Frenchman, whereupon the *Swiftsure* indicated her surrender. By this time the *Colossus* had suffered more heavily in killed and wounded than any other British ship in this battle.

The British *Achille* was following the *Colossus* closely. She passed astern of the *Montañez,* and then came up to engage her from leeward. About 12min later the *Montañez* sheered off and the *Achille* then went to assist the *Belleisle,* lying dismasted to leeward. Instead, however, she came into action with the *Argonauta* and fought her at close quarters

Above: Bellerophon in action at Trafalgar, a drawing said to be by her captain. This presumably means that it was by Lieutenant Cumby who took over from Captain John Cooke, who was killed during the battle. *Bellerophon* is the ship whose stern can be seen in the middle of the picture, with a large white ensign still defiantly flying above it. On her left is the stern of the *Monarca* and on her right that of the *Aigle*. Nearest to us is the stern of the French *Swiftsure* and the ship on the left of the picture coming towards us is presumably the *Bahama*. All these ships were simultaneously firing at the British ship. *NMM neg no: A7382*

for an hour. The *Argonauta* then tried to get away, but failing to escape, shut her lower-deck ports, ceased firing and apparently surrendered. Before the British *Achille* could attempt to take possession of her, her French namesake (the other *Achille* in this battle) opened fire in passing; and the *Berwick*, which had already been distantly engaged with the *Defence*, came in between the British *Achille* and her Spanish opponent, which then drifted off to leeward whilst the *Berwick* took her place. After more than an hour's fierce fighting, the *Berwick* surrendered and the *Achille* placed a prize crew aboard her.

The slow but powerful *Dreadnought* got into action with the already somewhat battered *San Juan Nepomuceno* at about 2pm and although that ship had some support from the *Principe de Asturias*, one other Spanish vessel and the *Indomptable*, she was taken in little more than a quarter of an hour. The *Dreadnought* immediately turned on the *Principe de Asturias* but failed to prevent her eventual escape.

The *Polyphemus* seems to have first fought the French *Neptune* and next the French *Achille*. She finally saw a Union Jack being waved from that ship's bows, in sign of surrender.

The *Revenge*, attempting to pass through the enemy's line so as to rake the *Aigle,* caught the French ship's jib-boom. From this position she fired a couple of broadsides into the Frenchman's bows. Having broken free, she was coming round on the port tack when the *Principe de Asturias* poured a heavy fire into her port quarter. She was also caught between three two-deckers, and suffered badly until more British ships approached and scared off her adversaries.

The British *Swiftsure* (another case of the same name shared between a British and a

French ship, both of which were present in this battle) having, as we have seen, passed round the stern of the *Belleisle*, began a warm action with the French *Achille* and set her on fire.

The *Defiance*, as she joined the confusion of the Allied line, exchanged some shot with the *Principe de Asturias* and, at about 3pm, ran alongside the *Aigle* and lashed herself to the enemy. Boarding parties charged on to the French ship with some success at first, even hoisting a British flag, but her crew then rallied and drove the British back. The lashings were cut and the British ship, still within point-blank range, opened so heavy a fire that, in about 20min, the *Aigle* surrendered. The *Defiance* subsequently also took possession of the *San Juan Nepomuceno*, which had struck to the *Dreadnought*.

The *Thunderer*, after first coming to the aid of the *Revenge*, then turned across the bows of the *Principe de Asturias*, raked that vessel and came round on the starboard tack. The French *Neptune* made a brief attempt to help the Spanish three-decker, but soon made her escape.

The *Defence* first came into action with the *Berwick*, before that ship turned away to her encounter with the British *Achille*. *Defence* then went on to an hour long battle with the *San Ildefonso* which then surrendered. The *Prince* did not get into action till late in the afternoon, firing upon the *Principe de Asturias* and (at 4.30pm) the French *Achille*. At that time the Frenchman's foretop was in flames. The *Prince's* broadside brought it down upon deck, and the flames spread. After firing for a while longer the British captain saw his opponent was doomed and sent boats to rescue the crew, as did other ships. Unfortunately heated guns were going off in the flames, making approach very dangerous, and the French ship blew up at about 5.45pm with most of her crew still aboard.

Collingwood's column had achieved its aim, having virtually destroyed the Franco-Spanish rear. We now have to turn to the other column, led by Nelson in the *Victory*, originally heading for the immense *Santisima Trinidad* though intending to engage Villeneuve's *Bucentaure*, which had the job of not only pinning down and destroying the Allied centre, but also of holding off any counter-attack that might come from the Franco-Spanish vanguard. Much would depend on how its commander, Rear-Admiral Dumanoir, reacted. If he moved quickly and decisively enough to the support of the rest of the Allied fleet his fresh ships might tip the balance towards a British defeat, maybe of

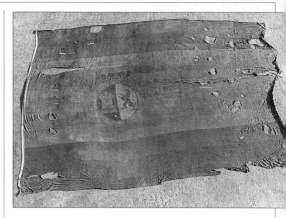

Above: A huge Spanish battle-ensign taken at Trafalgar at the surrender of the *San Ildefonso*. The flags in contemporary battle pictures may look absurdly large, but they really were that size. *NMM neg no: C1832/20A*

disastrous proportions. Nelson was gambling on the failure of French officers (and their Spanish allies) to react with the speed, initiative, effectiveness and degree of mutual support that he expected from his own captains.

At 12.20pm Villeneuve's ship began to fire ranging shots at his rival's flagship. One shot through the main topgallant sail showed that the range had been found and a very heavy fire was opened upon the flagship by a large part of the Allied van. There was no longer more than the faintest breath of wind and the progress of the *Victory*, now heading for the gap between the *Santisima Trinidad* and the *Bucentaure*, was slower than ever. During her long approach she suffered terribly. One of her guns went off by accident, but otherwise she made no return. As she neared the enemy, those ships immediately ahead of her closed together in an attempt to stop her breaking through the line. This in itself, plus the falling back of other vessels to support the *Santa Ana*, caused a considerable gap to open somewhat ahead of the centre of the Allied line. Certainly the *Redoutable*, and possibly *Intrépide* moved up to the support of the flagship. The *San Leandro*, however, joined the *San Justo* and *Indomptable* at the head of the rearmost group, which thus included about 20 ships, as against the 13 or 14 ships in the leading group. This produced a gap of at least ¾mile.

As the *Victory* closed on the *Bucentaure* a shot cut her mizzen topmast in two, and another knocked her wheel to pieces, so that from then on she had to be steered from below decks with relieving tackles. Every sail was in tatters. The French *Neptune* was on the *Bucentaure's* lee quarter, and coming up to close that gap was the *Redoutable*.

This particular ship had what was probably, physically, the smallest captain in the French navy. Under 5ft, Captain Lucas was, however, far from short of personality, energy or ability. Knowing the weakness of French gun drill he had concentrated on training his crew in the use of small arms and grenades. That training

was about to pay off, and claim an illustrious victim.

Looking at these ships ahead of him, Captain Hardy told Nelson that the *Victory* could not pass through the line without ramming one or another of those ships. Nelson's reply was 'I cannot help it, it does not signify which we run on board of. Go on board which you please. Take your choice.' Hardy headed as if to run on board the *Redoutable*, and at 12.59pm as the *Victory* began to pass under the stern of the *Bucentaure*, she fired her port guns, all double and many treble-shotted, in succession into the cabin windows of Villeneuve's flagship, the range being so close that, as the *Victory* rolled, her yard arm struck the *Bucentaure's* gaff. The salvo wrecked the stern of the French flagship, killed and wounded nearly 400 of her men and dismounted 20 of her guns. But the *Victory* was almost at the same time raked from ahead, and terribly mauled by the French *Neptune*.

Below: Victory and (on her left) Euryalus seen from astern approaching the Allied line at Trafalgar. The latter is the 'repeating frigate' acting as the communications link between the flagship and the rest of the fleet. She can be seen hoisting the same signal flags as Nelson's ship.
NMM neg no: X1896

However, this ship then moved ahead, out of danger of being rammed by *Victory*. Hardy, however, still intended to run on board of the *Redoutable,* which was on his starboard bow. He fired his starboard broadside into her as soon as it would bear and, putting his helm hard to port, made directly for her. She shifted slightly and the 100-gun ship ran alongside the 74. The rigging of both ships fouled. The three decker, with her greater height out of the water, should have had a decisive superiority over the smaller ship, but Lucas's men were so well-trained and their fire from the tops so deadly that *Victory's* upper deck guns were virtually silenced. The middle and lower deck guns continued to fire and to shatter the hull of the French ship, but a marksman from the French ship's tops had given Nelson his fatal wound. The French then succeeded in almost clearing the *Victory's* exposed decks, but attempts to board were frustrated by the 'tumble home' (inward slope of the sides) of both ships, and by fierce resistance from the British flagship's crew who emerged from the protection of the decks when it became evident the attempts were being made. This virtual 'stand off' was resolved by the intervention of *Temeraire* which appeared on the French 74's other side around 1.40pm. Shortly afterwards the *Redoubtable* stopped fighting, having taken up the attentions of two British three-deckers, the first of which she had fought to a standstill, thoroughly justifying her name. She would later sink, but she left *Victory* in no fit state to contribute more to the battle. The latter had lost her mizzen topmast; all her rigging was badly cut; her fore and main masts and bowsprit, together with their yards, and with the fore and main tops, were greatly knocked about; all her spare spars were too damaged to be of use; her hull was severely mauled; she had several shot-holes between wind and water (on the waterline); and she had suffered many casualties.

Her next astern, *Temeraire,* had some difficulty in staying in station behind her leader, having to take in some sails and to yaw a number of times. She was under a heavy fire as she approached the enemy. In an exchange of fire with the French *Neptune* and the *Redoutable*, she was eventually reduced by the former's raking broadsides to a nearly unmanageable condition, with the *Redoutable* on her port beam and the *Neptune* on her starboard bow. Finally, as we have seen, the drifting *Redoutable*, still fast to the *Victory,* fell on board the *Temeraire* with the French ship's bowsprit passing over the gangway of the British ship on the port side. The British crew lashed it there, and fired their guns into the enemy ship's bow as fast as they could. Shortly afterwards the *Fougueux,* which had already been attacked by the *Belleisle* and *Mars* of Collingwood's column, and then escaped them, appeared, steering for the starboard side of the *Temeraire*. She apparently thought she had an easy prey to attack. The British ship was badly damaged aloft, but she was well prepared for this new enemy. She had not yet fired her starboard broadside and, waiting until the Frenchman was less than 100yd from her, she poured the whole of it into the *Fougueux* with dreadful effect. At about 2pm, no longer under control, the *Fougueux* ran foul of her latest adversary, whose men instantly lashed the French two-decker by her fore-rigging to the British ship's spare anchor. Lieutenant Thomas Fortescue Kennedy then boarded her at the head of few men, and within 10min made her a prize. Soon afterwards the *Victory* pushed herself off from the *Redoutable's* port side, and the *Temeraire,* with the *Redoutable* and *Fougueux* still fastened to her, swung with her head to the southward. At almost the same time the *Redoutable* lost her main and mizzen masts, the main falling on the after-part of the *Temeraire* and smashing everything beneath it. However, it made a bridge between the two vessels which enabled the British ship to take formal possession of a ship which had for some time stopped fighting. The last offensive action of the *Temeraire* seems to have been firing of some of her foremost guns at the French *Neptune*, which quickly moved away out of range.

The British *Neptune* (at about 1.45pm), the *Leviathan* and the *Conqueror* arriving in rapid succession all fired their broadsides into the

Above right: Nicholas Pocock always put a lot of careful research into his paintings, not least by talking to those who had fought in the battles he was painting, as a seaman speaking to other seamen. This bird's-eye view of Trafalgar — seen from above and behind the Franco-Spanish line, some way forward from where *Victory* can be seen breaking the line — certainly seems to be as close to what actually happened as possible. In the background Collingwood's line is already heavily embroiled in the Allied rear, whilst the errant *Africa* is hastening down the outside of the Allied line — the ship going to the left at the right of the picture. *NMM neg no: 5785*

Right: Another pictorial print of Trafalgar, complete with a crude vignette of the death of Nelson. *NMM neg no: A7322*

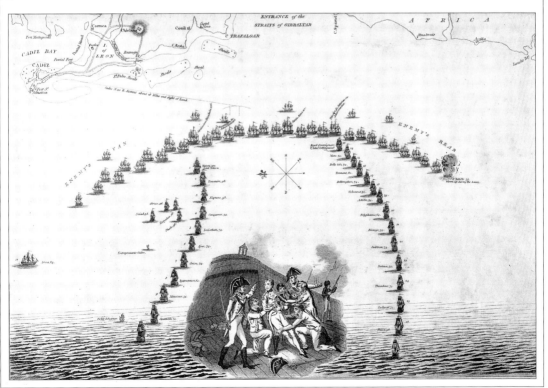

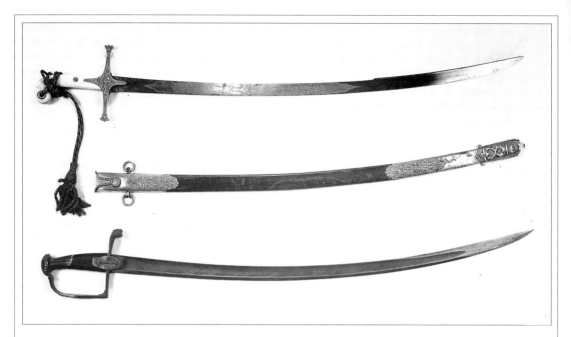

Above: Two swords associated with the Fremantle family, several of whose members served in the Royal Navy. The French officer's sword had belonged to Captain Magendie the captain of the *Bucentaure*, the French flagship at Trafalgar, and was surrendered to Captain Thomas Fremantle of the *Neptune*. The other sword is somewhat later, but is of the eastern, 'mameluke', type made popular by French and British involvement in Egypt in 1798. *NMM neg no: 3146*

already smashed stern of the *Bucentaure*. The *Neptune* then went alongside the *Santisima Trinidad*, already somewhat damaged by the fire of the approaching column, and fought her till she was totally crippled. The *Leviathan* chased off the French *Neptune* which had been attacking the *Temeraire* and then, seeing that the Allied van was coming down in an attempt to catch Nelson's column between two fires, boldly went out to meet them. She first engaged the *San Agustin*, which tried to rake her, but was easily outmanoeuvred. A single treble-shotted broadside into her starboard quarter brought down her mizzen mast. Captain Bayntun, who could not back his sails to stop his ship owing to the damaged state of his rigging, rammed the Spanish ship instead. She was boarded and captured without opposition. The prize was lashed to the *Leviathan's* port side. No sooner had this been done than the *Intrépide* came up, raked the *Leviathan* from ahead and then positioned herself along the British ship's starboard side. She did not, however, long remain there, as the *Africa* and *Orion* followed by others were coming up to help *Leviathan* cope with this threat.

The little 64-gun ship *Africa* always stands out on maps of the start of the battle, as she is off on her own. What had happened was that she had become separated from the fleet on the previous night and, when the action began, was quite close to the leading ship of the Allied van. Nelson signalled to her to make all possible sail, but her captain seems to have misunderstood the order, which was intended to keep him out of danger, as meaning that he should attack the enemy as soon as he could. The solitary 64 therefore sailed along the Franco-Spanish van, exchanging broadsides with it, and finally closed on the *Santisima Trinidad*. Thinking that she had surrendered, her captain sent Lieutenant John Smith (the fifth of that name in the Royal Navy at that time) to take possession. Smith reached the Spanish quarterdeck before he learnt that the Spaniard had not surrendered. No one, however, tried to stop him returning to his own ship, after what must have been one of the odder adventures of the battle. At about 3.20pm the cheeky *Africa* very gallantly took on the *Intrépide* and fought her for about 40min, until the arrival of the *Orion* upon the Frenchman's starboard quarter relieved the 64, which had been nearly knocked out of action by then. The *Orion* then came round the *Intrépide's* stern, and then attacked her port bow. After about a quarter of an hour of heavy

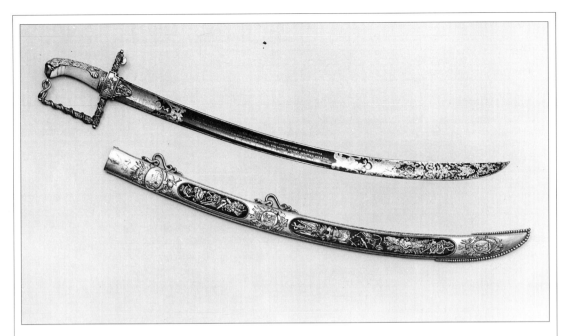

Above: The rewards of victory. Lieutenant Lapénotière of the schooner HMS *Pickle* brought home the news of the victory at Trafalgar and of Nelson's death. He was awarded this presentation sword and was also promoted to commander as a result. The sword was provided by Lloyds' patriotic fund which gave one of these £100 swords to all the captains of ships at Trafalgar. It was an accepted form of recognition of officers who had performed gallant deeds, though there was a hierarchy in this as in most other aspects of life at the time, for there were £50 presentation swords as well as the £100 ones. These were not, *pace* C. S. Forester's Hornblower, fighting swords. There was no edge to fight with. *NMM neg no: B1964*

fire from that position the French ship surrendered.

Meanwhile *Conqueror* completed the defeat of the *Bucentaure* which surrendered. Much earlier (just before 2pm) Villeneuve had signalled for all the Allied ships which had not yet become engaged to join in the battle. Unfortunately for him the very light winds did not assist such a move; some ships had to use boats to tow their heads round and others made no real attempt to join in the fight.

Ten ships finally came round, by which time Gravina with 11 ships surviving from the struggle in the centre and the rear was already retreating from the battle, but only the five that followed Dumanoir (*Formidable*, *Duguay-Trouin*, *Mont Blanc*, *Scipion* and *Neptuno*) seem to have made any real attempt to intervene in the battle. The others appear to have been trying to join Gravina. Some of these ships exchanged shots with *Britannia*, *Orion*, *Ajax* and *Agamemnon*. Dumanoir caused some anxiety amongst the crippled British ships as he skirted the battle and raked the British *Neptune*, but he was too late to affect the outcome of the battle and he knew it. He was eventually chased from the battlefield by the only undamaged ships enough to windward to intercept — the *Minotaur* and *Spartiate* — which managed to cut off the *Neptuno* from her colleagues and then batter her into surrendering at about 5.10pm.

As the battle drew to a close the sea was strewn with crippled ships. Many of the British ships had suffered severe damage. The *Belleisle* lost all three masts and bowsprit; the *Royal Sovereign* lost main and mizzen; the *Tonnant* all three topmasts; and the *Victory*, *Temeraire*, *Leviathan*, *Conqueror*, *Africa*, *Orion*, *Minotaur*, *Mars*, *Bellerophon*, *Colossus*, *Dreadnought* and *Swiftsure* had a larger or smaller number of important spars shot away. However, out of 33 Allied ships of the line, 17 had been taken, and one had caught fire and blown up. Of the remainder, four ships under Dumanoir, having sailed off to the southward, had got away for the time, though they never again entered a French port; and 11 under Gravina, had run to the northeast. Some of the latter had scarcely been in action; but others, having lost masts, were in tow of the frigates.

Left: The combination of crushing victory with the death of the national hero as that victory was obtained ensured that Trafalgar became an instant legend. This commemorative creamware jug is one of the first material signs of that legend. *NMM neg no: C3620*

Right: This Dodd engraving shows the scene at the end of the Battle of Trafalgar. On the right the French *Achille* is burning furiously. Standing by in the attempt to pick up survivors are, to her right, the cutter *Entreprenante* and, to her left, the schooner *Pickle*, shortly to become famous for carrying the news of Trafalgar to England. The mastless hulk in the foreground is the *Belleisle*, with, further to the left, the frigate *Naiad* coming to her assistance. *NMM neg no: B2582*

Below right: Engraving of the frigate *Naiad* coming up to take the disabled *Belleisle* under tow at the end of the Battle of Trafalgar. The frigate's log states: 'at 4, took the *Belleisle* in tow, she being without a mast or bowsprit. Observed one of the French line-of-battle ships on fire. At 4.20 out boats and sent them to take men from ditto. At 5, the firing ceased from all ships. At 5.10, observed the ship that was on fire to blow up.' This was the French *Achille*, seen blazing in the background. *NMM neg no: X1884*

Gravina's division was prevented by the wind from entering Cadiz that night.

Nelson had died of his wound knowing that victory had been won, but insisting to the last that the ships should anchor. Vice-Admiral Collingwood, who had succeeded to the command-in-chief, shifted his flag from the much-damaged *Royal Sovereign* to the *Euryalus*, which subsequently took the *Royal Sovereign* in tow and stood off shore. However, for reasons which have never been explained, he neglected Nelson's advice and did not anchor. This was almost certainly a mistake, with a storm getting up, a lee shore close at hand and many disabled ships. Of the 17 prizes, eight were entirely and nine were partly dismasted; and of the 27 British ships of the line, half were at that stage more or less unseaworthy. The fleet was in about 13 fathoms of water; the wind blew with moderate but increasing strength dead on shore; there was a nasty swell which greatly distressed the crippled vessels; and, only six or seven miles to leeward, lay the shoals of Trafalgar.

At 9pm Collingwood finally ordered his ships to prepare to anchor, but the wind then changed and the order was revoked. In the storm that followed, the gallant *Redoubtable*

foundered and the *Fougueux* was driven ashore with only 25 survivors. The *Algésiras* and *Bucentaure* were recaptured by their crews from bone-weary prize-crews, though the latter vessel then went aground and was wrecked.

The senior French naval officer at Cadiz, Cosmao-Kerjulien, with Admiral Gravina mortally wounded, took command of the five most seaworthy ships of the line left there and ventured out to sea to ascertain what he could recover. He was confronted by 10 British ships which cast off their tows and formed line and retreated, but his frigates managed to retake the *Neptuno* and *Santa Ana*. However, this was to prove an expensive sortie, none the less, as *Indomptable* went aground and broke up, whilst *San Francisco de Assisi* also grounded. *Rayo*, in danger of going ashore as well, anchored and rolled her masts out, only to be found by a fresh British ship out of Gibraltar (the *Donegal*) and forced to surrender. However, she then went ashore and was lost. Other prizes of the British were succumbing. The *Monarca* foundered, the *Santisima Trinidad* and *Argonauta* were ordered to be scuttled, the *Aigle* was wrecked, as was the *Berwick*, whilst the *Intrépide* and *San Agustin*

Left: Cuthbert Collingwood (1748–1810) as Vice-Admiral and Lord. A much more austere and remote figure than his ebullient old friend, Horatio Nelson. As a captain his contribution to victory at the Glorious First of June (1794) and St Vincent (1797) was important. He was second-in-command at Trafalgar, and has been blamed ever since for failing to follow the dying Nelson's insistence that he should anchor the fleet and the prizes. 'Anchor, I should never have thought of that' he is supposed to have said. He then took over command of the Mediterranean Fleet with all its enormous responsibilities, diplomatic and political as much as naval, and stayed afloat for the next five years till his death in harness, exhausted, in 1810. An admirable but slightly enigmatic and perhaps not very lovable man, though Nelson was very fond of him. The National Maritime Museum holds portraits of each man done by the other as young officers in the West Indies, and the locks of hair they exchanged. *NMM neg no: 6811*

Right: Euryalus, Victory and a damaged two-decker (as seen looking left to right) riding out the gale after Trafalgar. In the foreground one of the disabled prizes is foundering. Collingwood was aboard the frigate, and it is his blue ensign flying from the top of the foremast, indicating that she is now the flagship. This watercolour is by Nicholas Pocock, an excellent artist who had been a merchant captain himself and knew both ships and the sea. *NMM neg no: 8501*

were burnt as useless. Only four prizes were left: the *San Ildefonso*, the *Swiftsure*, the *Bahama*, and the *San Juan Nepomuceno*. This disappointment was somewhat lessened by the fact that on 3 November Dumanoir's four ships were caught by Sir Richard Strachan with five ships of the line plus frigates off the north of Spain. By the end of the action all four of these ships had fallen into British hands, and all were safely brought back to Plymouth.

The human cost of the battle to the British was 437 dead and 1,242 wounded. The combined total of dead and wounded for the Allies is not known but perhaps was in the region of 8,000 — of which all too many were dead thanks to the blowing up of the *Achille* and the losses in the storm.

As has already been made clear, Trafalgar did not prevent an invasion of Britain, as Napoleon's complicated scheme had already came to naught. It did not destroy French sea power or finish the Napoleonic War at sea. Napoleon till the very end, a decade later, continued to build up the French Navy; the Royal Navy had a very long and worrying haul before it in 1805, and the Nile marks a more decisive repulse to French naval aspirations

and is also Nelson's greatest masterpiece. Trafalgar did, however, knock Spain, once and for all, out of the first rank of naval powers. It was a great propaganda victory for Britain, and gave both country and navy a powerful and enduring legend. Its memory helped to cushion the blow of Napoleon's victory at Austerlitz shortly afterwards. It confirmed in no uncertain way that Britain was the world's leading sea power. However, it is interesting to wonder whether it would ever have happened had not Villeneuve reacted the way he did to the fact he was being superseded. As it was, the French admiral was a delayed casualty of the battle. Repatriated to France he then, allegedly, took his own life. The circumstances were suspicious, and the suggestion that Napoleon might have been the instigator of his death has never gone away. Nor, however, has it been proven. No more has anyone solved the question of just how much Nelson was actually looking for a hero's death or what would have become of him had he survived Trafalgar. What is sure is that a very large number of sailors died and several ships were lost because of the decision Villeneuve took to come out and fight.

Above: The *Victory* under jury rig lying to an anchor in the gale after Trafalgar, with no rest for the battle-exhausted crew. What the wounded were going through does not bear thinking about — Dodd engraving. *NMM neg no: 2788*

Fleets at Trafalgar

Three/four-Decker 130/140-gun nil/nil + one
British and French: nil
Spanish: *Santisima Trinidad* (taken, then lost — Flag of Rear-Admiral Don B. H. de Cisneros, Commodore Don F. X. de Uriate) — one

Three-Deckers 120/112-gun nil/nil + two
British and French: nil
Spanish: *Santa Ana* (taken, then retaken — Flag of Vice-Admiral Don I. M. de Alava, Captain Don José Gardoqui), *Principe de Asturias* (Flagship of Admiral Don Federico Gravina, Rear-Admiral Don A. Escafio) — two

Three-Deckers 100-gun three/nil + nil
British: *Victory* (Flagship of Vice-Admiral Lord Nelson, Captain Thomas Masterman Hardy), *Royal Sovereign* (Flag of Vice-Admiral Cuthbert Collingwood, Captain Edward Rotherham), *Britannia* (Flag of Rear-Admiral William, Earl of Northesk, Captain Charles Bullen) — three
French and Spanish: nil

Three-Deckers 98-gun four/nil + nil
British: *Temeraire* (Eliab Harvey), *Neptune* (Thomas Francis Fremantle), *Prince* (Richard Grindall), *Dreadnought* (John Conn) — four
French and Spanish: nil

Two-Deckers 84/80-gun one/four + two
British: *Tonnant* (ex-French — Charles Tyler) — one
French: *Formidable* (taken by Strachan 3 November — Flag of Rear-Admiral Dumanoir Le Pelley, Captain J. M. Letellier), *Bucentaure* (taken, retaken and finally wrecked — Flagship of Vice-Admiral P. C. J. B. S. Villeneuve, Captain J. J. Magendie), *Neptune* (Commodore E. T. Maistral), *Indomptable* (J. J. Hubert) — four
Spanish: *Argonauta* (taken, then sank, Don A. Parejo), *Neptuno* (taken then recaptured — Don H. Cayetano Valdès) — two

Two-Deckers 74-gun 16/14 + nine
British: *Conqueror* (Israel Pellew), *Leviathan* (Henry William Bayntun), *Ajax* (Lt John Pilfold — acting captain), *Orion* (Edward Codrington), *Minotaur* (Charles John Moore Mansfield), *Spartiate* (ex-French — Sir Francis Laforey, Bart), *Mars* (George Duff), *Belleisle* (ex-French — William Hargood), *Bellerophon* (John Cooke), *Colossus* (James Nicoll Morris), *Achille* (Richard King), *Revenge* (Robert Moorsom), *Swiftsure* (William Gordon Rutherford), *Defence* (George Hope), *Defiance* (Philip Charles Durham), *Thunderer* (Lt John Stockham, acting captain) — 16
French: *Scipion* (taken by Strachan 3 November — Charles Bellanger), *Duguay-Trouin* (taken by Strachan 3 November — Claude Toufflet), *Mont Blanc* (taken by Strachan 3 November — J. G. N. La Villegris), *Héros* (J. B. J. R. Poulain), *Redoubtable* (sank — J. J. E. Lucas), *Fougueux* (taken, then wrecked — L. A. Baudoin), *Pluton* (Commodore J. M. Cosmao-Kerjulien), *Aigle* (taken, then wrecked — P. P. Gourège), *Algésiras* (taken, then retaken — Rear-Admiral C. Magon de Médine, Captain Le Tourneur), *Intrépide* (taken, then burnt — L. A. C. Infernet), *Swiftsure* (ex-British, retaken by the British — C. E. Le Hôpitalier-Villemadrin), *Argonaute* (J. Epron), *Achille* (taken, blown up — G. Deniéport), *Berwick* (ex-British — retaken by them, then wrecked — J. G. Filhol-Camas) — 14

Spanish: *Rayo* (taken on the 24th, wrecked — Don Enrique Macdonel), *San Francisco de Assisi* (Don Luis de Florès), *San Agustin* (taken, burned — Don F. X. Cagigal), *San Justo* (Don M.Gaston), *Monarca* (taken, wrecked — Don T. Argumosa), *Bahama* (taken — Commodore Don D. A. Galiano), *Montañez* (Don J. Alcedo), *San Ildefonso* (taken — Commodore Don Jose de Varga), *San Juan Nepomuceno* (taken — Don Cosme Churruca) — nine

Two-Deckers 64-gun three/nil + one
British: *Africa* (Henry Digby), *Agamemnon* (Sir Edward Berry), *Polyphemus* (Robert Redmill) — three
French: nil
Spanish: *San Leandro* (Don Jose Quevedo) — one

Frigates four/five + nil
British: *Euryalus* (Hon Henry Blackwood), *Naiad* (Thomas Dundas), *Phoebe* (Hon
Thomas Bladen Capell), *Sirius* (William Prowse) — four
French: *Rhin* (Chesneau), *Hortense* (La Marre La Meillerie), *Cornélie* (de Martinenq), *Hermione* (Mahé), *Thémis* (Jugan) — five
Spanish: nil

Small Craft
British: *Pickle* (schooner), *Entreprenante* (cutter)
French: *Furet* (18), *Argus* (16)

Above: On 24 October 1805 the battered *Belleisle*, being towed by the frigate *Naiad*, approaches Gibraltar after surviving the storm. She has used what few spars are left to construct a jury rig to give her some steerage way. The dismasted battle ship had broken loose from the tow at the height of the storm the previous day. This picture shows her just after *Naiad*, having relocated her frighteningly close inshore, had managed to pass another tow. They were under fire from the Spanish batteries on the point with the flag that can be seen between the two ships. Fortunately neither was hit. *NMM neg no: X1886*

Above: Pocock's sketch for a painting showing Strachan's action, in which four French ships which had escaped Trafalgar were taken by Commodore (senior captain in charge of a group of ships) Richard Strachan. *NMM neg no: 3415*

Below: Naiad being attacked by gunboats off Cabrita Point. *Naiad* was one of the frigate force that joined Nelson's fleet just before the Battle of Trafalgar. *NMM ref no: A3571*

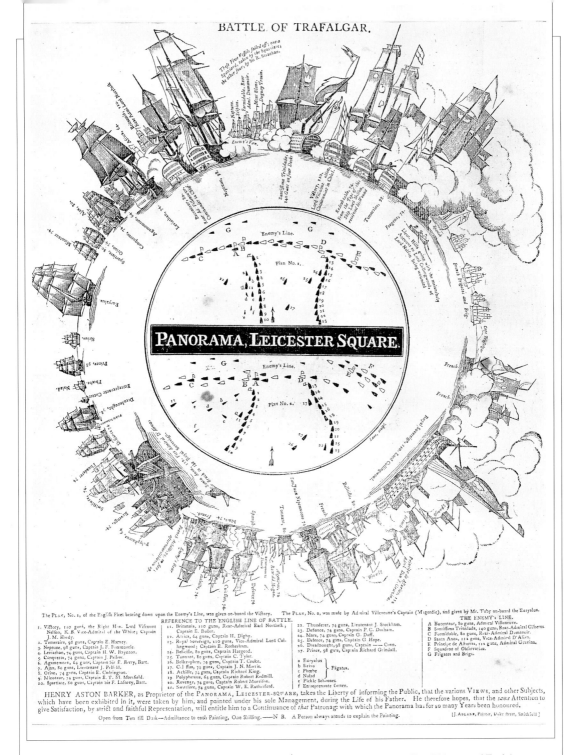

BATTLE OF TRAFALGAR.

PANORAMA, LEICESTER SQUARE.

Above: Trafalgar panorama at Leicester Square. A panorama was an immense continuous painting, originally, as here, circular. It would show the story of an event or a famous view and the public was charged an entrance fee. In effect this was the predecessor of the newsreel or feature film. This one of Trafalgar continued to earn money for its organiser and his family for a number of years.
NMM neg no: A7323

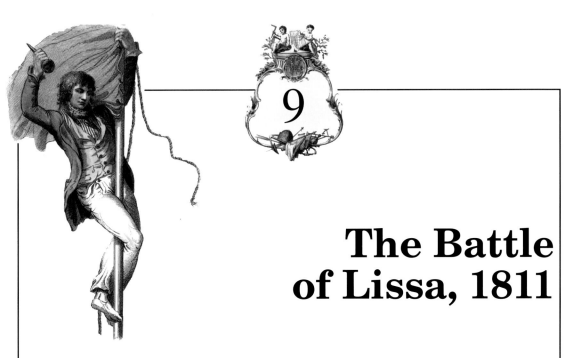

9

The Battle of Lissa, 1811

I f further proof were needed that Nelson's tactics at Trafalgar were an intelligent adaptation to particular circumstances, not a universally valid answer to the problem of obtaining decisive victory in sailing-ship warfare, it is provided by the Battle of Lissa. A French disciple of Nelson attempted to use a two column attack against a numerically inferior British squadron in line. He was consciously imitating what the British fleet did at Trafalgar, but he was confronting a protégé of Nelson, and, sadly for him, it was a fatal mistake.

In 1811 the British had for some time had a small force of frigates operating in the Adriatic Sea from the base they had established on the island of Lissa (now Lis, in what used to be Yugoslavia). They had been active in raiding up and down the coast of French-occupied Italy, under the direction of Captain Hoste in the *Amphion,* a 32-gun, 18-pounder frigate. He also had the 38-gun, 18-pounder frigate *Active* and another 32, the *Cerberus*, under his command. Hoste had been a favourite of Nelson's when he was a midshipman, being brave, bright and enterprising. He had caused a great deal of chaos. The French had a force of

Left: Portrait by Lane of Captain Sir William Hoste, the young frigate captain who raided and fought with great success in the Adriatic, and won the Battle of Lissa. *NMM neg no: BHC 2784*

French and Venetian frigates and smaller vessels, three 40-gun frigates, two 32s and two brig-rigged corvettes under the command of Commodore Dubordieu. This officer had studied Nelson's attack in two columns at Trafalgar and thought it might provide him with the answer to beating the smaller British force that confronted him. He had already had one confrontation with it in 1810, when he found Hoste with only *Active* in company with the *Amphion*, but had failed to bring him to action. Later that year he had raided Lissa when Hoste was not there, but did not stay to fight the British force when it returned.

On 11 March Dubordieu set sail from Ancona again, taking with him a force of troops to capture and garrison Lissa. He also now had four 40-gun frigates — of which at least one appears to have been armed with 24-pounder guns, two small 12-pounder frigates and an assortment of smaller craft. Before dawn on the morning of the 13th the British force sighted the French. On the face of it the French were decidedly superior, having four 40-gun frigates against one 38 and two 32s as far as ships with 18-pounders or more were concerned, and two small frigates or corvettes against one smaller vessel, without counting the brig and other lesser vessels on the French side.

This made four frigates of approximately 1,100 tons each and two of about 700 against one of 1,050, one of 909 (*Amphion*) and one of 796 tons, with another ship of 526 tons. It is

likely that the odds in numbers of men carried were much the same, if not greater, even if we do not count the 400 to 500 troops carried by the French squadron.

The British squadron was close to the shore of Lissa and immediately turned towards the enemy. Dubordieu seemed equally determined to close, and came down towards the British who had formed in a close line astern so tightly formatted that the bowsprit of one ship nearly touched the stern of the next ahead. They were in the order: *Amphion, Active, Volage, Cerberus,* the most powerful ships in the lead and the smallest in the middle. The Franco-Italian force was in two columns, like Nelson at Trafalgar, with the *Favorite* leading the *Flore, Bellona* and the brig in line astern against the head of the British line, whilst *Danaé, Corona, Carolina* and the small craft were moving against the rear of that line. Hoste signalled 'remember Nelson' to his line.

At 9am Dubordieu's ship was the first to come within range of the British force, and Hoste's well-drilled and experienced crew opened up on the French flagship, soon followed by the *Active*. Dubordieu was trying to break through the line between these two ships, but the combination of heavy and accurate fire with good station-keeping completely frustrated him. Instead he steered straight for the *Amphion*, joining the boarding party massing on his forecastle. He was, of course, completely unable to reply to the fierce fire sweeping his decks with his broadsides, and the vessels in his wake could not help him. He had closed to within a few yards when a brass $5^{1}/_{2}$in howitzer, obtained by some roundabout means and mounted on the quarterdeck of the *Amphion* for just such an occasion was fired, discharging its load of 750 musket balls into the packed mass of men on the French ship's forecastle. The boarding party was wiped out, and the French commodore killed, in this murderous blast.

Because the British line was moving at some three knots the enemy columns' line of approach was becoming more and more oblique, which meant that their nearer ships began to be able to fire their broadsides at the British ships. The *Favorite* was now trying to get round the head of the British lead ship in order first to rake, then to 'double' her enemy. This was the moment Hoste had been waiting for, and he signalled his ships to wear round, reversing their course. The *Favorite* which had been concentrating on going ahead of the line suddenly ran aground on the rocks off Lissa, lured there by Hoste's carefully maintained course. The French flagship was now out of the battle, to be set on fire and abandoned by her crew, and finally blowing up.

While the *Cerberus* was in the act of wearing, her rudder became jammed by a shot. This caused the *Volage* to get round before her, and that ship consequently took the lead on the port tack on which board, being close to the wind, the four ships fell into a bow and quarter line. Sheltered as she had been in some degree by her leader, the *Flore* was in much better shape for action, and now that the British line had stood away from the land, her captain found no difficulty in passing under the stern of the *Amphion*. She then opened fire, but her raking fire did little damage as the British crew were ordered to lie down between the guns as the Frenchman fired, thus protecting them from the hail of shot sweeping the decks. The *Flore* immediately afterwards hauled up on the port tack upon the *Amphion's* lee quarter. Almost at the same moment the *Bellona* came up on the *Amphion's* weather quarter and both ships opened a heavy fire on her.

Left: The larger type of frigate armed with 18-pounder guns in their main battery first appeared in the Royal Navy (which introduced the type) at the end of the 1770s. This is a slightly later example of the type, classed as a 36-gun ship — though, counting carronades, carrying another six or more large guns. The very similar 38-gun frigate was slightly longer, had another pair of guns in the main battery and, with carronades added, actually carried 46 or more guns. This very detailed model shows a frigate of the early years of the 19th century, but has not been identified with any particular ship. By that time most frigates being built were of this type or larger. *NMM neg no: A7432*

Below: Lissa at about 10.30am. *Author*

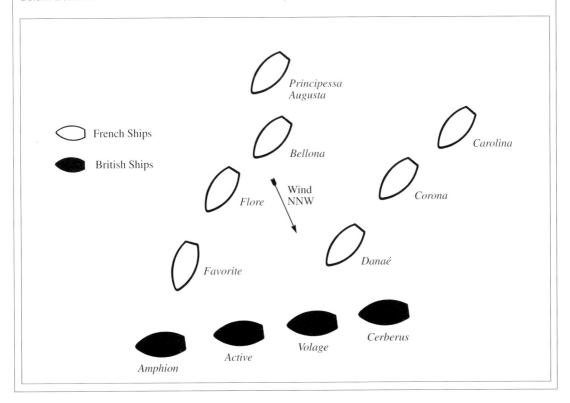

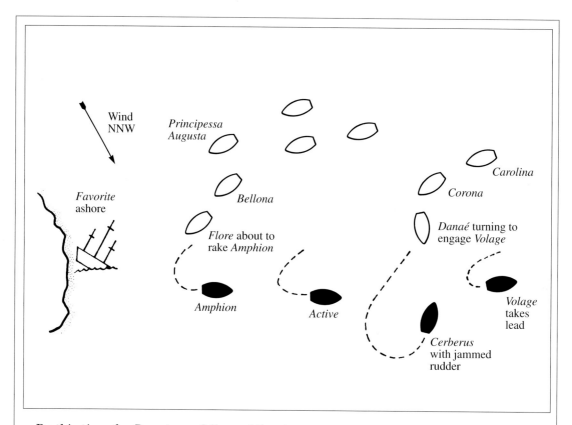

Wind
NNW

*Principessa
Augusta*

Favorite
ashore

Bellona

Flore about to
rake *Amphion*

Amphion

Active

Carolina

Corona

Danaé turning to
engage *Volage*

Cerberus
with jammed
rudder

Volage
takes
lead

Above: Lissa at 9.40am showing the the British line
wearing, *Favorite* going ashore, *Flore* about to rake
Amphion and *Danae* turning to engage *Volage*, which
has taken the lead in the British line because of the
temporary jamming of *Cerberus'* rudder. *Author*

Above right: Lissa at about 10.30am. *Author*

By this time the *Danaé*, carefully avoiding the *Active*'s line of fire, had also come on to the port tack, followed by the *Corona* and *Carolina*. Expecting the *Volage* to be an easy target, the *Danaé* took up a station abreast of her. *Volage*, splendidly justifying her position in the line with the frigates, poured in her 32-pound shot with steadiness and precision. Finding the unexpected weight of these, and soon discovering that they were fired from short-ranged carronades, the *Danaé* hauled off to a greater distance where her long 18-pounder guns could still produce their full effect, but where carronades could not reach. The *Volage* was now obliged to increase the charge of powder for her carronades and they, as a result, broke their breeching ropes and were dismounted from their slides. So that, at last, the long six-pounder on her forecastle was the only gun which this gallant little ship had to oppose to 14 long 18-pounders of her sensibly wary antagonist. Whilst this somewhat one-sided cannonade was going on, the *Cerberus* and *Corona* were firing fiercely at each other. It did not take long for the heavy and well-maintained fire of the *Corona* to begin to shatter the hull and disable the rigging of *Cerberus*, which was more than 90 men short of

complement. However, the *Carolina* seemed not very anxious to close, and gave little assistance to her companion or damage to her opponent. At length the *Active*, which had been striving her utmost to get to the assistance of her two friends in the van, approached under a press of canvas. The moment they saw her coming up, the *Danaé*, *Corona* and *Carolina* made all sail to the eastward, this being at some time between 10am and half past.

The *Amphion* was suffering greatly from the fire of the two ships that had placed themselves on her quarters. She gradually turned in order to close her heavier and most annoying opponent. Having passed ahead of the *Flore*, almost within touching distance, she then came up towards the wind again on her old, starboard, tack with her port broadside

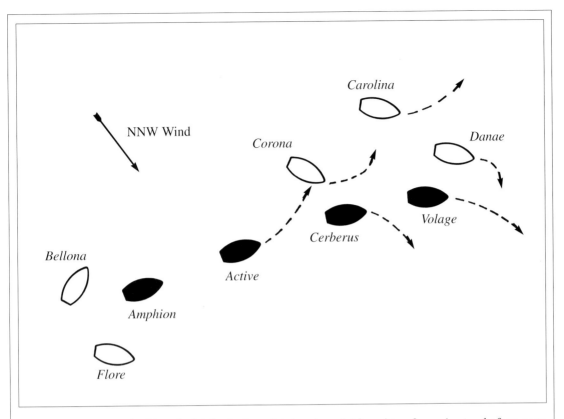

NNW Wind

Carolina

Corona

Danae

Cerberus

Volage

Active

Bellona

Amphion

Flore

pointing directly at the French ship's starboard bow. At about 11.15am the British ship opened such a heavy and accurate fire that in about five minutes the *Flore* ceased firing and struck her colours. However, *Amphion* herself had her own troubles as her other opponent, *Bellona*, had tacked immediately after she had, and, placing herself across the *Amphion's* stern, started a heavy and destructive cannonade. Although particularly careful not to fire into her surrendered squadron-mate, some of the *Bellona's* shot appears to have struck the *Flore*, which had imperceptibly crept forward in relation to the *Amphion*. Apparently believing the shot to come from the British ship, and to make the surrender clear, one of the officers of the *Flore* was seen to take the French flag, halliards and all, and, holding them up in his hands over the rail, as if for the *Amphion's* people to witness the act, threw the whole into the sea.

After an ineffectual attempt to hoist out a boat to take possession of the *Flore*, prevented by the damaged state of her rigging, the *Amphion* turned to close and silence the *Bellona*. She wore round on the starboard tack and taking a position on the *Bellona's* windward bow, the *Amphion* poured in one or

two broadsides. At a few minutes before noon she compelled the Venetian ship to lower her flag and surrender. In the meantime the *Principessa Augusta* brig had also been firing occasionally at the *Amphion*, but an 18-pounder was finally brought to bear upon her and the brig promptly got out the long oars known as sweeps and rowed herself beyond the range of either giving or receiving any damage. The one seaworthy boat aboard the *Amphion,* her flat-bottomed punt used for maintenance purposes in harbour, was sent with her first lieutenant and two seamen to take the *Bellona's* surrender.

Having done this, the *Amphion* came round on the other tack and, making the signal for a general chase, was a little to leeward of the *Cerberus* and *Volage* whose greatly disabled state had obliged them to steer down wind. The *Amphion* had now the mortification to see her first and most valuable prize, the *Flore*, out of gunshot on her weather bow, making sail for the French-garrisoned island of Lessina. The British, though failing to take the surrender of the *Flore*, considered this a dishonourable act, for the French ship had lain for some time at the mercy of the *Amphion*. However, the British ship was indubitably engaged with

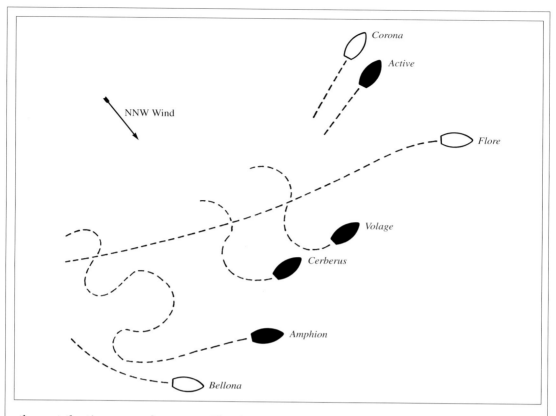

Above: Lissa between 11.15am and noon. *Author*

others at the time, as we have seen. The *Active* also, until she made sail after the *Corona*, might have sunk the *Flore*, and probably would have taken possession of her, but Captain Gordon had to consider the other Franco-Italian ships still unsubdued and the consequent danger to the two leading British ships in their disabled state. There is a slight air of sour grapes in British accounts of this part of the action; one might almost say of 'pushing their luck'. At this distance in time it is impossible to ascertain whether the *Flore* really had officially surrendered or not. In the heat of battle misunderstandings are more than likely. In any event Hoste (himself wounded) must have been very glad that he could ignore the *Flore* whilst dealing with the *Bellona*. It did not stop him demanding her surrender in a later letter to the new French commander — a demand which, predictably, was ignored.

Active's sails and rigging being in a more perfect state than those of either *Cerberus* or *Corona,* she soon passed to windward of the former, and at about 12.30pm, when just in mid-channel between Lissa and Spalinadon, came under fire from the *Corona*. *Active* could not bring any number of her own guns to bear without altering course and of course losing ground in the chase. At about 1.45pm the *Active* came up to leeward of the *Corona*. A fierce battle now ensued between these two frigates, and continued until 2.30pm when the *Corona*, having fought hard and gallantly till the end, surrendered. She had almost reached the protection of the batteries of Lessina. British accounts give very high marks to her captain, who made a distinct impression on his captors as a good fighter and skilful seaman. The *Carolina* and *Danaé*, having made no attempt to support their squadron-mate, were already in safety under the guns of those batteries, and just about to enter the anchorage. All the Venetian small craft also made their escape in different directions. Whilst all this was going on two British midshipmen and some privateersmen, who happened to be ashore at Lissa harbour, beat off an attack by the survivors of the *Favorite* by taking over a Sicilian privateer brig and using her guns against the attackers.

The *Amphion* had all her lower masts badly

shot through, particularly her foremast, and much other damage to her rigging. Her loss, out of a complement of 251 men and boys, amounted to 15 killed and 47 wounded, the latter including her captain. The *Active*, with comparatively slight damage, had four killed and 24 wounded out of 300. The *Cerberus*, although hardly damaged at all in her rigging, was a good deal battered in the hull, and lost 13 killed and 41 wounded. The *Volage's* main yard was shot away and she lost her fore topgallantmast, and was generally badly damaged in sails, rigging and masts. Her hull, especially on the port side, was completely riddled, and her loss of men was in proportion. Out of a crew of 175 she had lost 13 killed and 33 wounded, making the total British loss 45 killed and 145 wounded out of the total of nearly 900 men in the squadron. Another five lives were lost and four men badly burned in putting out a fire aboard the *Corona* after her capture.

As usual it is much more difficult to find exact figures for the other side. *Flore* was badly shattered and probably lost about half her crew or more, perhaps 200 killed and wounded, including her captain and most of her officers amongst the former. *Favorite* probably suffered much the same number. The *Corona* had her sails and rigging cut to pieces, her masts all badly damaged and her hull shattered — her total loss, again, may have reached 200. The *Bellona* had 70 killed and about the same number badly wounded, including Captain Duodo, who died of his wounds. Her hull was in a very bad state by the end of the action.

The Franco-Italian force lost three frigates in this extraordinary battle, two captured and one blown up, against a force just over half their size and power. With proper co-ordination of their forces they should have won easily. However, it was their opponents who were properly co-ordinated, better trained and in a higher state of morale. Lissa remains as a splendid little victory against odds, a Trafalgar played the other way round. Curiously, just over half a century later, another battle against odds in which Italian ships were on the losing side took place in exactly the same waters. This time it was Tegetthoff's Austrian ships that showed that excellent leadership, good training and high morale could more than cancel out numerical and material odds.

Below: The Battle of Lissa, 1811 — Whitcombe's picture shows a prize in the foreground (probably the *Corona*) being taken possession of as the battle draws to a close. *NMM neg no: 1217*

The Squadrons at Lissa

British — four

Amphion 32 — 26 x 18-pounders, six x six-pounders, six x 24-pounder carronades plus a howitzer — (William Hoste)

Cerberus 32 — 26 x 18-pounders, six x six-pounders, eight x 24-pounder carronades (Henry Whitby)

Active 38 — 28 x 18-pounders, 10 x nine-pounders, eight x 32-pounder carronades (James Alexander Gordon)

Volage 22 (design armament of 22 x nine- + eight x 24-pounder carronades + two x six-pounders) — actually entirely 32-pounder carronades — presumably 30 of them — apart from the forecastle six-pounders (Phipps Hornby)

French/Venetian (* indicates Venetian ships)

Favorite 40 (flag of Commodore Bernard Dubordieu, Captain A. F. Z. La Marre La Meillerie)

Danaé 40 (J. A. Péridier)

Flore 40 (Villon)

(All three of these French vessels were designed as 18 pounder frigates.)

*Corona** 40 — 24-pounders (taken and renamed *Daedalus*; wrecked off Ceylon — Pasqualigo)

*Bellona** 32 — 12-pounders (taken and renamed *Dover* — Duodo)

*Carolina** 32 — 12-pounders (Baratovich)

*Principessa Augusta** 16 (brig-corvette)

Also one 10-gun schooner*, one six-gun chebeck* and two gun-boats*.

Below: Illustration of an action in 1796 involving smaller French and British vessels. This illustration greatly exaggerates the size difference between the 26-gun British *Raison* beating off the larger French frigate *Vengeance* off Halifax, Nova Scotia. *NMM neg no: X2006*

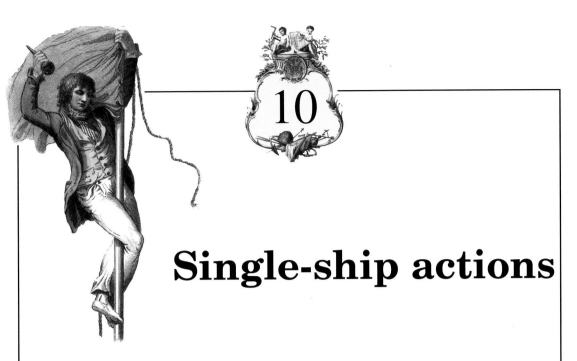

10

Single-ship actions

The period we are concerned with is the great age of the single-ship action; the battle between a pair of ships, usually more or less evenly matched with no other ships present or intervening. Earlier most naval actions were between larger or smaller groups of ships, fleet or squadron actions, and the same is true of the 20th century. It was during the 60 years between 1756 and 1815, when naval war involved more ships scattered further over the globe than ever before, that most of the battles between individual named ships occurred. This was also the age of the 'true' frigate, and the majority of the best known single-ship actions were between frigates, reaching a dramatic climax in the last few years of the period with the War of 1812. In this chapter we will look at a small selection of the most dramatic duels between frigates.

Quebec and *Surveillante*

This was the most spectacular, and the most portrayed, of the frigate actions of the American War of Independence, and one of which both the navies concerned can be proud.

At dawn on 6 October 1779 the British 32-gun frigate *Quebec* was patrolling off Ushant in company with the cutter *Rambler* when she sighted a French frigate of similar size and power, the *Surveillante*, also accompanied by a cutter, the *Expédition*. The British Captain Farmer of the *Quebec* was a distinguished officer, under whom both Nelson

and Collingwood had served, whilst Lieutenant Du Couëdic de Kergoualer, in command of the French 32, was an equally talented Breton who had sworn to conquer or die.

The two frigates stood eagerly towards one another, hoisted their respective flags, and each fired a long-range shot as a defiance to the other. Du Couëdic kept as close to the wind as possible, whilst Farmer rapidly bore down upon him. Some time after 10am the two frigates came within close range. The *Surveillante* had already been firing for some time, but at long range, and without doing much damage. The *Quebec* held her fire till she was within musket range (possibly about 100yd). The two then settled down to a broadside-to-broadside slugging match. After an hour of this Captain Farmer decided to rake his opponent's stern. He tried to drop astern, but the French captain had guessed what he was up to and foiled it by following his manoeuvre. Once more the two closed in on one another. Their masts and rigging were now damaged to such an extent that they could only go before the wind. The masts of both ships were tottering; both sides continued a murderous fire but neither, so far, had won any advantage. Twice, indeed, the *Quebec's* officers thought they saw the French crew running from their guns, but they were mistaken as the French ship kept firing. Casualties were mounting; the *Quebec* had had to reduce the original seven men to each gun to three per

Left: The frigate *Alarm* taking a Spanish prize into Gibraltar 1762 (if this date is correct, probably an imaginary incident as the ship was in the West Indies during this year). The prize is the two-decker, missing her fore topmast, shown in the background flying the British ensign over the Spanish. The frigate herself is shown with her fore topgallantmast struck and some damage to her sails. The hammocks stowed along her quarterdeck rails are conspicuous, as is the buoy hanging from her mainstay. She appears to be about to launch a boat from the spars amidships, or perhaps has just recovered it. The long lateen yard on the mizzen mast, with its sail only set abaft that mast, is a characteristic feature of mid-18th century rig. A later ship would have had a gaff and gaff sail in its place. *Alarm* was one of the first 32-gun frigates built, launched in 1758 and in service until laid up in 1802 (she was not broken up until 1812). This was an impressively long career, during which she took at least 13 small warships and privateers and sank a French 20-gun ship. This picture makes it very clear why the frigate made sense as a cruising vessel, with her guns mounted comparatively high above the waterline. The size of the figures emphasises that she was not a very large ship. The lateen-rigged light galley on the left hand side of the picture is probably from one of the North African corsair states, most likely Sale (Sallee) on the Atlantic coast of Morocco. *NMM neg no: 7170*

Below left: Print of a picture by Perrot which shows a slightly earlier stage of the *Quebec* and *Surveillante* action than the usually-pictured end. On the left hand side the two cutters are having their own fight. *NMM neg no: 9869*

gun. Captain Farmer was wounded in the finger and his collar bone was shattered. He did not leave the deck, but bandaged his wounds as best he could and called to his men, 'My lads, this is warm work, and therefore keep up your fire with double spirit. We will conquer or die.' The first Lieutenant, Francis Roberts, had lost an arm but remained on deck. Most of the other officers were killed or out of action.

The French captain was also wounded twice in the head, but he did not leave the deck. The masts of his ship, endangered for some time, fell overboard just before noon. They fell to port, her disengaged side, which was lucky as they were out of the way of the guns. Just after the fall of the *Surveillante's* masts, the *Quebec's* masts came down as well, but with a much worse result: they did not clear the ship, but, falling fore and aft blocked the gangways, and hampered the men trying to fire the forecastle and quarterdeck guns. The mizzen mast sails hung down on the engaged side and

were soon set on fire by the flash of the guns.

This was the moment at which the French apparently tried to board their opponent as the *Surveillante's* bowsprit was entangled in the wreckage of the *Quebec's* masts. However, Du Couëdic was now wounded a third time, just as he had ordered his three nephews to lead the boarding party. In any case it was soon obvious that it was too late as the British ship's sails were well alight and her quarterdeck was beginning to blaze. Despite his wounds the French captain was alert enough to cease fire and lower his boats. At the same time the *Surveillante's* bowsprit was cut away and the *Quebec* boomed off (pushed away with any spars that were available), for the French ship's rigging was already beginning to burn. The heat was intense. On board the *Quebec*, Farmer refused to leave the ship whilst there was a man on board. He ordered the pumps to be directed on the magazine, keeping the danger of an explosion at bay. The first lieutenant was by him. The crew at his orders jumped into the sea, saving themselves as best they could. The cutter *Rambler*, having fought her own little battle with the *Expédition* came up to the aid of the men in the water, though the explosions of the *Quebec's* loaded guns in the heat made the work of rescue very dangerous. Only one of the *Surveillante's* boats would float, and that one was damaged in hoisting it out. So the French crew threw oars and ropes to the drowning men. At 6pm the *Quebec*, with her colours still flying, blew up. Her captain was last seen sitting calmly on the fluke of an anchor, awaiting the end.

The loss of both ships was heavy. Of the *Quebec's* 195 men only 68 were saved; 17 by the *Rambler,* 13 by a passing Russian ship and 38 by the *Surveillante*, and of these, two died of their injuries. Those picked up by the French ship helped to put out her fire and struggle back to port at Brest. The French made a chivalrous gesture with these prisoners. In recognition of the gallantry of their fight, and as a thank-you for their help in saving the French ship, they were returned to a British port. The *Surveillante* had 30 killed and 85 wounded. Nearly all the officers were casualties of one sort or the other. The ship herself was in a sinking condition. She had been frequently hulled between wind and water and was leaking heavily. She was taken in tow by the *Expédition*. Later jury-masts were rigged, and she succeeded in returning to Brest.

The *Quebec* carried 26 nine-pounders and six six-pounders. She had struck a rock some

Above left: The end of the *Quebec* and *Surveillante* duel — an unsophisticated but dramatic version by Coqueret. *NMM neg no: 9870*

Left: This is George Carter's version of the conclusion of the *Quebec* and *Surveillante* duel, just before the former blew up. The representation of the British frigate, at least, seems very accurate. *NMM neg no: 9871*

Above: The disabled *Surveillante* and the blazing *Quebec* at the end of their duel, just before the latter blew up, as pictured by Dodd. In this engraving of the picture the cutter *Rambler* can be seen standing by off the bow of the British frigate, trying to pick up survivors but keeping out of the danger area from fire and explosion. *NMM neg no: 9865*

months before and, being compelled to throw all her 12-pounders overboard, she had only been able to replace them with the smaller nine-pounders. Her opponent probably carried 26 12-pounders and six six-pounders. The French ship was also rather better manned, with 255 men as opposed to the 195 of the *Quebec*.

Both captains were celebrated as heroes. Posthumous honours were showered on Farmer. Du Couëdic achieved the fame he desired and was instantly promoted to be *capitaine de vaisseau*, but he died of his wounds, three months after the action, aged 40.

Nymphe and *Cléopâtre*

This was the first decisive single-ship action of the wars of the French Revolution, and it set the pattern of much that was to come. War had broken out with the shots fired at the brig sloop *Childers* by the forts of Brest on 2 January 1793. It was an open question as to whether the new revolutionary fervour of the French sailors would compensate for the damage done to an officer corps half destroyed by terror and by emigration, so the results of the first encounters between British and French warships were eagerly, but apprehensively, awaited.

On 27 May 1793 there was an encounter between the British *Venus* and the French *Sémillante*. They inflicted considerable damage on each other, but the British ship had to break off the action when another French frigate appeared. This was the *Cléopâtre*. The British ship escaped and rejoined her companion, the *Nymphe*. This latter ship, captured from the French in the previous war, was commanded

by the man who would acquire the reputation of being one of the best of the British frigate captains, Captain Edward Pellew, later to be a distinguished admiral under the title of Lord Exmouth.

Early on the morning of 18 June Pellew, whilst cruising in the Channel, sighted the *Cléopâtre*, 36, commanded by Captain Mullon, and bore down upon her. The French ship shortened sail and waited for the British attack. The two vessels were within shouting range before either had fired. The *Nymphe's* men gave three cheers for the King; the French replied with republican cheers. Captain Mullon, standing in the gangway, waved his hat and shouted, 'long live the Nation'. At 6.15am, Pellew, who had been standing with his hat in his hand as a salute to the other captain, put it back on his head, as his prearranged signal for opening fire. At about 7am the *Cléopâtre's* mizzen mast fell, masking some of her guns on the engaged side, and just at the same time Israel Pellew, the captain's brother, who was on board as a volunteer, succeeded in shooting away the French ship's steering wheel. This caused her to collide with the *Nymphe,* poking her bowsprit against the *Nymphe's* mainmast. The bowsprit then broke,

Above: The *Quebec/Surveillante* action with its dramatic and tragic finale was a very popular subject for prints. This 'cheap and cheerful' version, evidently copied from other prints, appears to have been produced in what was then the Austrian Netherlands and is now Belgium. *NMM neg no: X1934*

Above right: Dodd's picture of an early stage in the duel between *Nymphe* (the nearer ship) and *Cléopâtre.* The British ship is already hitting her opponent much harder. *NMM neg no: 1051*

Right: Pocock painted the detailed, dramatic and probably accurate picture from which this engraving was taken to show the first capture of a French frigate in a single-ship action after the beginning of the French Revolutionary War. The *Cléopâtre,* with two out of three masts gone, has her bows caught in her opponent's side and is being boarded. *NMM neg no: B4021*

but the ships' rigging had become tangled and some of the *Nymphe's* had to be cut away to save her mast. The *Nymphe* then anchored in an attempt to shake the French ship off. Before this could happen, Pellew noticed that the French were gathering to board, and ordered his men to prepare to repel them; they were

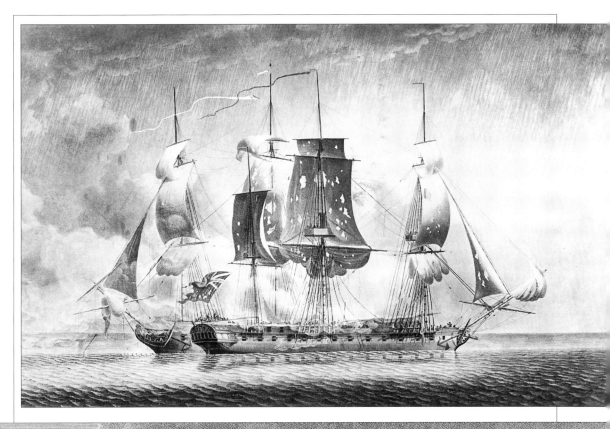

successful in this, and then swept on board their enemy and took the ship. Poor Captain Mullon was discovered in his death agonies, trying to eat or bite to pieces a paper which, he thought, contained French secret signals. He was too far gone to realise that it was his commission as an officer he was attempting to destroy.

The *Nymphe* was slightly the larger of the two ships (938 tons to 913), and had a slightly heavier broadside (322lb to 290) but carried a smaller crew (240 men to 320). The fact that she beat her enemy in 55min was fairly clear proof that British gunnery was still more effective than French, and that the skill with which the French fought had diminished since the previous conflict, though there was no diminution in their bravery and an increase in their fervour. However, the proportion of casualties (50 British, 63 French) was not as disparate as in many later actions. The action was notable because it was the first victory of the war. Many that followed were more impressive, and obtained against odds not present in this battle between equals, but few (bar the *Shannon* and *Chesapeake* action) were greeted with a greater feeling of relief or more rejoicing. Captain Pellew became a popular hero overnight, was knighted, and his brother, Israel, was promoted to captain. The foundations of the British naval 'habit of victory' were beginning to be laid.

San Fiorenzo and Piémontaise

This action must have been one of the longest drawn-out single-ship actions ever. In 1808, when it happened, British trade in the Indian Ocean was still threatened by raiders from the Ile de France (Mauritius). One of the more successful of these was the 40-gun frigate *Piémontaise* commanded by Captain Epron. She was lying in wait off the coast of Ceylon (now Sri Lanka) for three English East Indiamen when, on the morning of 6 March, she was sighted by the British 36-gun frigate *San Fiorenzo*. This ship was also of French construction, having been captured in Corsica (at the port after which she was named) early in the Revolutionary War. Captain Hardinge began a long chase of the French ship. During the subsequent night the British ship got quite close and her rigging was made the target of a couple of broadsides, after which her adversary drew away again. As day dawned on the 7th the *San Fiorenzo* began to get back in range. At 6.25am the French ship opened up at a range of 800yd, aiming at her opponent's rigging in the hope of slowing her down or crippling her

entirely. The French ship's mission was commerce raiding, and she wanted to escape to carry on with it. The gap slowly closed to 400yd, but by 8.15am the rigging of the British ship had been shot to pieces and she had to slow down. She had been firing at the French ship's hull, so the latter began to draw away again.

The *San Fiorenzo* then turned to the work of making good the damage done. So far she had only lost eight killed and 17 wounded. There were reasonable grounds for believing that the French ship must have suffered far more severely, but, being very strongly manned, she could afford such losses.

The repairs took all day. By the evening the *Piémontaise* had disappeared to the east. Towards midnight she was sighted again. From then onwards she was kept in sight, about 10 or 12 miles ahead. With the coming of day, the *San Fiorenzo,* now completely refitted by her crew's efforts, gained slowly on her opponent and was within range again by about 4pm. The *Piémontaise* could no longer escape without fighting an action. So she turned towards the British frigate, passing her on the opposite tack at 50yd distance and exchanging several broadsides. Captain Hardinge was killed by a grapeshot and Lieutenant William Dawson took command. The *Piémontaise* turned astern of the *San Fiorenzo* and came back to engage her closely. Her gunnery, however, did not match the British. At 5.50pm she surrendered, her masts and rigging cut to pieces and a great part of her crew killed or wounded. By this time she had fired away all her 18-pounder and eight-pounder shot. It was rare in actions like these

Above right: The exception to the rule. This French print shows a French success against the odds, and against the usual pattern of British success in single-ship actions. In 1798 the French 24-gun corvette *Bayonnaise* captured the 32-gun frigate *Ambuscade*, a larger ship (100 tons more). A combination of the bursting of a gun, another accidental explosion and the poor morale of the British crew was what gave the French ship her chance, which she took with both hands. This picture clearly shows the lower freeboard of the French corvette, and, unlike a more famous and artistically impressive picture of this action, does not exaggerate the difference between the sizes of the two ships. *NMM neg no: B9362*

Right: Another earlier (1797) battle, in which the *San Fiorenzo* took part, here battling with the French *Nymphe* whilst the *Resistance* chases another French frigate. *NMM ref: BHC0495*

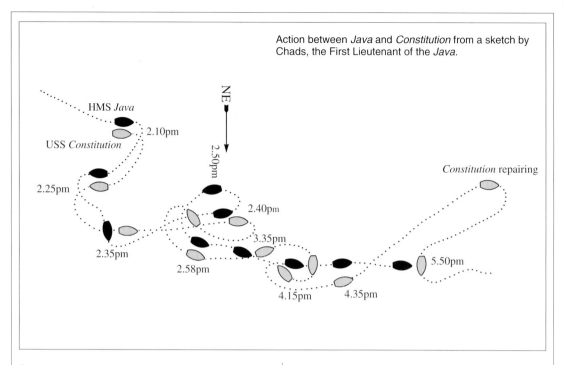

Action between *Java* and *Constitution* from a sketch by Chads, the First Lieutenant of the *Java*.

HMS *Java*

2.10pm

USS *Constitution*

NE

2.50pm

2.25pm

Constitution repairing

2.40pm

3.35pm

2.35pm

2.58pm

5.50pm

4.15pm   4.35pm

for ammunition to run short, but the vessel had been cruising since early in 1806 in the Indian Ocean with little chance of replacing this ammunition. She was also handicapped by her gun-locks being out of order at the beginning of the final action, and her slow match was extremely bad. So both of the conventional means of firing her cannon were in very faulty condition. Her masts were so badly damaged that they fell overboard the night after the action — thus giving the British crew yet more jury-rigging to do. Her British captors noted a crew of 366 Frenchmen and 200 Lascars (seamen native to the Indian Ocean region), but 50 of the French seem to have been absent in prizes. However, one of the British ship's lieutenants had been invalided ashore, and her crew was badly weakened by sickness. She only had 186 men aboard, probably under half the French total. The French ship was slightly bigger (1,093 tons against 1,032) and more powerful (46 guns firing a broadside of 533lb compared to 42 guns and 467lb). The French lost 49 killed and 92 wounded against the British 13 and 25 respectively.

By the time this duel was fought the Royal Navy, and even more the British public, had come to believe that British ships would, barring accidents, always win their battles. The 'habit of victory' had been established in many battles, where size, gunpower and numbers of men were in favour of the enemy, but the result was still a British triumph. It had become a statistical probability that any encounter between warships would be won by the British ship so long as the odds against were not very large indeed. Victories against the odds had become the norm. Such victories had been won time and again over the French, the Spaniards, even the hard-fighting Dutch and Danes. Certainly the morale element played a large part in this, and it cut both ways. The Royal Navy *expected* to win; its opponents *knew* they would probably lose. The full explanation of the 'habit of victory' is more complex, and has as much to do with, for example, the damage done to the French Navy by the Revolution, the excellence of British cannon, the training of British gun crews in rapid firing, and the longer time that British officers and men spent at sea. One must not forget the influence of other factors too: the malign influence on the French of their doctrine of the primacy of the 'mission' which often kept them from fighting battles, the political splits in the Dutch Navy during the 1790s, the enormous difficulties the Spaniards found in manning their ships with trained seamen. Whatever the reasons, the Royal Navy was getting dangerously complacent by 1812, when it came up against a small but wholly professional navy, more highly trained, very well equipped and quite capable of taking on

Above: Early in the War of 1812 the big American frigate *Constitution* was chased by a British squadron. For 60hr in light winds and calms the American ship was chased by four British frigates, none of them individually as powerful as her, and by the 64-gun line of battleship *Africa* (which had fought at Trafalgar) which was more than her match. *Constitution* by immense skill, activity, and some luck, managed to escape to fight another day. She would fight and capture the *Guerriere*, seen here chasing her in company with the *Belvidera*, *Æolus* and *Shannon*. NMM neg no: 1140

the biggest navy in the world on its own terms. The British were about to have a very salutary shock when they fought the US Navy.

Constitution and *Java*

The big American frigates had already scored two successes against British 38-gun frigates, capturing the *Guerrier* and the *Macedonian*, when this action was fought, but this was the hardest-fought and also the most interesting of the three battles in which the Americans showed their ability at single-ship frigate actions.

In late October 1812 the 44-gun frigate *Constitution* and the sloop *Hornet* sailed from Boston, Ma, with the intention of causing the maximum trouble to British ships. On 13 December the two ships reached San Salvador

in Brazil, where a British 20-gun ship, of much the same size and gunpower as *Hornet*, was lying with a load of treasure aboard. Her commander was not prepared to risk this even when Captain Bainbridge (who we will meet in the next chapter losing his *Philadelphia* to Tripoli) promised not to interfere in any action between his smaller consort and the *Bonne Citoyenne*. The American commander's attitude seems strange to us today — smacking more of sport than of war — but shows that, despite the changes produced by the French Revolution, many of the old 18th century attitudes to war, honour and chivalry were still alive and kicking. This seems to have been even more true of the American Navy than the Royal Navy. In any case the challenge produced no result and Bainbridge left Lawrence (later the captain of the *Chesapeake*) of the *Hornet* to blockade the British vessel.

At 9am on 29 December, while the *Constitution* was running along the coast of Brazil about 30 miles offshore, she sighted the British frigate *Java*, commanded by Captain Henry Lambert. This ship was carrying the new Governor General of Bombay out to his appointment, plus other material for India, which included the plans of ships of the line and frigates to be built for the Royal Navy at Bombay. The *Java* immediately set course in chase of the strange frigate, while the American led her away from the shore. The

Left: Java attempts to board *Constitution* over what is left of her bowsprit in this painting by Nicholas Pocock. The American frigate is still in good condition and easily holds off the attack, decimating the would-be boarders. *NMM neg no: A9308*

Below left: Java, having failed to board *Constitution*, is now a perfect wreck, almost entirely dismasted. The American ship moves out of gunshot to make repairs. The engraving from a painting by Pocock is the second in a set of three. *NMM neg no: 1041*

Right: The first lieutenant of the *Java*, Henry Ducie Chads. He was painfully wounded, then had to take command of an already beaten ship as Captain Lambert was more seriously wounded (he would eventually die). He had little choice but to surrender to the Americans, after a gallant and skilful defence against a more powerful, equally gallant and even more skilful opponent. *NMM neg no: 8438*

British ship (actually a captured French frigate in origin) was much the swifter of the two, and rapidly gained. Bainbridge was, however, merely gaining sea-room, not attempting to escape; not a very good idea in one of the comparatively slow though powerful American 44s.

At 1.30pm the American ship reduced the sails set to those usual in action (basically the topsails) and the *Java* did the same. At 2pm both sides opened fire at long range. Lambert scored a number of hits aboard his larger adversary, causing several casualties. He would probably have been well advised, given the accuracy of his gunfire and the comparative sluggishness of his larger adversary, to keep his distance until he could do some crippling damage. The fatal influence of the Nelsonic 'engage the enemy more closely' was in evidence in circumstances in which Nelson himself would probably have had the sense and intelligence to adapt his tactics to his enemy.

Lambert instead edged down towards his enemy, soon reaching a range where small arms and grapeshot could be bought into play. His faster ship was edging forward and finally came round in an attempt to cross Bainbridge's bows and rake him. The American anticipated this and came round at the same time. Shortly afterwards *Java* again attempted to come forward and rake. By this time the weight and accuracy of the American fire was beginning to tell at the very short range at which they were firing — 'pistol shot' (which was the range over which a pistol was considered accurate — a few yards at most). The British ship's rate of fire was beginning to fall off as she suffered more casualties. Most of the damage she inflicted on her enemy happened early in the action.

The danger of being outsailed and then raked was very apparent to Bainbridge, so he set more sails, caught up with his more nimble adversary and began to hit her very heavily indeed. The end of *Java's* bowsprit went and, deprived of the balance of her headsails, she was very slow in turning. This was the opportunity that the American had been waiting for and he raked the British ship with a powerful broadside as he passed her stern close-to.

After this manoeuvre the two ships were now sailing side-by-side before the wind, with the *Constitution* now inflicting damage with very little return. The men in her tops were sniping effectively at the British gun crews, already being decimated by the shot and grape from the big guns. Despite their casualties the British crew fought on bravely. However, they were clearly in a losing battle as far as the guns were concerned, so Lambert tried the desperate

Above: The finale of the *Java/Constitution* duel as portrayed by Pocock. *Java* having surrendered, her survivors have been taken on board the American frigate, which sets the shattered hulk of her adversary on fire and sails away as the British ship blows up. *NMM neg no: 1042*

expedient of turning to come down on his enemy, aiming to ram her amidships and board. This merely gave the American gunners the chance to rake the British frigate once again, whilst the steady small-arms fire of topmen and marines prevented any borders getting across. The stump of her bowsprit catching in the *Constitution's* rigging kept *Java* in this deadly position for a while until the two ships broke clear of one another. They ran parallel for a while, then the American came round again, raked her enemy and then fired at her from her other side. The British ship was badly hampered by the wreckage of sails and rigging lying over her starboard side, which kept catching fire from the flames of the cannon and having to be put out. One after another the masts went; then the captain fell, mortally wounded by an American marksman in the *Constitution's* tops. Chads, the first lieutenant, took over command, though himself wounded. Still the *Java* fought on, but with fewer and fewer guns till she fell silent. At just past 4pm the American ship lay off to repair her own damage. The British frigate lay dead in the water, hull riddled, deck a bloody slaughter-house. An hour later the *Constitution*, nearly as good as new, bore down again. At this stage resistance would have been a useless waste of life, and Chads surrendered his ship.

Java, nearly in sinking condition and far from any American base was burnt after her survivors had been removed. She had suffered 22 killed and 122 wounded, against the 34 killed or wounded of her larger and well-handled adversary. Both captains had fought a skilful battle, but the evidence is that the crew of the American ship, besides having been together in that vessel for longer (the *Java's* had only been on board for six weeks), had been better trained, with more practice at both the great guns and small arms. The rapidity and accuracy of the American fire was at least as important as their greater number of heavier guns. Given also that the sides of the American ship were thicker, giving her crew better protection, and that she had nearly 100 more men (475 against 377), the result is not particularly surprising. 'A good big 'un will always beat a good little 'un' in the language of the boxing ring — what was surprising, particularly to the shocked Royal Navy, was just how good the US Navy was. It should have been less of a surprise. In many ways the Americans were doing what the Royal Navy did in training officers and crews, only doing it better, following the older service's example but improving on it. They had the advantages of a small, high quality, professional service. The Royal Navy with its world-wide responsibilities had been strained to its limits, and expanded ever further, over 20 years of near-continuous war. A certain dilution was inevitable. Furthermore, there must have been a great deal of direct transfer of experience. One of the causes of the war was the pressing of American seamen into the Royal Navy, whilst many British seamen deserted or emigrated. The proportion of men who had served in the Royal Navy aboard US warships is not, as far as I am aware, known (it would be very interesting to find out, if it was possible) — but it was probably quite high.

Shannon and *Chesapeake*
The story of the frigate battles of the War of 1812 reaches its dramatic climax in an action which was the antithesis of the long drawn out battle of manoeuvre that has just been described. The *Shannon* and *Chesapeake* were in nearly all respects an evenly matched pair, and they fought one another in a straightforward slugging match with little tactical nicety. Both captains and their crews were determined to undertake a trial by battle on behalf of their respective navies; the British desperate to restore morale by regaining their habit of victory, the Americans to demonstrate that they did not need to have any advantage in size and firepower to win. The British captain sent a challenge by letter, having sent away his second frigate to ensure a fair contest. There is some question as to whether this letter reached the American captain, but he certainly acted in the same spirit. Both ships were of the same rate (38-gun frigates), though the American was slightly bigger (1,135 tons against 1,053). The main gun batteries were the same, 28 x 18-pounders in both cases. *Chesapeake* had two more 32-pounder

Above: The remains of one of the *Chesapeake*'s ensigns. The flags of captured ships were kept as trophies. A British visitor to the US Naval Academy at Annapolis often does a 'double take' on walking into a hall decorated with the familiar sight of white ensigns, which he suddenly realises are trophies from the frigate actions of the War of 1812. *NMM neg no: B169*

carronades, 18 as opposed to 16, whilst she had fewer but heavier long guns on the quarterdeck and forecastle: two long 12s and one long 18 as opposed to four long nine-pounders and one long six-pounder. Additionally the American ship had one 12-pounder carronade, the British three. If there was very little to choose between the ships as far as their armament was concerned, the American had a distinct advantage in numbers of crew: 379 compared to 330, nearly 50 men more. This advantage was counterbalanced by the fact that the British crew had served together under their captain since their ship was commissioned in 1806, whilst most of the Americans, including their captain, had joined their ship only in the month before the action happened.

This might not have mattered so much had the *Shannon* had a run-of-the-mill captain. She did not. Philip Broke was a gunnery enthusiast and a superb trainer of men. As soon as he commissioned the ship he started an incessant round of exercises with the guns and sails and practice with small-arms (muskets, pistols, pikes and cutlasses). The ship made a clean sweep for action every day, taking down all the obstructions on the gun decks and practising the crew at handling and firing the guns.

Competitions were organised between gun crews; emergency drills were sprung on the crew at unexpected times. Much of the training procedures of modern navies can be traced back to that commission of the *Shannon*. No ship in any navy at this time would have been better trained than this frigate, and very few would even begin to rival her. Yet this superbly trained crew had, in seven years of war service, no chance yet to show their worth in a serious action. After the news of defeat in the previous frigate actions with the Americans had reached the ship the crew had voluntarily renounced the chance of prize money and had burnt a

Left: Philip Bowes Vere Broke (1776–1841), the captain of the *Shannon*, whose victory helped to restore the Royal Navy's faith in itself. As befits such an enthusiast for gunnery, the cannon behind him is fitted with gun-lock and sights. He was appointed to the *Shannon* when she first commissioned, in 1806, and thereafter brought his crew up to an extraordinarily high standard of efficiency, particularly in gunnery. He was an excellent trainer of men. Though he never completely recovered from the wound he received whilst capturing the *Chesapeake*, his doctrines and training methods spread throughout the navy. *NMM ref: BHC2575*

Below: Butterworth's rather unconvincing impression of the *Shannon/Chesapeake* action. *NMM ref: BHC0601*

number of captures rather than lose the chance of winning a battle because of sending away prize-crews. This was a truly extraordinary decision, and reflects both the quality of Broke's leadership, and the feeling of distress at the American victories which permeated the Royal Navy at this time, in officers' wardrooms and on the men's messdecks alike.

Besides having trained his crew to the highest standards in both the handling of their weapons (and therefore speed of fire) and marksmanship (accuracy), and having got them to the stage where they could continue to fire without distractions, casualties and accidents breaking the rhythm of the broadsides, Broke also used his ingenuity to improve the standard of the weapons. Each gun had a sight fitted (at this stage this was unusual; in most ships gun captains just squinted along the barrel to aim, if they even bothered to do that). Arcs were cut in decks and angles marked so that when, in action, smoke concealed the enemy, a form of fire control could be used.

Lawrence, the American captain, had been promoted to command the *Chesapeake* after winning in a single-ship action between sloops with the *Hornet* (which we left blockading San Salvador a few pages back). He left no record of why he decided to take his ship out of Boston

Above left: An engraving by Lee and Webster showing the *Chesapeake* coming into action with the *Shannon*. NMM neg no: 393

Left: Schetky's dramatic print of the *Shannon/Chesapeake* action shows the latter 'crippled and thrown into utter disorder by the two first broadsides fired from HMS SHANNON' as the caption puts it. The one ensign flown at the peak of the gaff of the British ship in the background contrasts with the number of flags flown by her opponent. NMM neg no: 8608

Above: Schetky's picture shows *Shannon* and *Chesapeake* ranging up alongside each other and exchanging the first broadsides of their epic slugging-match. NMM neg no: 3570

Harbour to engage the lone British frigate blockading the port, nor of what he thought he might achieve. Probably it was enough that the British frigate was in sight, and he must have sailed out to attack her in the confident hope of victory.

This he did at noon on 1 June 1813. *Shannon* moved slowly out to draw him further from shore, and then, still in sight of Boston lighthouse, stopped to allow the American to close on her, which he did at a fine pace. He made no attempt to manoeuvre and rake, nor did his opponent. At 5.50pm the *Chesapeake* coming up alongside the *Shannon* at a distance of some 50yd, the latter opened fire with her aftermost gun followed in quick succession by each of the other guns on her starboard side. *Chesapeake* immediately replied. Both ships were firing furiously at a range at which they could scarcely miss. However, the training of the British crew told from the start; rate of fire and precision of aim were on their side. There are accounts of the men in the tops of the British ship having their view of the decks of their antagonist partly obscured by the sheer amount of shattered wreckage being blown across it. The concentration of fire on to the quarterdeck of the American ship was frightful. One helmsman was killed after another, officers fell dead or wounded. Small-arms fire from the *Shannon's* tops was also causing havoc, and a thrown hand grenade blew up an arms chest on the American quarterdeck. Rigging was also damaged, and the American ship began to turn, out of control, into the wind. This then caused her to be blown backwards, with her stern being forced against the side of the British ship just forward of the mainmast. By

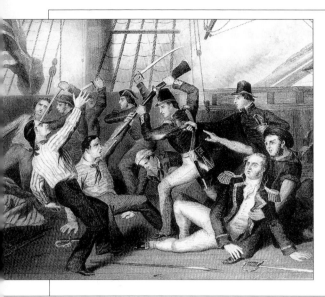

Left: 'Don't give up the ship' — an American print showing the death of Lawrence, as the British boarders storm the decks of the *Chesapeake*. Another stagey tableau which carries little conviction as a representation of what actually happened, but tells us much about the early 19th century taste for romantic heroism and deathbed scenes. *NMM neg no: 8898*

Below: Thomas Whitcombe painted the picture from which this engraving was taken. *Shannon,* mostly hidden behind her adversary, has sent her boarding parties across, and Captain Broke is leading them to victory on the American ship's deck. The flag proclaiming 'A free trade and sailor's rights', the slogan for which the USA had gone to war, still flies from the foremast head. *NMM neg no: B3792*

Right: The boarding of the *Chesapeake* — a contemporary British artist's impression published soon after the battle — too soon for it to show any close resemblance to what actually went on. However, it does give some sort of impression of the sort of grim, bloody, close-quarter, no-holds-barred, merciless scrimmage that happened when you boarded. *NMM neg no: 9216*

Below: Schetky's final picture of the frigate duel shows *Shannon* triumphantly leading her prize into Halifax harbour, to a rapturous welcome from the rest of her squadron. *NMM neg no: 8610*

this stage, only about six minutes after the firing of the first shot, training was telling even more. The British seamen were still working their guns like enthusiastic robots, ignoring the considerable casualties and damage being inflicted on their ship. Some of the Americans were beginning to show signs of flinching. Broke saw his opportunity and ran forward, shouting orders that the ships should be lashed together and his boarding parties go into action. His elderly boatswain successfully lashed the ships together, but as he finished doing so an American cutlass slashed down and cut off his arm. By this time both captain and first lieutenant of the American ship had fallen mortally wounded and been carried below, the former repeating 'Don't give up the ship'.

Broke stepped from the rail of his own ship on to the other frigate's aftermost carronade, and then down on to the quarterdeck, with about 20 boarders following him. The leaderless American sailors on the quarterdeck mostly fled below. The American chaplain fired a pistol at the British captain, missed, and was cut down. Other British boarders were now on board the *Chesapeake* and beginning to suffer casualties from fire from that ship's tops, but this was soon dealt with by shots from the *Shannon*. In the smoke, noise and general confusion the survivors of the gun crews on the upper deck of the American ship had not realised that they had been boarded until now. They then made a rush up at the British boarders and momentarily stopped them, but then were swept away. In a tussle on the forecastle, which may or may not have involved men who had apparently surrendered Broke was clubbed down, and suffered a bad head wound which would affect him till the end of his days. His assailants were immediately killed. There was a spatter of shots fired from below and the boarders replied with a volley, after which there was no more resistance. This was not immediately obvious from the *Shannon*, which had drifted off a little way, and a last shot from her killed the British first lieutenant in the moment of triumph. This bloody, hectic and ferocious action lasted only 12min from start to finish. During that time 61 Americans and 33 Britons were either killed or mortally wounded, whilst the numbers of wounded were 85 and 50 respectively. This was a very high 'butcher's bill' for any frigate action, and extraordinary for one that had lasted for such a short time. The British casualties are enough to show that the American crew had fought hard and well.

The Royal Navy had shown it could still win frigate actions, the US Navy had acquired another hero, and above all there was another indication that the most important factor in winning battles when there was not an enormous disparity in numbers, gunpower or luck, was training. Superior training had been at the root of the Royal Navy's 'habit of victory', it was the main explanation for the string of American victories, and it certainly lay behind the *Shannon's* victory in what otherwise was a contest of equals.

Below: The last days of Broke's *Shannon* are depicted here, serving as a hulk at Sheerness. This picture by Mends shows her dismasted, riding light and roofed over. This was a normal fate for old ships which were no longer needed or fit for active service. Many had long, useful, if unglamorous second existences as storage, accommodation or hospital hulks. *Shannon* herself was hulked in 1831 and not broken up till 1859. *NMM neg no: 8897*

11

Cutting out actions and bombardments:
Old and New Navies confront the Barbary Corsairs

Since the 16th century, trading voyages in the Mediterranean had to face a danger from the raiders of the North African shore, the area known as 'Barbary' (from the Berber peoples who lived there). The endemic state of war between Christians and Muslims had caused the growth of sea-raiding as a weapon in this war. On the Christian side the Knights of St John at Malta were the chief protagonists. The Muslims had the city states of Tunis, Tripoli and above all Algiers, as well as Moroccan towns, particularly Sale (Sallee). Older generations of historians tended to call these Muslim raiders 'pirates' — but they were rather state-backed privateers or, in some cases, state-owned commerce- and slave-raiders.

Newcomers to the Mediterranean in particular had trouble from these plunderers. In the late 17th century the Royal Navy fought a war, or rather a series of wars, against them. The usual practice of the European powers was a combination of subsidies and occasional hostilities. The French developed the first bomb-vessels in the 1680s in order to bombard Algiers. The Venetians, Portuguese and Neapolitans all sent expeditions against Algiers at one time or another in the 18th century. So also did the Danes, who bombarded the city in 1770. The Danes also sent an expedition to the Mediterranean in the 1790s because of trouble with both Tunis and Algiers, an expedition which had much the same sort of

experiences as the American one we are about to consider. These expeditions usually spent as much time in negotiating as in fighting. A powerful force which obtained some successes might be able to enforce concessions like the return of seamen who had been enslaved, or the signing of a treaty to respect the merchant ships which flew the flag of the country in question. More often money or goods were provided to the corsair states as ransoms or protection money.

After America had won her independence, her ships trading with the Mediterranean began to run into trouble with the North African states. They no longer flew the British flag, and therefore were no longer protected by the power and prestige of the largest European navy. American ships were captured or plundered, American seamen enslaved. This irritation was a major reason for building a navy. Initially, however, the Algerians were bought off, the Americans building them a frigate and two smaller vessels and providing other tribute. This was not very satisfactory, and in 1801 a force of the new American frigates arrived at Gibraltar. It would be tedious to recount the complicated story of blockade, negotiation and fleeting encounters with North African warships which makes up the story of the American squadron in the Mediterranean in the next few years. My purpose here is different, because the most spectacular exploit of that squadron, in what

Above: One of the most ferocious cutting out attacks of all: in 1797 the crew of the frigate *Hermione* had risen against their sadist of a captain in one of the nastiest and bloodiest of all mutinies. They had handed her over to the Spaniards who in October 1799 had her in the harbour of Puerto Cabello (Venezuela). Captain Hamilton of HMS *Surprise* led a night boat attack which, despite losing surprise, managed to capture the *Hermione* and bring her out of the harbour. The incredible casualty list was 12 British wounded against 119 Spaniards killed and 97 wounded. The artist responsible for this print appears to have had considerable problems with his perspective and sense of scale, as the miniature Spanish fort at the bottom left hand side of the picture demonstrates.
NMM neg no: A9969

was otherwise a mostly frustrating period, provides an excellent illustration of a particular type of naval action. This was the 'cutting out expedition' a raid, usually conducted in ships' boats and at night, with surprise usually a vital element, to attack enemy vessels in port. This was a form of action the Royal Navy, often faced by enemies who were reluctant to stir from the shelter of their ports, had made its own. At Tripoli in 1804 Lieutenant Decatur of the US Navy showed that this new navy was also skilful in this sort of daring attack. The previous year the American frigate *Philadelphia* had gone aground just outside Tripoli harbour when chasing a Tripolitanian raider. Captain Bainbridge had done his best to get his ship off, but was surrounded by enemies and forced to surrender. He and his crew were to remain in captivity in Tripoli, treated as hostages (shades of recent events in Iraq and Bosnia!) and not released until many months of negotiation and bargaining. Meanwhile, the frigate had been got off and taken into Tripoli harbour.

This was a constant irritation to the Americans, and it was decided to try and burn her where she lay, it being considered that it would be impossible to get her out of

the harbour. The squadron had just captured a Tripolitanian vessel, probably a local version of a ketch, called the *Mustico*. Her appearance was appropriate for entering Tripoli harbour without raising suspicions. Attacks of this kind needed some sort of disguise or a stealthy and undetected approach if powerful harbour defences were not to overwhelm it long before the target was reached. This vessel, retaining her appearance as a local craft, was

174

Above: Engraving showing the bombardment of Algiers — night having fallen, ships and forts are still battling away. *NMM neg no: C825*

commissioned into the US Navy as the *Intrepid*. To add to the illusion that she was a local vessel, the volunteer crew were given Maltese clothing.

Lieutenant Decatur sailed from Syracuse in company with the brig *Siren*, whose boats were intended to support his attack, on 3 February 1804. They reached Tripoli four days later but the weather was unsuitable to make the attempt and they withdrew to wait for better conditions. A gale then blew them eastwards, but they managed to get back into position on the 16th. The wind was light and getting lighter, and in the circumstances he decided not to wait for the *Siren's* boats. He did, however, have one boatload of the *Siren's* crew which had been aboard since the previous day, fortunately, as it turned out, with their boat, which seems to have been towed behind the *Intrepid*.

The ketch came sailing into the harbour with just a few men on deck, dressed in the Maltese clothes they had been issued with, and the rest of the crew gathered in mounting tension below, armed and ready to rush up once the word of command had been given. As she approached the moored *Philadelphia* someone from that ship hailed her and told her to keep away. The Sicilian pilot of the American vessel, however, replied that his ship had lost all her anchors, and therefore would have to make fast to the larger ship. At this he was given grudging permission to come alongside. At this crucial moment the wind shifted, and it looked as if the expedition would fail as the *Intrepid* came to a stop, just short of her target. It was then that the *Siren's* boat came to the rescue by taking a rope to the larger ship, assisted by a boat from the *Philadelphia*. The *Intrepid* came alongside, and as the alarm was raised, her boarding party rushed aboard the frigate. There was little opposition as the surprised Tripolitanians either jumped into the harbour or their boat. Careful planning and preparation now reaped their benefit. The incendiary material that the Americans had brought with them was placed where it would do the most damage and ignited. In less than 20min from the two ships touching, *Intrepid* was under way again, bound

for the harbour mouth, where the *Siren's* other boats were waiting to support her. By now the defences had woken up, and as the flames began to roar from the doomed frigate, a heavy fire was opened from shore batteries and the other ships in harbour. Fortunately for the Americans the defenders were surprised, rattled and inaccurate. The only casualty was a man slightly wounded, and the *Intrepid* got clear away. A combination of careful preparation, ingenuity, quick thinking and daring had won their reward. The blazing *Philadelphia* broke from her moorings and drifted ashore, a complete wreck.

This action happened in the same year as Trafalgar, when the major European navies were otherwise engaged and the North African corsairs could get away with a great deal, whilst waxing fat on subsidies from both sides in the Anglo-French struggle. The brief respite of the Peace of Amiens had enabled both French and Dutch to send fleets to participate in the usual business of bombardment mixed with bribes. The ending of the Napoleonic War, however, meant that the day of the corsairs was coming to an end. The Americans were the first to act. As soon as the signing of peace permitted, they sent Stephen Decatur, now risen to Commodore, with almost all of their navy, to confront the Algerians. He captured a frigate and destroyed a smaller ship and then made a satisfactory settlement (at least from the American point of view) with Algiers. He went on to do the same for both Tunis and Tripoli.

The British were slower to deal with Algiers, but when they did so, they could and did move with much greater force. A massacre of Italian fishermen was the excuse. It was unlikely that the premier naval power of the world, conscious of a role as the policeman of the seas,

Left: Stephen Decatur (1779–1820) — an engraving of the Chappel portrait. This American naval officer first distinguished himself in the burning of the captured USS *Philadelphia* in Tripoli harbour, an exploit for which he was promoted to captain. In 1812 he commanded the frigate *United States*, with which he captured the British frigate *Macedonian*. In 1815 he commanded the USS *President* which, attempting to break out from New York, first grounded and then was captured by a British squadron. He was killed in a duel with a fellow officer, a waste of the life of one of America's best naval officers. The strange drapes over the tops of the breeches of the guns in this picture are lead covers to stop damp getting into the charges through the touch-holes.
NMM neg no: 9215

convinced of the evils of slavery, would tolerate what was increasingly seen as the out of date and evil anomaly of corsair states. (The slave trade had been abolished at the beginning of the century, though it would be another generation before slavery was abolished in the British Empire, but already the Royal Navy had a small squadron cruising against slavers on the West Coast of Africa.)

Sir Edward Pellew, who we last saw as a young frigate captain achieving the first victory of the Great War against France, was given the job of leading the attack on Algiers. He was ideally suited for this post, having been a highly competent commander of the British Mediterranean fleet for the closing years of that war. He was given a force which included an 100-gun First Rate and a 98-gun Second Rate as his two three-deckers plus three more ships of the line, 74-gun two-deckers. He had three big frigates of the type recently built to counter the American 44s, one classed as a 50 and two as 40s. In addition to these three ships which were armed with a main battery of 24-pounders there were two more 36-gun, 18-pounder frigates. It was probably deliberate that all five frigates were fir-built. Ships built of softwood could be rushed out very fast in an emergency — taking perhaps half the time of their oak-built equivalents — but with equally short service lives. It was rare for a 'fir-built' ship (which were usually built of a variety of pine) to last much more than five years in service. It may well be that the Navy was happier to risk ships which would not last long and had been built for an emergency which no longer existed, rather than use ones likely to prove of more lasting value. Another factor may have been that fir-built ships were lighter, had shallower draft, and could therefore go closer inshore than oak-built ones. Two brig sloops of 18, and three of 10 guns were added. As the main purpose of the fleet would be bombardment, four bomb-vessels were included. Five gun-boats would be added at Gibraltar. They would be supplemented by the launches of the line of battle ships which were fitted with howitzers. A number of flat-bottomed landing craft were also acquired to be fitted to fire congreve rockets. There was also an ordnance sloop (a one-masted coastal vessel used to carry munitions, not a sloop-of-war) which was fitted as a floating bomb. Sailing out to Gibraltar the fleet practised their gunnery at every opportunity on newly-invented floating targets, urged on by their admiral, always a gunnery enthusiast and convinced that accurate and heavy fire was the only way of

Left: Beechey's portrait of Edward Pellew (1757–1833) shows him in his later years as Lord Exmouth. He was a brilliant frigate commander, his years as captain of the heavy frigate (cut down from a 64) *Indefatigable* being particularly notable, especially his harrying of the French 74 *Droits de l'Homme* to her doom in a January storm with another frigate in company. He was later C-in-C East Indies, and ended the Napoleonic War as commander of the Mediterranean Fleet, from which the command of the mission to bombard Algiers was a logical extension.
NMM neg no: 245

Right: Schetky's view of a cutting out operation as if seen from an approaching boat. This particular action (the cutting out of the French *Chevrette*) took place in 1800. He perhaps overemphasizes the size of the ship, but the impression of sudden violence exploding in the night is vivid and very convincing.
NMM ref: BHC0531

coping with the strong defences of the corsair base.

At Gibraltar the fleet received an unexpected, but welcome, addition. The Dutch Vice-Admiral, Baron van der Capellen, was there with four 40-gun 18-pounder frigates (of the standard French design, built for Napoleon), a 30-gun frigate and an 18-gun corvette. He had been sent by his government to deal with the corsairs, and immediately asked if he could add his force to Pellew's. He was welcomed and incorporated into the plan of attack. The brig sloop *Satellite* joined at Gibraltar, having just come from Algiers with the latest plans and details of the defences.

On 14 August 1816 the Allied fleet sailed from Gibraltar. On the evening of the 16th, some 200 miles from Algiers, the ship-sloop *Prometheus*, joined company direct from the port, with news of how the Dey (or Bey, the ruler of the city) had received the British ultimatum demanding indemnity for the massacre and his abandonment of slavery of Christians. The reception of this demand had, understandably, not been friendly. The sloop had on board the wife and daughter of the British consul. The two women, disguised in midshipmen's clothes, had with great difficulty been brought out, but the consul's baby was detected by its crying (or given away by its nurse) whilst being carried concealed in a basket to the boat. The Dey, besides the baby, had in his hands the surgeon of the *Prometheus*, three midshipmen, and the remainder of the crews of two boats, in all 18 persons. 'The child,' Lord Exmouth wrote, 'was sent off next morning by the Dey; and, as a solitary instance of his humanity, it ought to be recorded by me.' The consul himself was put in irons and confined in a small room on the ground floor of his house. Captain Dashwood tried to get the Dey to release his prisoners, but without success.

Captain Dashwood confirmed all that the admiral had previously learnt about the preparations the Algerians were making to resist his attack, of which they had apparently already received warning. About 40,000 men had been marched down from the interior, and all the soldiers from the distant garrisons. The Algerian navy was all in the port. It consisted of four 44-gun frigates, five large corvettes of from 24 to 30 guns, and between 30 and 40 gun and mortar boats. The fortifications of Algiers, for so small a place, were of considerable strength. Eighty guns plus six to eight huge mortars were mounted in various batteries on the north side of the city including a battery over the north gate, but the area of water they covered was too shallow for any large ships to approach close enough for them to have any effect. It was much the same for the 20 guns between the north wall of the city and the commencement of the 250yd-long pier connecting the town to the lighthouse. At the

north projection of the mole stood a semicircular battery, of two levels of guns, mounting about 44 in total and to the southward of that, and nearly in a line with the pier, came the three-level, 48-gun, round or lighthouse battery. Then came a long battery, also with three levels and mounting 66 guns, called the eastern battery. This was flanked by four other two-level batteries with 60 guns in all; and on the south head of the mole were two large guns, possibly 68-pounders and nearly 20ft long. This meant the batteries on the mole mounted about 220 guns consisting, except for those just mentioned, of 32-, 24- and 18-pounders.

Along the sea-front of the city from the small pier projecting into the mouth of the harbour were the 15 guns in three levels of the Fish Market battery. Between these and the southern end of the sea-front of the city, were two batteries of four or five guns each. Beyond the city in this direction was a castle and two or three other batteries mounting between them 60 or 70 guns. Besides all the batteries already described which constituted the defences of the port, there were various others on the landward side of the city and on the heights behind. There could well have been a total of 1,000 guns or more defending the city.

Having to tack up against a head wind until getting on for midnight on the 24th, when it shifted to the southwest, the fleet did not reach the western limit of the bay on which Algiers lies until noon on the 26th. At daybreak on the 27th the city was in sight. The fleet lying nearly becalmed, its admiral took the opportunity of dispatching a messenger, one Lieutenant Samuel Burgess, in one of the *Queen Charlotte's* boats, towed by the *Severn* to demand that the Dey agree to the following conditions: the abolition of Christian slavery and the delivering up of all Christian slaves in Algiers; the repayment of all the money that had recently been exacted for the return of Italian slaves; peace between Holland and Algiers; and the immediate liberation of the British consul and the two boats' crews of the *Prometheus*. As a calm stopped the progress of the frigate a signal from the flagship sent the boat on its somewhat unenviable mission into Algiers, flying a flag of truce. Arriving opposite the mole the boat was met by one from the shore with the captain of the port aboard. The demand was presented and an answer promised in two hours. Meanwhile, a sea breeze having sprung up, the fleet stood into the bay, and lay-to (came to a temporary stop) about a mile from the city.

At 2pm, Lieutenant Burgess hoisted a signal to the effect that there was still no sign of an answer, and the boat rowed out towards the *Severn*. The admiral immediately signalled to find out if all the ships were ready. Almost at the same moment every ship had the affirmative flag at her mast-head and the fleet bore up to the attack in the prescribed order. At 2.35pm the flagship anchored with springs out (ropes attached to her anchor so she could shift her broadside round) about 50yd from the mole. Just as the British three-decker was in the act of lashing herself to the mainmast of an Algerian brig, itself up against the shore at the mouth of the mole or harbour, and towards which Lord Exmouth had directed his ship to be steered as the guide for her position, a shot was fired at the *Queen Charlotte*, and almost at the same instant two other shots were fired from the opposite end of the mole at the *Impregnable* and ships near her as they were advancing to their stations. Scarcely had these three guns been fired when Lord Exmouth, with characteristic humanity, waved his hand to a crowd of 200 to 300 soldiers and artillerymen, standing on the parapet of the mole, gawking at the large ship looming up so near to them. As the greater part of these were in the act of leaping through the embrasures into the lower battery, the *Queen Charlotte* opened up with her starboard broadside. Thus the action commenced, each ship joining in it the instant she could bring her guns to bear. Next ahead of the *Queen Charlotte,* or rather upon her port bow, lay the *Leander*, with her after guns on the starboard side bearing on the mouth of the mole and her foremost ones upon the Fish Market battery. Ahead of the *Leander* lay the *Severn*, with the whole of her starboard guns bearing on that same battery. Close to the *Severn* was the *Glasgow*, with her port guns bearing on the town batteries. About 250yd on the starboard quarter, close to her intended station, was the *Superb*, with her starboard broadside pointing at the 60-gun battery, next to that on the mole-head. Her captain had intended her to be even closer, with her bowsprit over the stern of the flagship, because of the signal to anchor being made instead of 'prepare to anchor', as Exmouth had ordered. Close astern of the *Superb*, in a northeasterly direction, the *Impregnable* and *Albion* were to have taken their stations in line ahead, but *Albion* was not sufficiently advanced when the firing commenced. So the *Impregnable* had to bring-

to (stop) considerably outside, not only of her proper station, but of the line of bearing (about southeast from the south angle of the eastern battery) within which the attacking force had been ordered to assemble. The *Impregnable* therefore lay exposed at about 400yd from both the lighthouse battery of three tiers and the two-tier eastern battery. She soon opened fire on the first. Seeing the open space between the *Impregnable* and her second ahead, the *Superb*, the *Minden* stood on and took up a position about her own length astern of the latter. The *Albion*, following, brought up at first close ahead of the *Impregnable*, but finding herself too near to the three-decker, she filled her sails again and at about 3pm came to again, within her own length of the *Minden*. The latter, quickly passing a cable out of a stern port to the *Albion's* bow, pulled the two ships close together.

In this way the eight heaviest ships of the fleet took their stations: the *Queen Charlotte*, *Superb*, *Minden*, *Albion* and *Impregnable*, lined up from the mole-head in a northeasterly direction, and the *Leander*, *Severn* and *Glasgow*, curving from the Fish Market battery to the southwest.

The Dutch squadron was assigned to the station opposite the batteries to the southward of the city, and it appears to have been the intention of the Dutch admiral to place the *Melampus* in the centre of his five frigates; but the *Diana's* captain, not understanding exactly the orders given to him, did not go far enough to the northward. Seeing this, the Dutch admiral valiantly pushed the *Melampus* past the *Diana*, and at about 3pm anchored his frigate with her bowsprit's end over the stern rail of the *Glasgow*. The *Diana* and *Dageraad*

Above right: The scene on *Queen Charlotte's* quarterdeck during the bombardment of Algiers in 1816. The flagship's gun crews are firing slide-mounted carronades as fast as they can against the shore batteries. A good impression of the scene of frantic but purposeful activity amidst fearsome noise, blinding smoke and sudden death which was the gun deck of a well-drilled man of war in action. *NMM neg no: 3016*

Right: Another example of a careful sketch made by an artist to establish the position of ships in a battle, and as a basis for a painting. This one is by Joy and shows the position of ships for the bombardment of Algiers. *Superb* is on the left, *Queen Charlotte* is the big ship behind the two frigates to the right of centre, behind them Algiers rises up, and to the left is the line of the Dutch frigate squadron. *NMM neg no: A4447*

anchored one after the other astern of their admiral. The two remaining Dutch frigates anchored further out, and the corvette *Eendracht*, as she had been directed, kept under way, being a lighter and more vulnerable vessel.

The frigates *Granicus* and *Hebrus* and the smaller vessels (except the bombs), which were considered as a reserve force, had not had any particular stations assigned to them, but were to take advantage of any openings they could find in the line of battle. The *Hebrus* was becalmed (there seems to be some evidence that the heavy gunfire killed any wind there was) when trying to take advantage of such openings and was forced to anchor a little outside the line on the flagship's larboard (port) quarter. The *Granicus*, finding herself shooting fast ahead, hove-to, with the intention of waiting until her companions had taken up their positions. Thanks to the dense gunpowder smoke which rolled over the scene of battle,

hardly anything could be seen, except the *Queen Charlotte's* mast-head flag, so Captain Wise allowed 10min to pass. This meant the other ships had time to anchor. The *Granicus* then let her foresail fall, set topgallant sails, and soon with a combination of boldness and seamanship Captain Wise contrived to anchor his frigate in a space scarcely greater than her own length between the flagship and *Superb*; a medium-sized frigate in a position perhaps more appropriate to a three-decker.

Below: Chambers' huge and very impressive canvas of the bombardment of Algiers. In the foreground are the gun-boats. On the right is the bow of the *Impregnable* with behind it the fortifications of the mole. Further away, and in the centre of the picture, is the *Queen Charlotte*; the two-deckers to the right of her are *Albion* and *Minden*, with the Dutch frigates beyond, all seen against a backdrop of the city itself. *NMM ref: BHC0617*

The sloops attached to the squadron also took their posts: the *Heron*, *Britomart*, *Prometheus* and *Cordelia* remaining under way; the *Mutine* anchored off the port bow of the *Impregnable*. The four bomb-vessels were soon in their intended station, about 2,000yd from the fortifications, and began their high-angle shell fire. The 55 boats of the battering flotilla, commanded by Captain Frederick Thomas Michell, consisting of gun-boats, mortar-boats, launches with carronades, rocket boats, armed ships' barges and yawls, also began to bombard the batteries and forts.

The accuracy and destructive effect of the *Queen Charlotte's* fire was such that her third broadside levelled the south end of the mole to its foundations. She then shifted her broadside till it bore upon the batteries over the town-gate leading to the mole. Here gun after gun came tumbling over the battlements, and when the last gun fell, which was just as the artillerymen were in the act of firing it, one of the Algerian commanders leaped upon the ruined parapet and shook his sword at the ship whose cannon had so quickly demolished his post.

The *Leander's* excellent position and her rapid fire very soon cut to pieces the defending gun-boats and row-galleys, and any intention of boarding the nearest British ships was entirely frustrated. By the admiral's orders, towards 4pm the *Leander* ceased firing to allow the Algerian frigate moored about 140yd across the mole from the *Queen Charlotte* to be set on fire. This task was done by the flagship's barge, with an army officer (of the corps of miners — an engineer and specialist in demolition) aboard. A gallant but foolhardy young midshipman in rocket-boat No 8 followed, though not supposed to do so. His boat, being flat-bottomed, could not keep pace with the barge and as a result was exposed to a murderous fire that wounded himself and killed 10 of the others in his boat. In about 10min, Lieutenant Richards in the barge succeeded in boarding and setting fire to the Algerian frigate, and returned from the enterprise with the loss of only two men killed.

At 4.15pm the Algerian frigate in flames drifted out towards the *Queen Charlotte*, forcing the latter to move to let her pass. Ten minutes later the *Impregnable* signalled that she had lost 150 killed and wounded (a third of them by the bursting of a single shell), and requesting that a frigate might be sent to divert some of the fire from the ship. The *Glasgow* was immediately ordered upon that undesirable service. However, the wind had

fallen and after nearly three quarters of an hour had passed she was unable to do more than take up a somewhat better position for firing at the enemy. Here she was a short distance off the *Severn*, with her stern towards that ship. In that position the *Glasgow* became exposed to a severe raking fire from the Fish Market battery and other guns nearby. This dismounted two of her quarterdeck carronades, and in a few minutes did her more serious damage than any she had previously suffered. At 7pm the *Leander*, being badly hit by these same guns which lay off her bow, sent out a hawser to the *Severn* and pulled herself round to bring her broadside to bear upon them. By about this time the incessant and well-aimed fire of the mortar, gun and rocket boats had made certain that all the ships and vessels within the harbour were burning. The flames later spread to the arsenal and storehouses on the mole. Several parts of the city were also set on fire by the shells from the bomb vessels.

The ordnance-sloop which, fitted as an explosion-vessel, had accompanied the expedition from Gibraltar to be used against the ships in the mole, was now, as they were all destroyed, given another task. Lieutenant Fleming, who during the action had been commanding a gun-boat stationed close under the stern of the *Queen Charlotte*, proceeded, in company with Major Reed of the engineers, to take command of the explosion-vessel and to place her where an officer, sent by Rear-Admiral Milne, should point out. This officer, Captain Herbert Bruce Powell, a volunteer serving on board the *Impregnable*, indicated the circular battery to the north of the lighthouse. In a short time the sloop was run on shore, close under this battery. There, at a few minutes past 9, the vessel exploded. The 143 barrels of gunpowder aboard should have been a fairly effective diversion from the still-suffering ships.

The fleet kept up a tremendous fire upon the town and forts until about 10pm. By this stage the upper levels of the batteries on the mole were very heavily knocked about. The fire from the lower levels was nearly silenced. The ammunition of the attacking ships had almost all been fired away. The *Queen Charlotte* cut her cables and sailed away with a light breeze which, fortunately for the British, had just sprung up from the land. Following the admiral's orders the remaining British and Dutch ships began cutting their cables too. Owing to their disabled state, they made very slow progress, and the *Leander*, *Superb* and *Impregnable* suffered much in

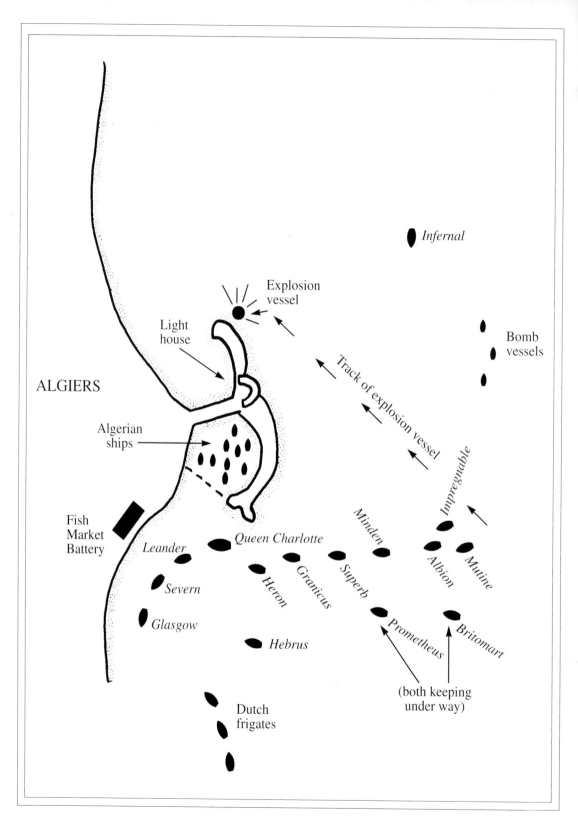

Infernal

Explosion
vessel

Light
house

Bomb
vessels

ALGIERS

Algerian
ships

Track of explosion vessel

Impregnable

Fish
Market
Battery

Leander

Queen Charlotte

Minden

Albion

Mutine

Severn

Heron

Granicus

Superb

Glasgow

Hebrus

Prometheus

Britomart

Dutch
frigates

(both keeping
under way)

consequence from the raking fire of a fort in the upper part of the city. Before 2am on the 28th every British and Dutch ship had escaped out of range of the forts. The blazing Algerian fleet and storehouses lit the way for this escape. As if the man-made turmoil was not enough, a three-hour thunderstorm now struck the bay.

A lot of damage had been done to the forts of Algiers, the Algerian fleet wiped out, and undoubtedly many men killed. The Dey had undoubtedly been taught a lesson about the increased power of modern artillery in the hands of experts. However, the Anglo-Dutch fleet had suffered many casualties and much damage, though fortunately no ship was lost. The British consul was freed, as were many slaves, and the Algerians paid an indemnity. They had received a warning and seem to have taken note of it, for we hear little of any raiding or plundering from then on.

However, it was not until 1830 that the threat posed by Algiers to European and American commerce was removed, and this was because the French, using steamships, mounted a full scale invasion and captured the city. They then went on to conquer its hinterland. The age of imperialism was well under way and Europe was on the march.

The bombarding force

Three-Decker (two)
100-gun: *Queen Charlotte* (Flagship of Admiral Pellew [Lord Exmouth], Captain James Brisbane)
98-gun: *Impregnable* (Flag of Rear-Admiral David Milne, Captain Edward Brace)

Two-decker line of battle ships of 74 guns (three)
             Superb (Charles Ekins)
             Minden (William Paterson)
             Albion (John Coode)

Large Frigates (24-pounders) (three)
50-gun: *Leander* (Edward Chetham)
40-gun: *Severn* (Frederick William Aylmer), *Glasgow* (Hon Anthony Maitland)

Frigates (18-pounders) (four Dutch and two British)
Dutch 40-gun: *Melampus* (Flag of Vice-Admiral Baron T. Van der Capellen, Captain Antony-Willem De Man), *Frederica* (Jakob-Adrian Van-der-Straaten), *Diana* (Petrus Zievogel), *Amstel* (Willem-Augustus Vanderhart)
36-gun: *Granicus* (William Furlong Wise), *Hebrus* (Edmund Palmer)

Frigate 30-gun (one Dutch)
             Dageraad (Johannes-Martinus Polders)

Ship sloops 18-gun (one British and one Dutch)
             Prometheus (originally built as a fireship)
             Eendracht (Dutch — classed as a corvette)

Brig sloops (five)
18-gun: *Heron, Mutine, Satellite*
10-guns: *Britomart, Cordelia*

Bomb-vessels (four)
             Belzebub, Fury, Hecla, Infernal

Plus five gun-boats, ships' boats, rocket boats and one explosion-vessel (ex-ordnance-sloop).

An impressive silver table-piece presented to Lord Exmouth after the bombardment of Algiers. It takes the form of the circular tower on the mole at Algiers, surrounded by figures of British sailors striking down corsairs and freeing slaves.
NMM neg no: B9054A

Above : The British 20-gun ship *Bonne Citoyenne*, herself originally a French corvette, towing in the French frigate *Furieuse* which she captured on 6 July 1809 in the Atlantic. This was less of a victory against odds than might seem at first sight because the French ship was partially disarmed at the time. None the less the smaller ship had done very well. The *Bonne* *Citoyenne's* lines were used as the basis for building a class of British warships. *NMM neg no: A1287*

Below: In another single-ship action HMS *Mermaid* runs aground off the coast of Grenada chasing the French brig-corvette *Brutus*. *NMM neg no: C627*

Above: The French 74 *Droits de l'Homme* driven ashore off Brittany, while carrying troops, by two British frigates in January 1797 and wrecked with huge loss of life. *NMM neg no: 1268*

Below: Fire was a constant hazard on wooden ships. The fate of Vice-admiral Sir John Jervis' flagship *Boyne* in 1795 is graphically illustrated in this picture of her 'on fire by accident at Spithead.' *NMM neg no: X237*

Index

A listing of the battles, ships and people mentioned in *Sea Battles in Close-up: The Age of Nelson*.
Page numbers in italics refer to illustrations.

190